The
COMPLE
RESTAURATEUR

Hugh Pitt, a former Fleet Street journalist and television producer, has spent much of his working life
travelling around the world. In the course of his
journeys he has stayed and eaten in some of the
greatest establishments known to man – and some of
the worst! After leaving the BBC, he opened his own
successful restaurant, and now divides his time between France and Sherborne, Dorset, with his wife
and youngest son.

For Annie
without whom nothing in this
would have been possible

The COMPLETE RESTAURATEUR

*The A–Z of Running
a Restaurant*

HUGH PITT

ROBERT HALE · LONDON

© Hugh Pitt 1989
First published in Great Britain 1989
First paperback edition 1991

Robert Hale Limited
Clerkenwell House
Clerkenwell Green
London EC1R 0HT

ISBN 0-7090-4675-8

Photoset in Palatino by
Derek Doyle & Associates, Mold, Clwyd.
Printed in Great Britain by
St Edmundsbury Press Limited, Bury St Edmunds, Suffolk,
and bound by WBC Bookbinders Limited.

Contents

List of Tables and Plans   6
Foreword by Derek Cooper   7
Introduction   9

1   Why Catering?   13
2   First Steps   21
3   Research   29
4   Pros and Cons   35
5   Some Not So Obvious Alternatives   43
6   With Notebook in Hand   55
7   Raising Money   62
8   Financial Forecasting   72
9   Legal Complexities   80
10 The Kitchen   93
11 The Dining-Room   114
12 Staff   127
13 Food   142
14 Loss, Break-Even and Profit   156
15 Behind the Scenes and Up-Front   174
16 From Crate to Plate   186
17 Public Relations   199
18 Expansion   217
19 Success?   225

Useful Addresses   233
Further Reading   235
Index   237

Tables

A	Cash-Flow Forecast	76
B	Profit and Loss Forecast	78
C	Gross Profit	171
D	Mark Up	172
E	Finding the VAT	172
F	True Income after VAT deduction	173

Plans

| Hugh Pitt's Kitchen in Scotland | 97 |
| The Troisgros Brothers' Kitchen, Roanne | 99 |

Foreword

by Derek Cooper

In 1979 on a warm spring day I drove over the summit of the pass from Glen Croe to Loch Fyne on my descent to Lochgoilhead. I was on my way to meet Hugh Pitt and his wife Anne for the first time. 'Come and see what we're doing,' they'd written; 'we could do with some encouragement.'

The further I drove down the single-lane track along the loch on my way to Inverlounin House the more I wondered what on earth had possessed a patently sane and creative couple to pour their life savings into a 'restaurant with rooms' in a remote place which had never seen such a phenomenon before and which didn't appear to be particularly grateful for it.

I was most impressed with everything the Pitts were doing. The food was fresh, seasonal and superbly presented; the wine list was carefully chosen. But when Hugh told me of the awful battles he'd had with planners and builders, of the financial millstone he'd hung round their necks and the dread fact that in the depths of winter the road to his dream hotel was blocked by snow I thought he must have gone off his chump.

I wrote a report enthusing over Inverlounin for the *Good Hotel Guide* and the place stayed in its helpful pages until the Pitts gave up the struggle and left. The *Good Food Guide* warmly commended it too but added, all too prophetically, '... let us hope they have got their sums right since the paddle-steamer no longer brings wealthy Glasgow commuters to peaceful Lochgoilhead'.

Despite the often inspired cooking, the idyllic lochside views and the reasonable prices, not enough people came to make the place viable. The sums were sadly wrong. By 1983 this unique little *logis d'Ecosse* had closed its doors for ever. Even the fact that, as one guest reported, 'what they present is almost *unrivalled* in the UK' the magic hadn't worked.

If *The Complete Restaurateur* had been around in the late 1970s for Hugh and Anne to read they would have looked at Inverlounin, realized it was a bummer and driven straight back down the road to Glasgow. But here at last is a book which could well save hundreds of similarly expectant couples from a great deal of heartbreak. For their is no industry more volatile, more strewn with bankruptcies, than catering. Its endemic instability, its high staff turnover and its manic unpredictability call for a high degree of resilience on the part of anyone brave enough to want to become part of it.

In Greater London alone the somewhat hazy statistics seem to indicate that fifty restaurants open every month – so presumably another fifty close. All the more reason to listen to Pitt as he points out the booby traps, the shock and sometimes the horror that lie in wait for those who just want to spread a little gastronomic happiness among their fellows.

I have never had a desire to run a restaurant but I read this book with fascination and mounting approval. Pitt proselytizes for high standards, integrity and a decent deal for the staff. The contemptuous way in which many cowboy outlets and chain hotels treat their employees explains why such places are so unrewarding to visit.

Consistently it is the small hotels, cafés and restaurants of Britain owned by 'amateurs' which steal the most complimentary mentions in the guides. The reason is that they are run by men and women for whom job satisfaction and enjoyment are more important than portion control and a company car. This book has been written for them and if it saves them one-tenth of the agonies and disappointments the Pitts went through in their apprentice days and encourages them to have a go at trying to create the best restaurant in the country, then it will have done the rest of us a great service too.

Introduction

Jean Anthelme Brillat-Savarin was a French politician and magistrate. He wrote many learned works on the law and politics. But it is as a gastronome that he is best remembered – his great work *La Physiologie du goût*, published just before his death in 1826, contained the following words:

'The pleasures of the table belong to all ages, to all conditions, to all countries and to every day; they can be associated with all the other pleasures and remain the longest to console us for the loss of the rest.'

This book is about providing those pleasures, for it is in itself a pleasure to do so.

I have no time for those without patience or appreciation for the table or the wine cellar. I have no time for those who regard eating as merely a method of keeping oneself alive. And I have no time for those in the catering trade – and there are many, alas – who are uncaring about food and uncaring about the enjoyment of their customers. I make no apology for this.

This book is not about the philosophy of food, delightful though I would find it, but about supplying it in your own restaurant. Neither is it a treatise just on setting up and running your own restaurant – it is very definitely an attempt to persuade you to set up and run a *better* restaurant than any of your competitors.

In my own case, my wife and I for many years had the idea of running a small restaurant and, admittedly, we were lucky enough to be able to travel extensively because of our jobs. The exact sort of operation, however, was a little hazy in our minds until one day we found ourselves at a small *auberge* in France which was so perfect from our point of view – in its position, the way it was run, the food and service it offered and the type of customer it attracted – that we knew we had found the exact model for ourselves. I am not claiming that we were able to achieve that particular excellence, but at least it was a goal towards which we could work, a pattern for our determination, a tangible illustration of what was possible.

When we eventually took the plunge, by converting an old property on a sea loch in the West Highlands of Scotland into a 'restaurant with rooms', as the French call it, there were no books to guide us. We had, it is true, tried as much as we could to study the subject, apart from having had a life-long interest in it, and we went to endless trouble in taking advice and so on. Nonetheless, it was a sobering experience. We made a lot of mistakes. We learned the hard way. We still had much to learn when we moved south to another restaurant.

That learning process was not at all easy.

We did not necessarily want to run a bigger restaurant, a more financially successful one, a more 'up-market' one, a more specialized one than anyone else. Just a better one – better in every way. No matter what the goal is – a small shop doing coffees, lunches and teas, or a sandwich bar aimed at the 'take-away' trade, or a concession in a pub or hotel or office block or factory; or whether it is a roadside café or a full-blown, smart eating place for the 'carriage trade', open all day and serving the very finest dishes. Even the humble fish-and-chippy on the corner can be made 'better' than another one down the road. And therefore more successful and appealing to you and your customers.

This book is not intended for the experienced or the wealthy, well versed in the ways of 'food and beverage' and money-management. It is strictly for those people who wish to run their own, personal, small business, where good food and service are more important than quick profit, but who nevertheless quite properly hope for a reasonable return for the staggering amount of work and hours their investment will require.

You will find mentioned early on in this book, and the theme will be reiterated throughout, the need to 'stick to what you think you can do best'. And alongside will be stressed the need for detailed research, leg-work and homework, before committing yourself to anything. But I do hope that this book is going to go quite some way in helping you, because I have kept in the forefront of my mind the anguished memories of crying,

'If only someone had told us' when we came across yet another obstacle, yet another hurdle in our path. I am going to endeavour to 'tell' you – I hope entertainingly and without too many dreary facts and figures – all the things we had to find out for ourselves. And I also hope to convey some of the great fun and satisfaction to be found in running your own, *better* restaurant.

1 Why Catering?

Tell me what you eat, and I shall tell you what you are.
Brillat-Savarin

More than 2 million people now work in the catering and hotel industry in Britain – and on present estimates about 50,000 new jobs will be created every year for the foreseeable future. By its very nature, it is a fragmented industry and does not always get the attention or appreciation it deserves from the government or local authorities – yet it is of increasing importance to the country, not only as a source of employment and revenue but also as a source of foreign currency earnings.

Within this vast 'leisure and service' enterprise, there are a great number of men and women who run a huge range of catering outlets on their own or with the help of one or two staff, some of them only 'casuals' or part-time. They receive even less government attention and official recognition, yet their contribution towards the national wealth is enormous. The number of these people increases steadily, attracting to their ranks all manner of men and women with all manner of backgrounds and experience.

Not surprisingly, an unfortunate number of these businesses 'go to the wall' within a year or two – the figure is set as high as 10,000 annually. Not everyone attracted into the catering trade is in reality suited to it when it comes to weathering the first storms, nor are they prepared mentally or physically for the sheer exhaustion of running their own restaurant, however small it is at the start.

This book, however, is not about failure, though I hope it will do much to prevent it. No, it is to help the fittest to survive and prosper and to give them a better chance of the success they undoubtedly deserve.

And in this respect, there can be only one simple, glaringly obvious but all too often ignored piece of advice: define – at the start, at the very start, even before you have looked at advertisements, seen any property, talked to anyone in the trade or consulted any experts – exactly and specifically what you believe you are good at and therefore what sort of place it is that you want to run.

I say that this is all too often ignored, and I say it with considerable foresight – and hindsight too. And I shall go on saying it. So many people who consider themselves a dab hand at the odd omelette, in their own kitchen at home, mysteriously and frighteningly suddenly become possessed with delusions of grandeur once the idea of running a commercial kitchen enters their heads.

'If I can cook an omelette,' I have heard them say, 'I can have a go at anything else.' Well, the short answer is: 'You can't!' Not without a lot of learning, and even more practice. Cooking at home is completely and utterly different from cooking for people who are going (you hope) to pay you for the experience.

But, first of all, let us take a look at the five principles without which no one will ever succeed – not even you! They should be written down at the head of your own notebook, the importance of which we shall discuss later, and they should be inscribed indelibly in your own brain and in its thinking.

The five are: FLAIR, TOUGHNESS, LUCK, CAPITAL, CAPABILITY.

Yes, all of them. And do not confuse flair and capability – they are quite different. But let us consider these two, the first and last in the list, right now.

Flair

Flair, when it comes to running a restaurant, has more to do with your own personality than with anything else. Are you, you must ask yourself, the right sort of person in the first place? Are you an extrovert, do you like people, do you get on well with them, does hard work and what are now termed 'unsocial hours' worry you? Are you physically and mentally fit, do you panic easily or do you sit down and think things out carefully without rushing into some instant decision or conclusion? Are you a born leader? You are going to need this attribute if you ever need to employ staff and keep them loyal and (another modern jargon term) 'well motivated'.

You see, flair is not just the invention, or creation, of great dishes in the kitchen, the ability to work 'front of house' with charm, dignity and that *savoir-faire* you perhaps so much admired in a toast master at a fashionable wedding or banquet, or in the way a head waiter filleted a Dover sole at your favourite, up-market restaurant – it is much more than all those things, important as they may be. It is the ability to learn quickly, to have a great amount of common sense and to be able to apply it to the myriad problems that will confront you – and to apply it quickly, sensibly and, above all, correctly and properly. Whereas flair seems to most people a good thing to have in, say, an architect or a schoolteacher, you do not, alas, hear it said very often of people who run restaurants, yet it is just as important an attribute, if not more so, for restaurateurs as it is for those in occupations such as architecture.

Alas, having said all that, it must be admitted that it could well be, for most people, well nigh impossible for them to know with any certainty whether they have flair for running a restaurant of any sort until they are actually doing it and experiencing the problems at first hand.

Somewhat later in the book we consider the actual need to do the job before committing yourself to it as a way of life – job-experience, even part-time or 'casual', is of enormous use and can often mean the difference between burning one's boats and then regretting it or forging ahead secure in the knowledge that the restaurant trade is definitely the one for you. In the meantime, sit down and have a good think: 'Do I, in all honesty, really believe that I have the necessary flair, or even just some flair, for a job like this? Or do I really not like people very much, or working weekends, or working possibly seven days a week, or having to be pleasant to people at a time when I least feel like it?' Flair for the business includes all these things and an awful lot more. I hope much of this will become apparent during the rest of this book.

If your answer has been an emphatic 'no' to all the questions I have posed, then (much as it goes against the grain) I suggest you shut this book, put it back on the shelf and forget all about a career in the catering trade. But I hope you will want to go on.

Capability

Capability is, perhaps, easier to define than flair, for you can be capable in a great many jobs, and if you are, there is little reason why you should not be capable in the catering business. Because capability, I believe, is largely a matter of the 'nuts and bolts'.

Later on, you will find whole chunks of this book devoted to the awfulness (or the pleasure) of administration, paperwork, accounts, budgets, cost control, portion control and a host of other things that will mean long hours for you at a desk in an office and not in the kitchen or in the dining-room. There is no way you will be able to avoid these hours and succeed. Indeed, if you do not spend the necessary hours at the necessary tasks, you will most certainly fail, for in this day and age, sad to say, the problems of running your own business, especially the catering business with its constantly multiplying rules and regulations (whatever the politicians may say!), will rapidly become all too obvious.

You can therefore have flair for catering but, without the sort of capability I have just mentioned, it will be set at nought. Of course, to encourage you, it works to a certain extent the other way round – though not perhaps as much as you would like to think. It is a simple fact of life that good business men or women can run anything, including a very successful restaurant, and make money, sometimes quite a lot of money, at it. The success or failure of a catering establishment has, alas, very little to do with one's ability to wield a wooden spoon in a saucepan or being charming and deft in a dining-room.

Anyone in the trade knows all too many (often *very* many too many) business people who run restaurants and make more money at it than they perhaps deserve, yet have hardly ever been into a kitchen, let alone know what a *bain-marie* is. But you may console yourself that these places are often pretty soulless, more often than not they are part of a 'chain', and, anyway, that is not the sort of place you want to run, is it? But it could also be said that, whereas you will never run a great restaurant on business acumen alone – it takes flair to do that, you can at least hire some of the business acumen you will need, in the shape of lawyers, accountants and so on, though it may cost you more than you expect. Some form of business capability, therefore, has to be learned by the ignorant – at least enough for them to see the pitfalls before they occur, or to know when, and in good time, to get expert help and guidance. But this learning process is not all that difficult: a great many agencies, both governmental and local, now exist to help, and very useful they are too. But we shall deal with that aspect later.

So to sum up on capability, remember, it is something which, for the most part, you can learn. You cannot, I believe, learn flair. You can take, perhaps, some comfort from that.

Toughness

To be tough in the catering business does not mean that you have to be a 'bouncer' in the night club sense. Nor does it necessarily mean, as I mentioned earlier, that you have to be physically fit, though that helps. No, toughness in catering is more a trait of personality – determination, if you like, to stick to an idea or a plan of campaign and have the courage to see it through. 'Pig-headedness' is a dangerous word to use, because it tends to connote stupidity and blindness in the face of clear evidence that you are wrong. I do not mean any such thing. What I do mean is, do not be swayed by what everyone tells you you ought to do – remember, it is your money and skill and judgement involved, not theirs. It has to do with being the sort of person you are.

If you set up a restaurant of any sort, and you plan your menus, and you decide the sort of place you want to run and the type of clientele you want, there will always be someone – probably an acquaintance or even a close friend – who will come along and tell you (in the strictest confidence, of course) what you *should* be doing. The advice is, naturally, well meant. You would do well to heed it – by that, however, I mean certainly listen to it. Advice, whether it is informed or even uninformed, is always worth listening to, but in the catering trade you will get a lot more advice than you need – and, although you must always listen to what people say, it takes toughness to ignore it.

It also takes toughness, very often, to take it all in, think about it and then accept the really important piece of information that is worth bearing in mind. I say this advisedly: whenever, or whatever, people – friends, acquaintances or just casual customers – say, it is *always* worth listening to; there is always a grain of truth in it. You would be ill-advised to dismiss it out of hand, even if you do not, immediately, take it to heart and put it into practice. Indeed, you must be tough enough *not* to put it into practice, either at once or ever. Just bear it in mind, think about it, store it away, think about it again and then act on it – but only if you, yourself, actually and truly believe in it.

Now I seem to have laboured this point, and I can hear you saying, somewhat restively, how many more times, and in how many other different ways, is he going to go on about it? I make no apology. I shall probably refer to it again, and I shall certainly refer to the absolute necessity of seeking advice not only from ordinary people but also from experts, people in the same business. And (here I go again) having the toughness to decide which bit is right for you and what is irrelevant.

You are about to become your own master: you might fail, it is true, because you were too pig-headed to heed good advice while accepting bad – but you will never prosper if you chop and change and cannot make up your own mind. It is going to be *your* restaurant, not a mixture of other people's.

Luck

How do we assure that luck will look on us kindly? The simple answer is that we cannot, no more than anyone else can. But what we may be able to do is to try to ensure that luck is encouraged as far as possible. For no matter how 'lucky' you may feel you are, as a person, it will never, ever appear to favour you in business if you just leave everything to such fickle chance. That is fairly obvious, I know, but opportunity (another name, perhaps, for luck) can be encouraged by good homework, good research, careful preparation and meticulous planning. Having mastered, so far as possible, these details (actually they are massive details, all of them), fortune may smile on you, give a helping hand, and you will not only deserve it, but be in an excellent position to make the best use of it.

I shall spend some time and space in the next chapters on research and planning, but bear in mind throughout this book that, although luck is mentioned in particular only here, it is lying about waiting for you to pick it up, dust if off and reap some of the benefits. 'Opportunism' is yet another name for it, really. The ability to recognize something as being there, available for the asking if only we can capitalize on it. Some people, it is said, are 'born opportunists'. In fact, they are the people who see the main chance and take it – you must do the same. But no one can ever actually 'grab a chance' without being in a position, first, to see it and then have the time and ability to make use of it.

Capital

Thus we come to perhaps the trickiest, the thorniest problem of all. It is a problem that will never leave you alone in your early days as a restaurateur and, however successful you become, will still be discussed, agonized over, thought about. It is the problem of capital, the last point of our five that we must now consider. It has been said, and with doubtless good reason:

You can never have enough capital.

Later on, we shall discuss this in great detail but for the moment this may be another reason for shutting this book and forgetting all about the whole project; without capital, either your own or someone else's, be it a bank's or funding from another source, you will inevitably fail. The 'generation' of money in the catering trade is notoriously slow and subject to vagaries of which you could, at this stage, have no idea. However meticulously planned your new operation is, however well thought-out in terms of cash-flow forecasts, spend-per-head, overall costs, fixed head costs, profit margins and so on, the idea of putting up, say, as an example, £100 and reckoning you will have got back £150 in one month's time when the first bills become due means that you are living in a Cloud-cuckoo-land so profound that you must abandon hope from this moment. Whatever the paperwork may say to the contrary, it simply is not going to happen! For a start, by the end of the month, I can guarantee there will be more bills coming in than you first thought, more problems which need money in their solution. I am not being gloomy. I am being very practical.

So let us leave the subject for now – after all, why blight your life so early in the proceedings? But remember the warning above: capital is going to occupy an enormous amount of your time and effort. Better be prepared to take the unwholesome medicine now – there will be no more bitter a pill than this that you will have to swallow! And one final barb: if you have plenty of capital, remember pundits greater than I who say: few people would be foolish enough to invest money in the catering trade; there are much better (and certainly easier) ways of using your money than this.

*

It occurs to me that a somewhat gloomy view has emerged from the very start of this chapter, and I should be, and indeed am, sorry about that. But you could be embarking on an absolutely hare-brained scheme, and if what I have written so far has put you off or put serious doubts in your mind, perhaps you are not the sort of person who should go into the restaurant business in the first place. But it could be that I have whetted your appetite, caused you to say, 'It just cannot be as *bad* as all that.' In that case, so be it: welcome to a super way of life, a lot of fun and an experience you would not miss for all the world!

2 First Steps

One can learn to cook but a restaurateur is born.
                                        Brillat-Savarin

The highly questionable aphorism at the top of this chapter, from a man whose sayings and actions were for the most part very far from being questionable in any way, could well have been a despairing wail at the British catering trade. I believe that a good restaurateur can become good even though he is far from being born to it – but it takes an enormous amount of self-criticism and study, not to mention a degree of intelligence not necessarily found in other trades. I do not mean that all good restaurateurs are, or need to be, candidates for a Brain of Britain quiz (though it could well help) or that they are any more intelligent than any other successful business man or woman – just that the degree of intelligence is a special one devoted to studying the needs and likings of your fellow creatures (customers, you hope).

Alas, not all restaurateurs understand this, and few practise it. But you are going to be a good one, a *better* one, so let us look first at the special attributes you will need.

Start As You Mean To Go On
In the first chapter I mentioned the absolute importance of defining what you want to do and what you think you would be good at. It is no good at all thinking great thoughts of building massively impressive classic menus when your only experience of eating out is the local hamburger bar or, on a special occasion, a steak house. Not that you cannot acquire over a long period of intensive study and practice the necessary skills for a classic menu, but it would be foolish, I would suggest, to start out with such an intention when you lack everything to achieve it.

21

In this connection, therefore, it is important that you start as you mean to go on: you *must* decide from the word 'go' what you intend to do, and you must decide to stick to it. You cannot, and must not, open, say, a fish-and-chip shop with a few seats in it and then expect it, magically, to develop into a high-class fish restaurant serving fresh turbot and lobster instead of cod and chips. The 'image' you created in the first place is going to take years to eradicate, whether your fish-and-chip shop succeeds or fails. This precept applies to everything you do.

It may seem rather curious, at first sight, that you cannot change a business gradually. Well, you can, if you are very skilful and the change is very gradual, but I am afraid that it sounds very much easier than it actually is. *Development* along natural lines is one thing, *change* is something quite different: it gives a bad name to a place which already has some reputation in so far as you lose old customers while taking a long time to attract new ones. Hence the absolute importance of deciding what you intend to do, and then sticking to it.

This decision is the first and possibly the most important decision you must make. The British customer of any eating-place is among the most conservative animals ever evolved – he or she is bedevilled by 'class', by preferences for one type of food or another, by one type of service, décor, 'image'. The customer simply cannot imagine, or feel comfortable in, anything that he or she does not expect in advance. Why, I do not know – if all restaurateurs knew the answer to that question and could translate it into action in a practical way, there would be very many more rich caterers than there are today. It is, sadly, a fact of life, and you would do well to believe it from the outset.

Therefore we have established that development is good, change bad. Once again, it is a question of starting as you mean to go on. And having decided what it is you are going to do, what *exactly* you are going to do, the *type* of food you are going to serve, the *type* of place you want to open, you can move on to the whole, exciting (and at times, admittedly, depressing) next stage of finding the right property. But one last warning: remember – do not over-reach yourself: stick to what you know about and think you can cope with. I have said that a number of times, and I make no apology for saying it again.

Decision-Making

To buy that restaurant of your dreams? To open one from scratch? To take a partner – either your spouse or a friend or a business person of your acquaintance? To employ a chef or do the cooking yourself? There are simply dozens of questions you will need to answer. And on top of all of those, there is the thorniest problem of all, which you will remember from Chapter 1 – finance. Capital. In other words: money.

At the moment let us assume that you are not totally stupid about finance, that you have some sort of idea how much you can raise yourself, how much you may be worth; some 'target'.

But there is a good reason why we should leave money to a later section: the search for a suitable property often leads to ideas about 'bending', or juggling with, the money you do have. It is too self-limiting to have very strict, rigid ideas about finance before you have been out and about in the market-place, both property and financial, to see what is there. You will find you can stretch money in various ways to go round, to encompass what you wish to achieve. Let us take an example or two.

To buy or rent the property of your dreams? To 'live over the shop' or look for a lock-up? It is obvious that from the start the money available can be used in different ways, 'stretched', if you like.

Perhaps the most extreme example of this would be to remain where you live, in your present house, flat, and buy, somewhere in the neighbourhood, the sort of thriving business you have always wanted. This course is obviously going to cost you a whole lot more money than 'selling up', going somewhere else and living 'over the shop'. On the other hand, the fact that you will still own your own house (and, however badly you may do financially in your new business, it will still retain some worth if you have to sell up) could well mean that at the very least a roof over your head is secure.

For those with enough capital, or with sufficient collateral and 'free' money of their own, this may well be the best course: the initial outlay will be very considerable but the immediate-future expenses will be very much less. And if you are buying an established business there is possibly very much less risk, unless you have been very foolish. Even then, you would do well to carry out a bit of research first, because, however much money you have or however little, to hazard any of it is hardly the best way of starting off any enterprise. This whole question of 'research' is fascinating, time-consuming and wholly essential.

There is an old-established military rule which states: 'Time spent in reconnaissance is seldom wasted.' There is more than a grain of truth in it: the phrase is *completely* true – whether you are about to fight a battle or set up a restaurant venture, whether you are saving lives or money. Reconnaissance, or research, call it what you will, is going to do two things for you: in the first place it is going to help you decide what exactly you want to do and what you can afford, and in the second place it is going to increase your knowledge and experience.

However, perhaps it would be better to set out some parameters first.

What Do I Want?

To start with: where? Have you a very defined area in which you intend to search or can you go anywhere, following your own wishes and ideas on where it would be nice to live and work?

Within reason, setting up a restaurant, especially if you are going to 'live over the shop', gives you enormous freedom. No longer are you going to be tied to someone else's factory, office or shop, but to your own – and your own, subject to family ties, *can* be anywhere.

Many would-be caterers have always dreamed of certain areas – perhaps where they have been on holiday or on business, or just thought they might like to live and work with a friend or family. There is nothing wrong with this; it is an unadventurous man or woman who has not had such dreams, and many put them into practice, often very successfully. But dreams do not, on the whole, make money, and this is where reconnaissance comes in – whether it is for a place 'just round the corner' or much further afield. In either case, it is essential to get 'out and about', and the money you are going to have to spend on this research will never be a bad investment, however time-consuming or depressing it may prove to be.

Let us first consider the buying, or the leasing, of a catering business already established. We shall look at the problems involved in starting a completely new restaurant in Chapter 4.

Do not be put off by the idea of leasing, which we shall consider in greater detail later. Remember, a great many good restaurant sites are in popular shopping streets in towns and villages throughout the country, and these tend to be leasehold rather than freehold. This is no bad thing, providing the terms are attractive, and, more often than you might at first think, sites exist with very low premiums attached to them by the landlords and with very reasonable prices asked by the incumbents.

So, having decided on one or two areas, get down there and literally 'trawl' through the whole place – go to every estate agent and business agent there is, read every advertisement you can find in both trade and local papers, journals and magazines – including the 'freebies' which are so much a part of publishing life nowadays. Visit as many restaurants, cafés, pubs as you can. This will increase your knowledge, magically, of the locality and its advantages and problems, its attractions and drawbacks, and will also increase your knowledge of the catering trade if you are observant enough – two slabs of research in one! Do not, ever, be afraid of saying, 'No, this area is not for me.' Just go on to another one. Whatever you do, 'Keep at it.'

At some time, sooner or later, you will come across, even stumble on accidentally, a property which attracts you. It will not necessarily be the sort of place you had in mind when you set out. Again, do not be worried about changing your mind – after all, you would never have known of such a place if you had not set out to find something there in the first instance. I am not saying you have to change your mind; I am not saying that single-mindedness and determination to find exactly the place you wanted originally is a bad thing, far from it. But much of life is compromise, and what matters is the place's appeal to you and to no one else. Take no notice of the inevitable remarks that will be made if you do come back with a sort of establishment different from the one you intended when you set out. Once again, it is going to be *your* money and *your* life, not those of your critics.

My wife and I set out to buy a hotel in Scotland, we ended up by buying a huge house and converting it. Sometime later we decided to move back to the south of England. The last thing we ever wanted was a pub, yet we found ourselves eventually setting up our new restaurant in just such a place. In both instances, the attractions of the area and our new ideas succeeded in changing our minds.

'And Why Are You Selling?'

So, having found the sort of place which appeals to you, what next? 'More research' is the answer.

Why is that particular establishment up for grabs? That is question number one. Do not let that question out of your mind for an instant.

Perhaps a pleasant, but insistent, cynicism is the correct attitude. Everyone trying to sell something is going to paint a rosier picture of it than the one that exists. We all do it and in so doing are not necessarily venal, dishonest or deliberately misleading. After all, a prospective buyer is pretty keen on the idea even to be there in the first place; if he knows anything about hunting for a restaurant, he should have done some homework beforehand, even down to having had a meal or a drink there more than once!

The asking price, assuming you know it, should be a good enough guide to whether the business being sold is on the way down or up. Other enquiries in the area, comparing like with like, will give any prospective buyer a very good idea of the 'going rate' for most businesses. Similar rules apply for private property as well; there is no special formula for one or the other. But beware of businesses which are running, or have run, down.

Now, I am the first person very seriously to encourage others to consider run-down businesses. There are a number of advantages: they will be cheaper than those which are successful; they often give you, the new buyer, a lot more scope to do what you have in mind with them, rather than have someone else's success imposed upon you from the start, and you will not be handcuffed to a whole lot of customers who will see every change you make as a change for the worse, encouraging each other to say, 'This is not the way old so-and-so did it before you came along!' This will be said anyway – and it will take toughness to ignore it, but you can always take comfort by saying in return, quite politely, 'But I'm not old so-and-so. It's *my* business now, and I'm just different!'

But be careful just how run down the business is, and remember, it is a sad fact of life that taking over a bad reputation is far, far worse than taking over no reputation at all. It can take years to overcome in people's minds, just as a business that is always changing hands so very often proves a graveyard for all those that follow, be they ever so hopeful, efficient and skilled. A little 'historical' research never comes amiss.

Good reasons for an ailing business to be looked at seriously are numerous, but some are worth mentioning here.

Increasing age of the present owners, if they have been there some time, along with a possible lack of children to 'take over', is very often a quite genuine cause of giving up. In many instances their lease may be coming towards an end, and a new lease may be negotiated favourably with landlords; or, if there is plenty of lease left to run, an elderly couple may wish to get rid of the place while their lease still has some value. In any case, the value of the business will have been depressed if trade has been slipping for some time, and this will show in the asking-price. Older people very often want less hassle than younger ones; they may be keen to retire, get rid of what has become a burden to them without too much fuss. Local enquiries in any area will reveal the truth about such a situation quite quickly.

Marital disharmony is a very common cause of places being put up for sale. It is often that restaurants, pubs and hotels provide customers for lawyers and the divorce courts quicker than they provide customers for their owners. Again, judicious local enquiries and quite simply 'nosing about' will often reveal this, if you do not spot it for yourself soon enough.

If you come across any establishment in which partners operate, and by this I mean two families or married couples who went into the business together, two men or two women, again disharmony is almost certainly the cause for pulling out. In the licensed trade, for instance, the brewery representatives will always tell you gloomily that such partnerships are doomed to failure – it is inevitable, merely a matter of just how long they hang together, not whether they will or not. This may, perhaps, be rather a cynical view, but I am afraid it is based on solid knowledge and years of experience. Very often one partner buys the other one out, but the actual business will always suffer, along with its trade. Customers in any establishment are quick to sense uncomfortable 'vibes' between partners and feel they are intruding into people's private affairs – so they stay away, more and more of them. It is very rare that the partner, or partners, who remain as sole owners will stay very long – the damage has been done, and everyone knows it.

Sheer lack of suitability to the trade, exhaustion and depression by reason of character or temperament are yet another reason for putting the 'For Sale' notices up.

A great many well-meaning people go into the catering trade to find eventually that it is far too exhausting, or too full of problems, or just simply unattractive to them. There is nothing wrong with that – all sorts of people 'have a go', and I, for one, would award them nothing but praise. After all, it is better to have tried and failed than never to have tried at all. The world is full of the 'if onlys' – the people we all have met who keep on saying they should have done something else (even written a book) 'if only' they had had the time or the money or the encouragement or no family. They are full of excuses. Personally I think they deserve little sympathy. They are very often lazy, too content with a 'safe' job and easy hours and always unadventurous. Yes, if you do go into the catering business, you may well fail but, as I said before, the world would be a poorer place, and a lot of great and famous names would have been lost to it. The 'if onlys' would almost certainly fail, but there is no reason to suppose you will, otherwise you would not be reading this book – you are already too far down the road, I hope, to consider anything but success.

So much for some good reasons for buying a certain type of business. How about some bad ones?

3 Research

The science which feeds men is worth at least as much as the science which teaches how to kill them.

Brillat-Savarin

There are far more reasons for *not* buying a business than the other way around – at least, so most people seem to believe. But the initial research that I am so insistent upon will do away with many prejudices and should reveal to you a great many positive facets.

As I said in the last chapter, we shall study in due course the whole question of raising the money you will need, but once you have started your researches in your chosen area, and have possibly found something which interests you, it is often a good idea to make your way to the nearest bank and ask for an appointment with the manager.

Now, I know that in Britain the local bank manager is rarely acknowledged or famed as a gourmet – unlike his opposite number in France. As a matter of interest, whenever my wife and I are in France and completely ignorant of an area, we always ask the local bank manager, or one of his cashiers, where the best place to eat is. They always know. But to continue: the local manager in Britain may not know a lot about food, but he almost certainly knows an awful lot about local business. He might even know very well the actual business you are enquiring about (it may be a customer's) and, although he will obviously not divulge any confidential information, he can be a tower of strength to you as a stranger.

There is no need to go to a branch of your own bank – any will do, and our experience is that a local manager is only too pleased to help. In the final instance, just before you leave, ask him if he, as a banker, would lend you money on the place you are enquiring about. If he says no, on the whole leave it alone. He may be right, he may be wrong, but if he will not lend money, it is almost a dead cert that no other local manager will.

When I have property-hunted, I have always first gone to a local bank. The answers I have received have either put me off completely or made me very keen indeed. So far as I know, the information has been absolutely right in every case. Local bank managers for the most part get the 'feel' of a place and the properties in it; they do not need to know a particular one to pass on useful information to you.

Town or Country?
Of course, a great many people who want to go into the catering trade often dream, as I mentioned earlier, of far-away places, deep in the country, perhaps in some lovely 'olde worlde' village. No reason why not, but beware of what I call 'the green wellie syndrome'. The picture of life in the country so often painted by those chic women columnists in the better Sunday papers and in the classier magazines are not, actually, very true. Those word-pictures may be true to them, perhaps, but for the most part they are 'weekenders', unused to the real business of living all the year round away from towns, buses, taxis, garages, Underground systems and the like. Life, real, everyday life, throughout the year in the country is quite, quite different from what townspeople believe, however much they think they know, or romanticize.

It is very difficult, of course, to persuade people about this before they have learned it, often the hard way. I am a Londoner, born and bred, yet have lived so long away from London (often in very remote areas of Britain) that I know that, if I went back to London or any other big city to run a restaurant, I would very quickly become extremely unhappy and very bad-tempered. I would also take it out on my customers, which would not be good for trade! The point is that the over-crowding, the pace of life, the difficulty of transport, parking and so on would very soon take its toll. Some people would find this exhilarating; some people would not change it for the world. I would find it acutely depressing, and I also find life in cities stultifyingly boring, compared with that of the country. So, if someone like me finds cities boring, just think how townspeople may react to the country!

Even country towns are different, certainly those picturesque 'postcard' ones with graceful churches, cathedrals or abbeys, filled with antique shops and tea-rooms. They are quite, quite different from the great conurbations and life in them can be a 'ball-game' very different from that of industrial towns, even of a similar size.

In my own local country town, yes, certainly picturesque, there are many catering-places, ranging from fish-and-chip shops, tea rooms, cafés and so on to a considerable variety of pubs and one or two expensive hotels. In a place like that, everyone knows everyone else's business. One or two are constantly changing hands, one or two are so 'snobby' that local people, however well-heeled, find them irritating – they are for tourists only. Like most others in 'the trade', I know almost at once which is up for sale, which is not doing too well, which is prospering. But if I were in a big city, or a different type of town, I would certainly not have the 'inside information' which I have now. People in such areas are far too busy minding their own shop to know very much about other people's. You, as an individual, may like it that way, but if you do, the countryside, town, village or wherever, is certainly not for you, for it would irritate very quickly, and the catering trade has too many irritations to add others which you can best avoid if possible from the start.

Now all this comes under research, initial decisions to be made by you alone, after a very considerable amount of cogitation and soul-searching. Only you can make such a decision and, having made it, set out to do something about it.

Location Research

So, then, we have already got somewhere. You have decided the sort of area you would like to live and work in. To this must be added a very great amount of extra work. Say you want to stay away from the bigger cities, even then some matters are very important.

It is one of the great truisms of the trade that Conrad Hilton, when asked for the three most important factors for success, said, 'Location, location and location.' That was many years ago, before the motor car changed the face of society, along with other forms of easy access and travel.

But Charles Forte, when deciding to set up his first milk bar (and a subsequent one) stood in the street outside the premises he wanted and counted, literally, the people who walked by at particular times. He studied the sort of people they were and where they worked, and he looked at other catering places in the immediate vicinity. He spent a very long time doing just that, and he put his finger unerringly on a gap in the market – there was no place where the ordinary office-worker could nip out and get himself something to eat in a clean, decent place at a very reasonable cost. Naturally enough, everyone told him he was crazy, and they went on telling him even when he opened the second one. I often wonder if anyone tells him that now.

Having decided on your area, take a look at the map, ask at the public library about local populations, catchment areas, if you are unsure. Study the *sort* of people who live there, in the immediate vicinity, in nearby areas. Study traffic flow, look at buses, trains or any other form of transport or undertaking which might affect you and your possible trade. Take a wander around a local car-park or two – is it full of Range Rovers and Volvo Estates or is it full of clapped-out old Fords with pink dollies hanging in the windows? I am not putting down one or the other – both sorts of owners have a certain amount of money to spend, but is it the sort of money you want to attract and know how to deal with?

Next, remember estate agents – I have already mentioned them, but in a research context they are useful for another reason: they put 'For Sale' boards outside private properties. Are there a lot of those signs? Are there streets full of them? If so, why? Always ask why, why, why. A great number of 'For Sale' signs can mean that the area is becoming depressed or a new by-pass is to be built in the immediate vicinity. Perhaps a major employer, a factory say, may close. The local paper will almost certainly tell you about that.

Within the catchment areas which may affect you, especially if you want to set up in the country but near a large town, spend some time looking at local businesses. As an example, are there branches of, say, Marks & Spencer, Safeways, Tescos, Boots? If there are, remember that the operators of big stores like those are smart cookies – they have already done *their* homework, and if you are clever, you will realize they have done a lot of homework for you too.

As an example, I remember not so long ago wanting to run a

restaurant in a village near quite a large town. Some years beforehand, the main industry of that town had collapsed but another industry, completely different, had risen. It had attracted a skilled workforce, earning good money. Then Government 'cut-backs' in defence contracts, coupled with high inflation and a poor national economy, threatened this new industry too. The outlook was gloomy, to say the least. Inevitably there were rumours of the railway's being closed (there are *always* rumours like that!). Yet what actually happened? Not only did one or two of the big retailers I have already mentioned enlarge their premises but others came along too, opening huge new shops. A new precinct was built, enormous new car-parks were provided alongside.

Why? You might well think that the big operators were reckless gamblers, but that is the last thing they would be, especially if they have shareholders. No, their massive, painstaking researches – very much greater and more thorough than anything an ordinary individual could undertake – had led them to believe that all was not as gloomy as many people thought, and they leapt in, seized their chance when land values were depressed and quite rightly are now reaping their rewards. Remember what I said in Chapter 1 about opportunism, or, as I called it, luck?

Finally, there are your competitors. Take a look at them.

It has been said by a great many restaurateurs of note and success that a restaurant without competition is simply not in the right place. Now I confess that I do not know why this is, but I do know it is right. I suppose it should not be all that surprising – after all, those huge retail chains I mentioned above more than once must in all honesty feel that competition is better than none, otherwise they would not be there, often literally side by side on the same street or in the same shopping precinct.

I am not, however, suggesting that you tempt fate too much.

There are peculiarities in the catering trade which may well make it foolish to have similar restaurants too close together, but to believe, as many people do, that you can set up, miles from any other restaurant, a place of your own and expect people to beat a path to your door is unwise, to say the least. Not that such a course is *always* silly – I can think of a number of eating-places, with or without hotels attached to them, where no one in their right mind would choose to set up shop, yet they have prospered. This is particularly true in the north and Highlands of Scotland, where some famous places seem to do very well and achieve accolades: their very remoteness actually becomes the attraction! But be careful about this; your researches will have warned you about 'seasonal' places – they appeal to some caterers (a nice long winter off) but not to everyone if only because of the problems of keeping afloat, so to speak, during long winters, with money going out and none coming in.

I suppose the supreme problem is that the British public are extraordinarily fickle in their tastes, habits, fads and fancies. Why, exactly why, one place succeeds and another fails is unbelievably difficult to define. You simply have to hope that you have done your homework properly and got the formula right. At least you are not alone – everyone in the trade hopes they have, as well.

4 Pros and Cons

The pleasant hours of our life are all connected, by a more or less intangible link, with some memory of the table.

Monselet

Your Work Book

We have spent some time considering the whole question of preliminary research, or reconnaissance, but before continuing, your attention should be drawn to the importance of using a notebook. Get into the habit of carrying one with you. I have what I call 'work books' dating back years and years, and very good and amusing reading they often make. They also serve a practical purpose: unless you are blessed with a superhuman memory, they do far more than jog your senses; they act as a present record and a future reference as to what you intended to do, or thought was a good idea at the time or simply did not carry out at that moment, for reasons which should also have been recorded. The first 'work book' is merely the precursor of the endless lists I shall shortly be urging upon you.

Many people, it is true, do not bother with work books, nor do they bother over-much with lists. I think that is wrong, and I also think it foolish. I believe it is important to be as ordered as possible: it makes for being a better restaurateur and also for a much easier time all round. On top of that, I shall also urge upon you in Chapter 15 the necessity of blackboards – but putting into your mind the whole idea of a work book suffices for the moment. If you adopt my idea, you will discover fairly rapidly how useful the book is – into it will go not only the properties and various details you have seen or noticed as you have been out and about but also all your ideas and the many questions you forgot to ask, or those questions which later occur to you as important.

There are some in the catering trade whom I have met who have been openly disdainful, or faintly amused, at the whole idea of a work book. So be it. They are different people, and perhaps their own system (if they have any system at all, which I doubt) is better than mine. I have, however, noticed how unobservant such people are (you will meet many such in this business), and I have reached the conclusion that they wished they had thought of the idea but were too dishonest to admit it. Certainly, others have praised the concept.

Pros and Cons
So, armed with your new work book, filled already as it is with notes and queries, you may well have come across the sort of property which interests you. I know it has been a tedious, exhausting but often hilarious business, but never fear, if you are determined upon the whole idea, you will find just such a property eventually – and I say 'eventually' with wisdom. It can take months, but never, never be tempted into something of which you are not one hundred per cent sure.

Although *excessive* caution is not desirable in every case – if it were so, few of us would ever actually do anything practical or concrete, especially when it comes to buying a property, moving house, changing jobs and so on – there are quite a few checks yet to be made, a lot more questions to ask. And, it has to be admitted, these could still lead to disappointment and the resumption of the search.

Let us leave aside, for a moment, the obvious questions of legal acceptability; we shall come to that later. I mean the checks you can make yourself, and only you.

'Research' and 'observation' are both words I constantly use. Well, the same words have to be born in mind once more.

Is the place right from a practical point of view? That is question number one – and if it is not, start looking again.

'Practicality' embraces all manner of things. If you fail to consider it dispassionately, you can be in for a very expensive shock.

Accessibility
In the first place, take a close look at the actual position of your new-found property.

If it is in a town, are there double-yellow parking lines outside it? A catering place very often stands or falls just on this point. No matter how picturesque, no matter just how 'right' the place seems, looks and feels to you, double-yellow lines are an instant drawback.

Now I know some places where it does not seem to matter, where it does not seem to affect business. For instance, in a busy town, full of tourists in the summer and with a large office block nearby, a café-cum-tea-room, with a 'take-away' facility, may not suffer at all, even less so if there is a big car-park not too far away and the premises are on a main street, easily spotted by someone going by in a car. Indeed, I know of just such a place in a country town not far from where I live. It is a very successful business indeed, but I suspect only for day-time trading. For the fact remains that there are double-yellow lines outside and, although this seems to have little effect during the working day, 'after hours' you still cannot stop a car there, and people out for the evening are just not going to walk back 200 or 300 yards having parked their car.

So, once again, define what you are going to do, the sort of place you are going to run, and having decided that, look at all the circumstances which can effect it.

Let's consider one or two further examples, all of them existing in towns I know.

Some very nice premises (converted and decorated to the highest standards, just off a very busy trunk road through an historic town, overlooking the main road at a slight angle, and adjacent to a very pleasant open area with lovely houses, offices, shops and residences for a public school) are constantly changing hands. They have been sold at least three times in about five years. Each subsequent owner has made slight alterations; one even changed the name, and a recent one catered in a very 'up-market' way, with excellent food and service. Why do they never seem to 'make a go' of the property? I think I know.

It is true that the property has a car-park and that the facility is well advertised – but the car-park is miniscule, taking only about four vehicles for a seating-area in the restaurant for about thirty people. Visitors are often told that they can park, in the evenings, in the car-park of a nearby public building, but it does not seem to matter: owners of the restaurant still seem to come and go, because the customer tends to stay away – the fact remaining that, whereas motorists will park in the street when permitted to do so, they do not like the idea of parking on someone else's property, even if it does belong to a public utility, especially in small country towns. Needless to say, outside and all around this particular restaurant there are double-yellow lines.

Now, I am not saying the successive owners were foolish to buy such a place; it is just that I, personally, would not do so. To run a successful restaurant, you simply have to make it as attractive as possible to the customer, in every single way. Just one obstacle and that customer is likely to be off to your competitor, however good you are at your own job.

Take another example, again in an ancient country town. No double-yellow lines this time, only single ones – but a very narrow street. Yes, you can park there in the evenings, but people out to spend a relaxed evening, and quite a lot of money, are not overkeen on leaving their (perhaps expensive) motor car in a narrow street which serves two-way traffic in a town's busy through-route.

There is another disadvantage too. This restaurant is situated in a delightful courtyard, standing back through an archway from the pavement. It is very difficult to spot if you are a stranger and do not know the area, and because parking is not permitted in the street during working hours and there is no car-park anywhere near enough to make it attractive, this particular restaurant caters largely for local townsfolk, mainly the elderly, who can walk there. But the town has a number of such establishments and is too small to have all that number of 'specialized' clientele available. A question of 'catchment area' again, very local this time.

Finally, one more nail in the coffin, a psychological one this time, and most curious: the restaurant is on the first floor.

Quite why such a factor makes so much difference to the success or failure of some operations is not fully known, but it does. For some odd reason people often do not mind going *downstairs* to eat, sometimes through a door immediately off the pavement, but they simply will not go upstairs. In the case of this particular place I have in mind, the reason for its continuing difficulties – again, a constant change of ownership and type of food – is not so much that most of the customers it does have available are elderly, are often carrying shopping-bags and therefore find a flight of stairs daunting, but simply the psychological barrier of having to go up some stairs. I have asked a number of psychologists for an answer to this, but it seems to puzzle them as much as it does me – and the rest of the trade.

Of course, some of these factors – yellow lines, parking and so on (but not the problem of the stairs) – are less serious in big cities and towns. It all has to do with the size of the 'catchment area'. Obviously, people who live in large conurbations are more used to such problems, and there are certainly more people, anyway, more choice of customer. Public transport is often available too, and walking some distance a perfectly normal thing. You just cannot apply one set of principles in one place to a completely different place. Odd, I know.

Again, yet another set of principles applies in villages or remoter areas. People are even less likely to walk anywhere here, unless they are hikers or the countryside attracts ramblers and holidaymakers in sufficient quantity who enjoy strolling from a holiday let, caravan park or something similar. Parking is essential, and preferably on your own ground or at least in an area of public ground which is sufficiently large so as not to cause problems to anyone – certainly not complaints of bad parking, noise and so on. Customers with cars are curious: they like to feel safe and secure in themselves when they come into your restaurant, but they also like to feel that their vehicles are too. And nothing is going to get you a bad name locally quicker than complaints from other landowners, neighbours and so on about bad parking or noise (even if it is not directly your fault). In fact, the British countryside is notoriously full of very tetchy people, and if you are to live among them pleasantly and happily (and, you hope, attract them as customers too), you are going to need an expertise in public relations which even Saatchi & Saatchi would envy.

Hidden Extras
As I said before, beware of 'the green wellie syndrome'. There are other problems as well.

Some years ago my wife and I were very much attracted to a property deep in the country and seemingly ideal as an out-of-the way restaurant. The catchment area was good; although it was well 'off the beaten track', the lanes were wide

and without awful blind bends; the surroundings were particularly beautiful, and the building itself, a private house, was very
easily convertible to the sort of operation we envisaged.
Planning-permission for change of use did not seem to be a
terrible problem, as a polite phone call to the local council
indicated. To add to the allure, there was a well-kept tennis court
and room for another, along with a swimming-pool and very
beautiful grounds, with a spacious terrace outside. In our mind's
eye, we could see our customers crowding the outside tables on
fine summer evenings, having enjoyed their swim or tennis. The
only problem was going to be the money.

Nevertheless, we were uneasy. It seemed *too* perfect for the
price. A careful recce of the surroundings seemed in order. The
'snag' very soon manifested itself. Virtually surrounding the
property was a huge dairy farm. Idyllic, even better, the green
wellie brigade might say. But we knew that dairy farms mean
silage pits, and the huge silage pits we discovered lay just beyond
the boundaries of the tennis courts, swimming-pool and terrace.

Dining *outside*? You would not even be able to have guests
inside once that silage pit was opened. There would be no escape
from such a nuclear holocaust of a smell.

No wonder the owners of the property we so much liked
wanted to get rid of it.

Officialdom
Whether your ideal place is in town or country, however, certain
things will be common as to its suitability. Unless you are made
of money, construction work is prohibitively expensive and you
would do well to bear in mind that the sooner you can 'set up
shop', the sooner some money will come in and the sooner your
name will get around. Therefore try to choose a place which has
certain basic things: an adequate dining-area is one, an adequate
kitchen is another. Storage space too is important, as well as
easy access (for both customers and goods). If the place is a
going concern, Health and Fire Regulations may already be
satisfied, but be careful about this – there may be a list as long as
your arm (and costing an arm and a leg) waiting to be done.
Failure to comply with the many regulations which will affect
you is one of the main reasons for people wanting to sell, often
quickly – they just cannot afford to pay for the demands being
made.

If it is to be a new venture, in a property not hitherto used as a restaurant, you are into all sorts of other problems. And the very first thing you have to do is to ring, or preferably call in to see, the planning officer or one of his assistants.

Planners live in County Hall, as the Americans say, and they, and the planning committee which is meant to watch over them, have the main say as to whether you can change the use of a property from one sort of thing to another.

In some areas, you will remember, I said that there is unlikely to be much opposition to change of use. In others, mainly residential, in a conservation area or just simply 'very rural' by nature, there could be much trouble if, for instance, the planning department either gave an emphatic 'no' to your first query or seemed just a bit uncertain.

It is rare that planning officers are overruled by their would-be mentors, the planning committee (and vice versa), and you do have the right of appeal in cases where you feel they are all wrong. But this is a long, expensive and complex process, and by the time an inspector is appointed to hear your case, you will be old and grey and probably have gone off the whole idea anyway.

In the main, the local government officers are reasonable, polite and helpful. You will undoubtedly come up against one or two whom you (among a great many other people who have had dealings with such a person in the past) would gladly throttle, but that is a fact of life wherever you go. It is far more practical, therefore, to approach your local planning officer personally and discuss with him what you propose to do. If he seems doubtful, you should talk to your local councillor to sound him or her out. Miracles can happen.

If change-of-use permission is needed, plans will have to be drawn up for any structural alterations. Unless you are skilled at plans, drawings and specifications or are an architect, builder or connected with that trade, you will swiftly find yourself out of your depth. So get hold of a good local builder (by making judicious enquiries in the neighbourhood) and leave it all to him. He may well feel he should bring in an architect if the job warrants it. So be it. Either the builder or the architect, but probably both, will know the planning officer personally. You could well be saving money in the long run by turning over the whole problem and getting on with something else. Remember that building-work is extremely expensive, so get good estimates first. The architect's fee, if not included in the builder's account, will anyway seem small by comparison.

The builder and architect will also know the building control inspector, whom you are bound to meet eventually, although he is concerned less with you personally than with ensuring that work complies structurally with the myriad regulations surrounding building-work in Britain, that the drains are properly laid and run the right way and that the building is not unsafe either to yourself or to the public.

In any event, planning, building and your local builder and architect will be inextricably entwined with environmental health. For the most part, environmental health officers are helpful and understanding. It is their duty to ensure that all catering premises meet certain standards of hygiene, so that the public at large may be the better protected against the hazards of eating therein.

But unlike the planning officer, the building control officer and your own builder and architect, the environmental health officer is going to be with you for the rest of your days, whether you are opening a completely new restaurant or taking over an existing one. (I shall deal with him in Chapter 9.) And even then, you have only just put a single toe into the water when it comes to officialdom.

5 Some Not So Obvious Alternatives

Those who have a profound indifference to the table are generally gloomy, charmless and unamiable.

Lucien Tendret

So far we have considered the search for your ideal and what you can do on your own, without spending money on anything other than the occasional meal or drink in a place which interests you, and in its possible competitors, and on car mileage or over-night stays if you are looking a long way from your present home. There has been no need to use a solicitor or an accountant (though these will be necessary in due course), and your preliminary enquiries of the local planning officer, or environmental health department, providing they have been courteous and reasonable, will have been free. And I have asked that these are kept to a minimum, the enquiries being made *only* when absolutely necessary about a place in which you are truly interested.

But at this point it may be well to mention that there are all sorts of ways to get into the catering trade without necessarily buying or leasing a 'place of your own'.

Let us look at one obvious one and at another which is not so obvious but becoming increasingly popular.

Franchising
Now, it should be said at once that the whole franchise scene is surrounded by pitfalls in many people's minds, and it was certainly true some years back, when it first came into Britain from the USA. A number of very smart operators set up dubious

operations which cost innocent people a lot of money, largely because the ideas that were being peddled were in themselves not good ideas at all from a business view-point: they often cost large sums of money, there was very little back-up in terms of national marketing, advertising and so on, and the franchises were over-sold, in that too many people in any one area were allowed to buy their way in and found themselves in competition with the same franchise schemes locally when they had been promised exclusive rights to one district or centre of population. Since those days, however, matters have dramatically improved.

To find out more about the whole background of franchising schemes, it is better to start with your own bank. Most of the Big Five produce customer packages on franchising, and certainly the Royal Bank of Scotland and the National Westminster Bank are among the best such. You do not, obviously, need to be a customer of one of these banks – the packages are freely available in most branches of any bank.

In addition there is the *Franchise Opportunities Directory*, published by Franchise Concepts Ltd, which is published every six months. You will normally find a copy of this in your local Job Centre, and it is well worth looking at before you contemplate taking out a subscription, as any edition gives you an excellent idea as to whether franchising is right for you.

The first thing you will find surprising is just how many high-street businesses are, in fact, franchised – apart from the host of other ideas which are advertised in your local paper, normally under 'Services'. Some truly 'national' names (such as Little Chef) are franchise operations.

So what, briefly, is a franchise and how does it work?

A franchisor is a company which 'sells' to a franchisee (someone like yourself, perhaps) the right to offer the public a product or service. That 'sale' is in effect a 'down payment' initially and a 'royalty', or share of the turn-over, thereafter. In return, the franchisee agrees to abide by certain standards and operating-procedures – often rigidly laid down – and also to buy his prime products from the franchisor. It actually sounds more complicated than it is.

There are a great many advantages in being a franchisee – or franchise-holder, to cut the jargon.

In the first place, you often have a guaranteed product of

some quality to sell to the public, and it is backed by a nationwide marketing and advertising organization. Most banks not only recognize this but are prepared to lend money just on a 'name' – in other words, once you have secured a franchise, the name of the product is enough to reassure the banks as to your credit-worthiness. (This is hardly the case when you open your own restaurant for the first time – you will have a hard job convincing a bank to lend you money if you have no track record in the catering industry, as we shall see later.)

In addition, the franchisor, once he has accepted you, will train you and your staff, oversee the whole operation for the first few weeks or so (to satisfy himself that all is on the right lines, as well as to help you) and provide you with the site, the equipment and the general 'know-how'. Obviously no franchisor is going to take just anyone onto their books and launch them without making quite sure they are suitable. A number of interviews will take place, a number of references will be required, and close enquiries as to your suitability will be undertaken. A reputable franchisor has his nationwide name at stake, as well as quite a lot of money, so you must expect him to be very careful indeed.

Now all this is not going to be cheap! So the disadvantages start with the finance. You are going to need quite a few thousand pounds to put you into the running at all. Just how much, however, will be very carefully explained to you – there will be very few, if any, 'hidden' expenses if you are dealing with a good franchisor and are well advised by your bank and the columns of *Franchise Opportunities*.

Exact 'start-up' costs vary, and it is not possible for me to dwell on them here, but most banks are prepared to lend up to £15,000 (1988) as a Small Business Loan to applicants who have been properly 'screened', by a franchisor, or more under a Business Development Loan. There are few franchises available, however, which would cost less than £20,000, and some may be as much as between £70,000 and £100,000. Most solidly based companies are members of the British Franchise Association and are not coy about the sort of money they require: Burgerking, established in 1954 and claimed to be the second largest restaurant chain in the world, with more than 5,000 units worldwide and sixteen in Britain, requires a minimum investment from its franchisees in the region of £400,000 to

£600,000, depending on the site. The Spud-U-Like baked potato fast-food outlets, with more than forty units in the UK, require a minimum of £20,000 investment. And the well-known Wimpy chain, with 122 counter-service and 305 table-service outlets, requires a minimum investment of £450,000. It is highly unlikely that any individual will have available such huge sums of money of their own, so borrowing (and the ability and courage even to contemplate so much debt from the start) puts the larger chains beyond the reach of 'first-time' operators.

In fact, the outlets of the larger chains are in the so-called 'investment franchise' category, and they simply employ managers and staff as any other employer would. As you do not want to be a manager but want to run your own business, this is hardly for you, but it *is* good 'hands-on' training for a future expedition into the catering trade, and we shall be considering the whole question of necessary and desirable job-experience in a later chapter.

Let us, however, sum up what of necessity must be a very truncated appreciation of the franchise business:

Advantages: You will be your own boss.

You will be buying a tried and tested business formula.

You are buying a ready-made image.

You will have the back-up of a team of business experts.

Disadvantages: You will have to conform to the franchisor's rules.

You are largely dependent on the franchisor as the main supplier.

Part of your profit must be paid to the franchisor.

You must work very hard indeed.

However, do not be too despondent if you feel that franchising *is* the world for you. I have already mentioned the help that is available, and it is up to you to pursue all the various sources, not only of finance but what is on the market – it is a market which is constantly expanding, with new opportunities constantly being offered. Go and see the franchisor if one project interests you – he will normally be only too happy to give you an appointment. But do not waste his time by professing ignorance not only of the franchise scene but also of his product – that is tantamount to downright rudeness and presumption of his time. Get as much information and background as you can from existing franchisees – most of them will be pleased to help, because they know you are not likely to be setting up in direct competition. And finally, do not approach a franchisor until you are pretty certain it *is* the sort of thing you want and have done all the homework possible. A fully 'clued-up' and enthusiastic applicant is much more likely to impress than someone who has no idea what he or she is talking about! But that goes for anything and everything in this life – if only more people would realize it.

'Private' Franchising

The second method of opening your own restaurant is, in effect, a 'private' type of franchising. It is taking over an existing kitchen and dining-area in an existing business and running it as your own. Typical of this idea is the local pub, especially in the country.

A great many publicans have neither the interest nor the expertise to run their own commercial kitchen. In fact, and not being too cynical, very few publicans do, whatever they may say. Very often it is the wife who struggles to cope with a lunchtime food trade. She is often ill-equipped to do so, lacking any form of training or enough time, especially if she has children. On top of this is the problem of staff. We shall discuss this later on; here it is enough to say that staff are particularly hard to find in country areas, and much of the hard, often heavy work devolves upon the publican's wife. Not surprisingly, inn-keeping is also one of those occupations with a remarkably high matrimonial disaster rate.

The steady but sad, rise in pub food (it was Miles Kington, I think, who said that Britain must be the only country in the world which considers the sign 'Pub Grub' actually to be an inducement to go in and eat) has led not only to an enormous increase in domestic problems but also to a total 'sameness' of all food to be found in such places. For the most part, the local landlord (i.e., publican) is both ignorant and uncaring about the pleasures of the table. It used to be true also, years ago, of the quality of his beer, but standards have improved enormously over the years, and well-kept beer is now the norm rather than the exception. The publican's dining-room, however, is another matter.

There is, normally, in most such premises, plenty of suitable room. Indeed, without food sales many pubs would go out of

business. In 'tied houses' (those which belong to the big brewer-
ies), it is customary for proceeds from food sales not to be
considered in fixing the rentals – such proceeds are strictly
landlords' 'perks', whereas in 'managed houses' there is no rental
to be fixed, the licensee being merely the direct employee of the
brewery.

It is important to understand the complications of the licensed
trade before you embark on any enquiries along these lines. You
will normally be wasting your time in considering managed
premises, and you will have to find out, either directly or by
'asking around', whether a particular pub is 'tied' or 'managed'.
And then there is the 'free house', normally owned by the
licensee himself. Literally 'free' of all 'ties' to a brewery.

Now I mentioned earlier the problems of staff in the kitchen in
pubs. The serving of food, even poor food and even 'bought-in',
ready-portioned food straight from freezer to micro-wave, causes
many headaches to licensees (or, more particularly, as I said, the
poor wife), and if evening meals are being served or considered,
thus again helping turn-over, the problems become even more
insistent. Thus it is not surprising that in some instances a
landlord has a millstone round his neck – something he cannot do
without but which is dragging him down nonetheless.

To put it in its simplest terms, renting a pub kitchen is definitely
one way into running your own restaurant.

Naturally, there will have to be legal safeguards, a water-tight
contract drawn up by a solicitor and agreeable to both parties, but
this is not an insuperable problem and can be couched in quite
simple terms.

The rental too will have to be fair. But it should not be very
much – after all, you are taking over many of the licensee's
problems, and although he is entitled to a proper return for his
space and equipment, you are entitled to a proper return for your
expertise and hard work. Each encourages and benefits the other.

It is true that you do not see many advertisements for this type
of arrangement and, indeed, very few landlords have even
thought of the idea themselves. So for the most part it will be up
to you to seek out a suitable place and put the proposition, asking
the licensee and, especially, his wife to consider it in their own
time. You can then go back after a few days and discuss it further.

There are a number of advantages in this idea which are
obvious to all concerned, chief among which is the fact that your

'ingoings' will not cost very much. Indeed, why should there be *any* cost if the publican already has a workable kitchen? And most such places do, even if they are a little primitive.

You can always arrange a trial period, to suit each of you and to see how things work out, and it is important, too, that very definite guide-lines are laid down. For instance, will you be expected to feed the landlord and his family or just his customers, and when is the kitchen yours and not theirs? But providing *always* that these matters are worked out in advance, after due consideration by both parties, there should be no real problem apart from the normal personal relationships, which may seem strange at first but should not, one hopes, become 'strained'.

As a putative renter of the premises, or part of it, you will obviously have to bear in mind how the licensee 'sees' his own operation and how you (and he) see yours. It is no good installing a sumptuous menu in a country pub more used to bread-and-cheese. The landlord will obviously be concerned that his own 'image' will suffer, however low that image in fact is. You will have to remember that, whatever you think of him, he is still the owner of the property, and he has the most to lose if anything goes wrong or if your type of food discourages the trade he already has, instead of building on it. It is this building-up of trade that could well be your trump card, that and removing from his shoulders a whole load of worry.

There are no problems which cannot be solved by intelligent and frank discussion, providing they are discussed in advance and that a clear and contractually viable agreement can be worked out.

Equipment too has to be taken into account, even crockery and cutlery. Who is to be responsible for breakages, replacements and so on? In effect, it is better if the licensee deals with this, in agreement with yourself. As owner of even a knife and fork, he will, after all, be better off should you leave.

Concessions
Pubs are not the only source of possible entry to the catering trade for a newcomer. Even some smaller hotels, especially in country towns, experience similar problems – so much so that I know of one or two which have dispensed with their kitchen and dining-facilities altogether and gone over completely to the

French 'sans restaurant' concept. This is not because the hotel owners do not care or do not want dining-rooms and kitchens – far from it, they always have the room, and they certainly need the cash; it is just that they cannot cope with both sides of their business – and the business of letting rooms is very much easier (and more profitable) than the business of feeding the guests who stay in them.

Again, such opportunities are rarely advertised, but they do exist and they can be discovered by anyone prepared to do the necessary research.

New leisure complexes, new shopping precincts (though these will often entail considerable sums for equipment and so on) offer opportunities, but so do staff canteens, especially in small companies, and all manner of enterprises, if you only take the trouble to keep your eyes open and just think about it. I know of at least one private airfield which has a small restaurant doing a roaring trade, to both flying-club members and outside customers.

It would be wrong to use the term 'franchise' in connection with this sort of operation: they are normally described in the trade as 'concessions'. I feel they will become more and more common. The business of feeding people is getting more and more complex, more and more 'big business' – but where there is complexity, there is opportunity for the specialist like yourself, and where there is big business, there are always smaller people making their own way, and being successful too.

Starting Small
As you have probably already realized, there are more ways of entering the catering trade than just buying a restaurant of your own, or leasing one. It just needs a bit of what Edward de Bono calls 'lateral thinking'.

In most towns now there is a delicatessen, and I know of at least one which extended into a small restaurant, serving simple food, wine, tea or coffee and so on. This could well be a 'way in' – you may care to consider the possibility of buying an established business of a similar sort, or even opening one in a town which does not possess one. If the premises are adaptable as a food retailing business, it may be but a short step to opening part of it to take tables and chairs. A small shop, with room to expand eventually, in a good place, will give you a steady income fairly quickly (probably far quicker than a newly opened restaurant), and you can take your time about changing the operation slightly.

Small premises suitable as 'take-aways' (or 'carry-outs', as they call them in Scotland), perhaps with one or two stools at a counter top for people who want coffee and a cake or sandwich while there, can be a very good way to start up and get to know the industry at first hand. Again, in my own experience, I know of one man who started in just such a way, prospered and became popular, then moved further up the street to much bigger premises where he has not only a very much larger 'take-away' trade for lunchtime but also quite an extensive seating-area open now for Sunday lunches as well as during the week. I wonder how long it will be before he opens in the evening?

The tea shop is also making a come back today – whether it is ye olde worlde type in a lovely country town or village or in a larger town. Start-up costs here are often very much less than for a full-blown restaurant operation. These places are well worth bearing in mind: they are a good introduction to the trade in general; there are often suitable lease-hold properties in many towns, either as a going concern or worth converting; they are comparatively easy to run, opening at, say, 9.30 a.m. serving coffees, light lunches and teas, and closing at 5 p.m.

Some of them, unfortunately, perpetuate the 'feather-in-the-mouth' image of amateur gentleladies not really knowing much about what they are doing. These places seldom prosper for long and can often be bought over at a very reasonable cost – the owners being only too happy to get rid of them. On the other hand, they are well on their way to becoming a restaurant in their own right, with proper work and attention, and many of them also have a large lunchtime 'take-away' trade, which again helps turn-over.

But beware of certain ideas.

The first is turning your own home into a restaurant. This is different from buying a property suitable for conversion and in particular tends to apply only to people living in the country, in a nice house or cottage, perhaps. Wanting something to do, they think a small tea-room or cosy restaurant might be the thing. This rarely works. In the first place, it is often too 'cosy', too cloying from the customer's point of view, and in the second place it is difficult, psychologically, to adjust yourself to the fact that *your* home is being used by all and sundry, even though you are charging them for the privilege. Of course, as with most things in life, there are exceptions, but they are very few and far between, and unless you are absolutely certain, the whole idea is best left alone.

Specializing

Similar doubts apply to highly specialized operations, 'ethnic' restaurants and the like.

The catering trade is a curious one in that it attracts people of very little ability in the course of action they have chosen. For instance, no one would ever think of setting themselves up as, say, a blacksmith, when they had absolutely no idea about forging iron or wielding a hammer. Such a thing is not only ludicrous, it is also unthinkable. Not so with the catering trade.

Very often as a result of a holiday somewhere, people reckon they know all there is to know about French or Mexican or Italian food. It is the old 'If I can cook an omelette, I can cook anything' syndrome. Yet people actually do it – and fail. And feel surprised. Of course, if you are Chinese, or Mexican, or Indian, you are more than likely to know something about your native *cuisine*, but unless you are a 'native', leave it alone – there is much more to running a Mexican restaurant, I can guarantee, than strolling off to the local supermarket for some packets of tacos and bottles of chillies! Not even a library book on such cooking will be of much use in the long run, yet people actually do it – and all on the strength of a holiday or some other such ludicrous 'experience'.

As that ubiquitous American Bob Peyton said: 'I go into lots of places in Britain which call themselves American, and they just are not American in any way. It is hoodwinking the public.'

There are other specialist places, I know, which can be embraced within reason by people able and willing to study and broaden their expertise, providing a good, sound basis is there. Fish, for instance, is becoming more and more popular, and many people consider specializing in just this one sort of raw material. But supplies in Britain (unless you live virtually next door to Billingsgate Market) are extremely difficult to obtain, most of it going directly to France, and once away from London it becomes virtually impossible to guarantee a continuous menu, however much you are prepared to pay – and charge – for the product.

Then there is the vegetarian restaurant. This again is highly specialized, and even those with considerable knowledge of this type of food often fail after a few months – for all the publicity surrounding 'healthy eating' and the latest food-fad craze, there just does not seem to be enough people around to support such a concept, except in the larger cities. I have some friends who are virtual vegetarians while at home but when they go out for a meal demand the choicest game or cuts of meat! For a vegetarian restaurateur, people like that are a despair. And there are an awful lot of them.

The simple fact is that, whereas vegetarians will happily embrace a restaurant serving their sort of food exclusively, the carnivores among us will not.

This means that vegetarians will often choose non-meat dishes from a normal menu when dining out with carnivorous friends, but those self-same friends will never choose to go to a vegetarian restaurant, and neither will the vegetarians insist upon it. This means that a vegetarian restaurant has to have an enormous catchment area through which it can trawl for custom, unless it is attached to a centre of attraction such as, say, a national monument, where there is nowhere else to eat for miles and the 'audience', so to speak, is a captive one. Then eating in such a place is not out of choice through a sudden conversion to vegetarianism but simply out of sheer hunger.

Outside Catering and Supplying

Outside (or 'outdoor') catering is difficult for newcomers – there are a great many efficient firms already in the market, and the mobile equipment you need (all of which has to be bought, or leased, in advance) will cost a great deal of money. The return on your investment will take a long time to materialize. On the other hand, outdoor caterers of various sizes and specialities, do come on the open market and you can see them advertised for sale, occasionally, in the trade or local papers.

Some enterprising people have, however, entered this field by converting double-deck buses into mobile restaurants for race meetings, agricultural shows and so on. And yet others have bought caravans or vans for sites on the sides of main roads, or for serving food at private parties, village fêtes and the like. In most cases a reasonable 'concession fee' is payable to the organizers or by means of a licence from local councils.

The schemes are attractive because the capital outlay is comparatively small, but there is, nevertheless, a substantial element of gamble, because it could well take some time to see any return on your money as it can take a year or two to get established and know that you will be guaranteed an increasing number of bookings or a continuance of licence.

Another popular *entrée* to the trade is that of the small, private cook who specializes in producing high-quality merchandise for local retail food shops.

Many of these enterprises have turned into quite large businesses with plans of expansion, but for the most part they remain on the outskirts of the catering trade, a sort of dilettante operation thought suitable for gentleladies or those requiring only 'pin-money' or, as they say, 'something to do', often in their spare time.

But care should be exercised over thinking about such operations. It is illegal to sell food to the public at large without the necessary permission for premises or sites, and inspections by environmental health officers will certainly be necessary. Many such small concerns do get away with it, I know, but there is no point in wilfully breaking the law.

One final point: if you want to get into the trade but lack certain experience and possibly have some doubt as to whether you are prepared to find all the cash necessary for your own place (perhaps you are none too sure about the trade being just the right thing for you), many works canteens are actually run by someone on their own, someone who does the cooking and, with help, the serving but is nevertheless 'employed' by that company or organization, or is self-employed and charges a fee for the work involved. It may seem like putting your head into the lion's mouth but one of my friends runs a very successful dining-facility in my local Inland Revenue office! As I said, there are all sorts of opportunities if you care to look for them.

6   With Notebook in Hand

Cuisine is both an art and a science.

Monselet

You will remember my insistence on a notebook, and also, perhaps, my mentioning the need for some work experience before committing yourself, your family and, possibly above all, your money to your new venture.

Your notebook alone by now should have convinced you of all the problems and questions needing answers, and you should already have decided on exactly the sort of operation which appeals to you, the sort of operation which you reckon you can run with confidence and profit.

But the notebook is only just beginning to come into its own: you now have to get out and about and do a lot more research – by going to see anyone in the business (the type of business in which you are interested) and, quite simply, 'picking their brains'.

Advice from the Experts
Now, though this sounds problematic it is, in essence, a very simple task. Getting people to talk about themselves is the easiest thing in the world!

As a former Fleet Street newspaper reporter, I suppose I am lucky in that I had a vast experience to call upon in approaching people, and I was certainly not shy, as you can imagine. But I assure you there is nothing special about the technique: you simply ring up the person of your choice, or write to them, asking if you can come to see them, as you would like the benefit of their advice and experience. There are very few men or women who have made a success of their lives who are not obligingly flattered by such a request. There is no need to be dishonest about it either: their sense of their own importance will make you welcome when you tell them you are wanting to set up in business on your own – but not, of course, directly in local competition with them.

Do not be afraid of their secretaries either. In fact, seek to get them on your side not only by being polite but by asking them to help you get to the 'great man' and explaining why. Flattery works just as well with secretaries as it does with their employer. I cannot think of any occasion when I have been rebuffed – but, mind you, you must not waste anyone's time and you must do your homework first. There is no point in asking to see Lord Forte and then starting by asking him what, exactly, his business is.

Ask cogent questions. If necessary, have a list of them, say you have a list and go through them. He or she will be impressed. And because you know what to ask, and the questions are pertinent, he or she will expand and even help you along by providing all sorts of hints and tips which you probably had not thought of yourself. Do not be afraid to write down, or make a quick note of, things that are said to you. Again you are creating an air of flattery – what is being said to you is so important that you must not miss the point!

Now, I know all this sounds pretty obvious but I am afraid that, if it *was* so, a lot more people would adopt it. Unfortunately they do not. I have had many people come to me to ask advice and (because I am flattered) I have always been happy to help but, like most people, I get very irritated at silly questions and at people who are using me as a short-cut to save trouble in looking things up themselves. After all, why waste time (yours and his) by asking Anton Mosimann what sort of balloon-whisk he prefers when any catering suppliers can show you a range and let you make up your own mind? Yet people do just that sort of thing. I find it extraordinary. You have gone to see a particular person for one particular reason – because of his own expertise in that particular field. So stick to it.

Before my wife and I set up our first hotel and restaurant, we spent hours travelling about talking to successful people, and some unsuccessful ones. That is not to say we acted like Pavlov's dogs, slavishly, on every crumb of advice. Far from it. We picked and chose that which we felt suited us and our type of operation. But without all that advice – and the most tremendous amount of help and encouragement – we would have been much the poorer in our ideas, and much the less skilled at our chosen business.

Observation

Earlier in this book I mentioned 'observation' along with research, and I commented on how unobservant so many people are, how they do not seem to make use of the free information and help there is all around them, how whenever they go into a restaurant or hotel they fail to see (and make a note of) the bad things as well as the good things.

For a long time before we set up our own first business, we had kept notebooks and journals into which the smallest matters were entered. We were lucky to spend much time in Europe, and as our intention had always been to open a small 'restaurant with rooms' in the French style and we had been fortunate to come across in France exactly the sort of place we wanted to run ourselves back in Britain, we knew we had gained enormously from 'observation'.

Of course, the note-taking did not stop just there. Every time we went into a restaurant, we noted the things we liked and the things we disliked. Every year, when we closed our restaurant during March and went to France, our journal was filled with comments and queries, ideas about recipes, about making people more comfortable, about lighting in restaurants, arrangements of tables or room-dividers, the small touches which pleased us, those things of which we said, 'How simple! If only we had thought of that!' Into the notebooks it all went. They are to hand now. They are the very stuff of which this book you are reading is made.

Job-Experience

To all this research should be added a little first-hand experience, if at all possible.

Now, I know how much you will want to 'get on with it', but even so, some caution should be exercised. So, if it is at all possible, you really should go out and get a job, however 'casual' or temporary, in the sort of establishment you wish to run. You will never regret it. It can be difficult, I know. You might have a good job which you do not want to hazard until you are ready to set up your new business. But the new business you are contemplating is pretty hazardous in itself, remember, so you may find some extra 'risk' money to spend on teaching yourself at first hand some of the ins and outs of your new life. If at all possible, you must do it, even if it means giving up precious weekends or evenings while still at your present job. After all, you are going to have to get used to giving up leisure time, so you may as well start now. Or, if it is simply not possible and if your spouse is going into the business with you, could he or she get some first-hand experience?

There are many chances in the catering trade for 'casual' staff. Those in it are notoriously poorly paid, and there is constant difficulty finding anyone – as we shall learn in Chapter 12. You will not earn a lot of money, therefore, but you will learn a lot about the business.

There are courses, too, you can go on. For a start, enquire at your local college of further education. There are not only evening classes in many subjects to do with catering but very often day courses. And remember, catering is not just about food – it is about management, accountancy and a whole host of other things.

The organizations which deal with training or 'job-experience' tend to change names, if not purposes, and mushroom all the time. Any list would be out of date before you can read this book, but apart from your local college, and the pamphlets or books in your public library, the Job Centres in every area really are very helpful, and they really do know what is available for any particular career you have chosen. They are also, nowadays, very much more 'local' in their outlook and can save you a lot of time and trouble in letter-writing or on the telephone. There is also, at the end of this book, a list of the names of the major organizations which deal with the catering trade, and they, too, are always ready to give advice and guidance.

But courses, however helpful, are still only courses, and they still put off the day of actual, real practical experience. I do not in any way wish to 'knock' such pursuits but I do want to make a personal plea for real-life experience, in however humble a capacity. Working as a *plongeur* or washer-up in any commercial kitchen is going to do more for you in one hour than a whole day could at college, when it comes to seeing what the steamy side of life can be like. And working behind a bar in a pub is going to tell you more about people than you ever thought possible, let alone learning about drink. The modern phrase is 'hands-on training' – not a bad term for the catering trade.

I am a firm believer in any form of experience being better than none. If it does nothing more than acquaint you with the public, if you work in a bar or a dining-room, and with all the problems that is going to entail, it will be useful. And working behind the scenes, in a kitchen, for instance, might not let you meet the public but *is* going to let you meet those who one day might be your fellow-workers, and that in itself can be quite an eye-opener.

Whatever the experience you gain, you are going to be very surprised. Not until you have actually worked in the trade do you have any idea at all of what it is really like – and that goes for a great restaurant or ye olde worlde tea-rooms. Either you are going to hate it or it is going to enter your soul, never to leave. And that is not a bad reason for gaining some experience. If you do hate it, you will have saved an awful lot of your own money and time. But if you like it, well, think of the bonus. Either way it will be a good investment.

Now, as I mentioned before, you may not think you necessarily need this 'hands-on' experience. After all, many businesses are run by accountants and so on, and successfully, but this book is not aimed at them, it is aimed at you, who, I assume, want to be a real restaurateur and not just a good juggler with figures.

This job-experience will not only help you in setting up your own restaurant, it will go a long way to helping you with finance. As I shall mention later, in Chapter 7, a bank manager will be a lot more impressed if he knows you have at least some working knowledge of the trade you are proposing to enter. And so will those people whom you approach for advice. It is part of your 'homework' and displays your seriousness.

I think it will also help you in a much broader way. In company with many people in the trade, I know a great many men and women who had absolutely no experience at all when they first set up their own operation. Not even a few hours casual work in a local pub. Virtually everyone found their lack of experience, their lack of *expectation* of what it might be like, more or less disastrous, and a great many found themselves in serious difficulty before many months – not just financially but psychologically too. Actual day-to-day working, the pressures of the long hours and the constant demands of staff and customers exhausted them mentally and physically.

Yet, as I said before, people still keep coming into the trade, opening their own restaurants, coffee-shops, wine bars and so on – be they fresh from a village shop, a department store in town, the police force or, yes, even a bank.

In their previous jobs they would have been the first to tell you the necessity for experience and training, but here they are, all leaping into the deep end, because they somehow assume it is all so easy. The omelette-at-home syndrome tiresomely once more.

Reading Up on It

There are, too, quite a number of books about running restaurants, and your local librarian will doubtless be pleased to help you find the lists of publications under 'Catering'. There are actually more than you think, and many of them so esoteric that they are hardly worth bothering with.

You will not, I would have thought, actually want to read highly specialized books on the 'art' of waiting at table and so on, although they exist, and I shall have more than a little to say on cookery books later on. But many publications are a help, and you should steep yourself in as much of the literature as you can manage, if only to get the 'feel' of the industry as a whole.

The weekly magazine *Caterer and Hotelkeeper* is normally available through your local newsagent, and apart from being a source of news, it also has columns on various aspects of running a restaurant and is very useful for properties, for sale or lease. Sensible reading of these columns will give you very good parameters in which to work in valuing the property which interests you.

But apart from the solid books on 'how to' subjects, I would also like to urge any newcomer to take a look at such authors as Ludwig Bemelmans and John Fothergill or even the biography of Lord Forte, which is quite fascinating about how *he* started his own business – a lesson to be learned by us all.

Bemelmans (born in Austria, died in 1962) spent many years of his life in the hotel and restaurant trade, which he actually observed and wrote about wryly and lovingly. I was fascinated by the books as a young man, never realizing that one day I would tread, however humbly, in some of his footsteps. When I did so, I was surprised and delighted that much of his wisdom, and above all much of his joy, had rubbed off on me, and I was able to detect a 'Bemelmans story' heading my way in my own experience. Life seemed to repeat itself, even though I was hardly in the same class as Bemelmans, with his 'grand' hotels and luxury-loving guests and customers.

I am sure Fothergill should be just as well praised as Bemelmans, but to me he lacked the sheer apparent *happiness*. Although his writing is instructive not only about the trade but particularly about his customers, one wonders why, sometimes, he stayed in the catering business when so many of his visitors proved to be so tiresome. On the other hand, to be fair, the essential 'flavour' of the trade is there in his books about his inns and about innkeeping in general.

7 Raising Money

My method is the fruit of late nights and innumerable experiments.

Nicolas Appert

There will, perforce, have to be some chapters in this book dealing just with finance.

Money – how to get it, how to keep it, how to stop it leaking away, how to store it, how to nurture and care for it and allow it to bloom into a tree of golden loveliness.

It sounds extremely boring unless you are a banker or a businessman. But, alas, it is absolutely necessary, for the truth of the matter is that, however fine a chef you become, however marvellous a host you will make, very much more of your time is going to be spent at an office desk than coping with your customers. Money is going to bedevil everything you do – the lack of it is going to keep you awake at nights for months on end in your early days – and perhaps for a long time after; even if you start actually to make some, to have that marvellous word 'surplus', you are going to worry again about losing it, or too much of it, to the eager hands waiting for it – be it the Revenue, Excise, light-fingered staff, builders and decorators or what-have-you.

We have already mentioned both buying an existing business, or leasing one, and setting up a new operation completely. In any event, raising the money presents the same, or similar, problems.

I am assuming that you are not totally ignorant about finance and that it is therefore fairly obvious that your chances of raising *all* the money necessary by borrowing it is not only remote but undesirable as well. You will therefore need some capital of your own – at least fifty per cent (certainly not a lot less) of the total costs involved in any new project would be a workable proposition.

Now, raising money is not very different whatever the business you are proposing, with the serious exception that, because of the failure rate of catering outlets, you are going to work much harder at convincing any lender that yours is a worthwhile investment, especially if you are new to the game and have no track record in the industry.

However, it is not impossible, and you must not become too despondent. You just have to set about it in a very serious, organized and persuasive way. It is on this point that many people fail before they even start.

'That First Small Sum'
Look first at your **assets** and tot them up:

> Value of house
>> contents
>> any personal possessions
> Second car, caravan etc
> Second home
> Building Society account
> Any form of investment (i.e. National Savings, stocks
>> and shares etc)

Then take a look at your **liabilities** and tot them up as well:

> Mortgage
> Overdraft or bank loans
> Hire purchase
> Outstanding debts, bills etc
> Other commitments, e.g. school fees etc.

A simple subtraction will give you an idea of how much 'unattached' money you might have towards your new venture.

I said earlier that you can never have enough money. Having done that initial sum, you probably put your head in your hands and wonder why on earth you are so damn poor.

But having done even that first small sum, you have done something that will stand you in good stead. Write it all down, neatly, in appropriate columns, nicely laid out, preferably typed, with as much cogent information as you can add. (For instance, you may have some jewellery, or some antique furniture, or a picture or two. Get such things valued and attach the valuation to your first piece of paper.)

This exercise is not just for your benefit and discipline: you are going to use it as the first page in your 'presentation' to the man or woman who is going to provide the necessary borrowing-facilities – be it a bank, another source of lending or even a rich relative. (Lord Forte started, doubtless, by doing simple sums, and doubtless, too, the rich relative who lent him his first money wanted some persuasion along such lines.)

Then prepare a second sheet of paper: a list of your projected needs and the costs thereof. Include *everything* you can possibly think of. It will look something like this:

Ingoings

Cost of property/lease
Fixtures and fittings
Goodwill (if a separate sum)
Legal charges
Other costs (e.g. oil, coal, garden machinery etc not necessarily included in F & F)
Your own removal expenses
Rates/water charges
Rent (if leased)
Estimated annual cost of gas, electricity, telephone, water (if metered)
Projected staff costs
Projected food/liquor costs for, say, first three months
Estimates for *necessary* building/decoration, alterations etc
Anything else (and there is always something else, so list it)
Insurances

The table is not quite the sort of thing that an accountant would present – but you are not an accountant, you are going to be a restaurateur, and although you are going to need a properly qualified accountant in due course, there is, as yet, no point in spending what little money you have on using qualified people for something you can do yourself or, at any rate, something you should be doing yourself if only to introduce you to the disciplines and understandings you are going to need.

For instance, from an accountancy point of view, some of this list is capital costs and some ordinary running-costs, as well as 'start-up' costs which are not necessarily going to repeat themselves. Even so, by listing *everything* that is going to need money, you are not only helping yourself to see the problems which lie ahead but also helping a putative lender. Many borrowers seem to forget that they are, in effect, trying to 'sell' something to a bank manager, say, who in turn is in the position of being a 'buyer'. If you ignore this fact, you are not likely to be very good at selling anything else to possible buyers, whether it be food and drink, heavy machinery or a new idea for a mousetrap.

Once again, make all the notes you require, but do type them, or set them out, cleanly and decently – someone else is going to read it all, you hope.

Approaching a Bank
Your first recourse is going to be a bank manager, and the question whether it is the one you have always known (but not necessarily loved) or to a complete stranger in the area in which you are choosing to settle and set up your new business, is at the moment worth considering.

There is a saying in the banking business that 'long-distance' banking is undesirable. On the other hand, just turning up at a branch, not even of your own bank, and asking for a good few thousand of what used to be called 'the long greenies' is not very desirable either. There is less of a problem if you are setting up your new business locally, where you have been known to your bank for some years and have some sort of 'track record', even if only as a company employee with a monthly wage cheque being paid in.

In those cases you may find the process easier, or less harrowing, but even so you will still need a disciplined and orderly approach to your manager, whether you know him (or her) quite well or not at all, as may be the case in a large branch in your own town or city. You are going to stand or fall by the way in which your plea for money – I call it the 'presentation' –

is made, and the neater it is, the better set out it is and the more obvious the necessity not only for the money but for the money to be lent to *you*, the more chance it stands. Hence my advice to leave no expense out of your reckoning – the very fact that you have thought of it will impress the banker no end. And, better still, if one or two matters are left (preferably one or two of less importance) and the banker does ask you about them, if you have the answer at your fingertips he (or she) will be even more impressed. Now perhaps you are beginning to see the use of your notebook, for into that will have gone all your jottings about your expenses, as well as about the property, and somewhere the answer is going to appear.

But now we have mentioned it (yet again), let us stay with the notebook for a moment. In it you will have all the details of the actual property you are after and what you intend doing with it. This will mean yet another page for the presentation.

Set out details of the property and, if possible, paste in a colour picture or two. The bank manager may even know the place if it is already a restaurant or catering establishment, but even then he (or she) will appreciate the trouble you have taken and the seriousness of your approach. Bank Managers are Very Serious Indeed when it comes to Lending Money.

The purpose of this is to reassure the banker that the place is suitable (if a new venture) or worth some value as collateral. Remember that the banker, too, will be interested in catchment area, accessibility, parking problems, position and so on – if only to be reassured that you have taken them into account too. A copy of the estate or business agent's details should be included, along with information about fixtures and fittings you think of interest. The only person who can help the bank manager make up his (or her) own mind, and come down on your side, is you, yourself, so why make his (or her) job harder than it need be? Put yourself in his (or her) shoes and try to answer questions you think the manager is going to put or need answering.

Always remember this: the bank manager is not on your side but on his (or her) own and that of the bank. The banker is in the business to make money, not lose it, and stands or falls on that ability. If you can persuade him (or her) that by lending you money he (or she) is going, in due course, to make money for the bank out of it, that any loan is going to be secure not only (and not necessarily) in terms of collateral but in terms of a sound investment, you will probably succeed. But you are wasting your time, and the banker's, by a sloppy, unthought-out approach, by woolly thinking, woolly presentation or woolly ideas about what you propose doing.

And, of course, you may have got the wrong bank manager. But let us consider that in due course.

Now turn to thoughts about you as a person. If the manager does not know you, he (or she) would like to have some idea as to the sort of man or woman you are. A potted biography will not come amiss. Yet another page for the presentation.

There is no need to write a heart-wringing eulogy – you are not (anyway, not yet) at your own funeral. But some idea as to your background would be in order, and some ideas as to experience both in your previous working background and possibly in your new one would be helpful. Married or not, family or not and, most important, if you do have a family, how do they view the new project and what part will they play in it? There are few 'small' restaurants run without family assistance, and it would not be a bad idea to take your spouse along to the eventual interview if he/she is going to play an important role in the business or give moral support.

In this connection it will be of interest to the banker if you are envisaging a partnership, for which a solicitor will eventually be needed to draw up the necessary deed. Or whether you are going to be a limited company, for which an accountant will be needed. All these things have to be thought about and considered for the banker to make up his (or her) own mind and also to offer you (free) advice on the best course to take.

It is also important that you seek to answer the prime question – why? Just why are you wanting to run a restaurant of your own?

It is obviously no good being half-hearted at opening a new business. You should, a long way back, have questioned your self-motivation. Just a change of scenery, or because you are bored with your old job and want to try something new, is simply not good enough. Nor is unemployment any excuse, or reason. That may sound hard-hearted but it is merely practical. Unemployment is a very good spur to branching out on something new; it is rarely sufficient excuse. Anyone asked to lend you money is going to want to know the answers to these questions and to be satisfied by them.

Not a bad starting-point is financial, the desire to make a decent living. Job satisfaction is another. Thus the desire to make a decent living doing a job you have long wanted to, on top of which working for yourself is an added attraction, whatever the hours or the problems, is already building up a picture that a banker, or anyone else, needs to have of you.

It is a mistake to set your sights too low, to say, in effect, 'I would rather be poor and happy than rich and miserable.' That sort of thing belongs in fairy stories, and bank vaults are not full of fairy stories but of gold bricks. The manager can never have enough of those, so he (or she) does not understand people who disparage them.

Now, I have been conscious once or twice while writing the foregoing pages that I am almost certainly trying to teach my grandmother to suck eggs. If this is true in your case, I should have warned you at the start not to bother but go on to something which does interest you or which you do not know about.

The reason, however, why I have so far dealt with the presentation in such detail is simply because of the number of people who go in to see their bank managers without the slightest idea of what they are doing, without written information, without any form of financial expectation or ideas as to how much everything is going to cost. If you do not believe me, ask at any bank. Not for nothing does at least one of them publish a special pamphlet called 'Help the Bank Manager to Help You'.

So I make no apology: I like to think I am trying to help you help yourself. And if you need further help – and you do, start by getting all the relevant 'start-up' business brochures from your local bank.

So far we have looked at the first three sections of your presentation and considered what it should contain. But in the case of your buying or taking over an established business, it is essential that it contain a fourth section. The financial position of your new interest.

Your own observations (however acute) of the property you are after stand as nothing compared with the accounts. No one can possibly hope to sell a business without accounts and, in any event, accounts are required by law, as we shall see at a later stage.

I say no one can possibly 'hope' to sell a business without such information. It is not strictly true – you, as a possible buyer, have no absolute right to inspect the accounts if, for some reason, the seller does not wish you to see them. It would be foolish of anyone to take such a stand, as refusal would almost certainly be taken to mean there was something radically wrong. And it would certainly put you, the buyer, into a very difficult position as regards borrowing any money.

Now a word of warning here.

It is extraordinary but true that no catering business, pub, hotel, bar, restaurant or anything at all is ever doing badly, if you listen to the present owner. It is a bit like gardeners who are always telling visitors that they 'should have seen the garden last week' when it was at its best. If you go into any pub, hotel or restaurant and it is empty, you will always be told, 'You should have been here last night/week – you just couldn't move!'

I do not know why this is, but I do know it is a fact. However gloomy present, past or future is, to outsiders you are always 'doing well'.

It is certainly not because caterers are mendacious, seek to mislead. Not at all. It may be because they have to be like white-faced clowns, tears behind the grease-paint and all that. And there are a lot of tears and there is an enormous demand for grease-paint in a great many establishments.

One of the reasons may well be that the public (even, or especially, if there are not many of them) do not like a gloomy owner or staff – and they certainly hate it if the place is half empty. For many people it is in their nature to paint a rosy picture for their customers, friends and possible buyers. So there is an unconscious, or conscious, urge to reassure customers that tonight happens to be an exception, for reasons you cannot fathom. It is the same with the weather. The weather is meant to have an effect on all catering establishments – if it is wet, people stay indoors; if it is sunny and warm, they like to stay outdoors. Whatever the weather, they very often stay away from your establishment and, incidentally, you hardly ever actually know why. The catering trade is the most casual and haphazard trade in the world.

Believe me, you can be packed out and turning people away, or totally empty and then your single booking cancels. There simply is no rhyme or reason to it. I only wish there were – in company with a great many other caterers, I could have done with such 'inside' knowledge many times over.

Now why am I mentioning all this slap in the middle of a chapter on 'Raising Money'? Because I want you to be careful with all your plans and forecasts, not only financial but in ambition. And that will have an effect on what you say to the bank. Although cheerful enthusiasm is always the order of the day, coupled with calm confidence, do not overgild the lily, otherwise not only the bank, but a lot of other people will think you rather 'wet behind the ears'.

And do not be chary about asking for sufficient money – under-capitalization kills businesses. You will not get a loan just because you ask for too large an amount. Indeed, you may be refused a loan because you have asked for too little – and thus neatly demonstrated your own ignorance.

So whatever you feel about the business you have your eye on, be cynically detached until the vendor comes up with the accounts. And then be even more so when you inspect them.

In an ideal world you should present to your bank the accounts for the past three years of the business you are proposing to take over. They should always be laid out and attested by a qualified accountant whose professional reputation is just as much at stake as the caterer's. Even if the accounts do not mean much to you, they will certainly mean a lot to the banker, who will be readily able to 'read between the lines' if there is anything slightly doubtful. The most upright and proper accountants can be economical with the truth, if asked, and vendors very much more so. Bankers know this. They are a very cynical breed.

Your Solicitor and Accountant
As you would imagine, inextricably linked with buying any established business is not only a banker, but also a solicitor and an accountant. Whereas much of the preliminary research work can be, and should be, done by you yourself, you simply must not imagine you can put off for too long the day when you have to start paying for expert advice. And that time is now.

I dare say that, if you are buying close to where you have been living a number of years, you will almost certainly know a solicitor, or at least a firm which, perhaps, dealt with the house you bought. But if you are moving away, you are very much on your own, and you will have to use your now well-developed nose for research in finding one.

Although this chapter is devoted to raising money, we are not actually all that far off the point. Both solicitors and accountants have considerable knowledge about raising money, and many of them have clients willing to invest in well-thought-out schemes. The trick is how to find just the right sort of adviser for you and your new business.

The local Citizens Advice Bureau, as well as the library, has lists of local professional people, but staff are not allowed to suggest any particular name. In a small country town, this is very little problem. Any bank manager will normally suggest to a stranger that he go along to see someone whom the bank regards as 'sound', and there is no harm in that. You can always change your advisers later on, if you do not get on with them, but it is necessary to have some advice immediately, and any solicitor (unless you are desperately unlucky) will do. But it is important that you use someone with local knowledge, whether you are in a big town or a small one – you will get a better deal for your money in the long run, and they will certainly know a lot more about local matters, and business prospects, than you do.

And incidentally, because you have already worked on a good presentation for a bank manager, you can use this too to impress a solicitor or accountant, and the information you have laid out will save them a lot of time and also help them to advise you properly.

8   Financial Forecasting

When there is no more cookery in the world there will be no
more pleasant, easy relationships.

Carême

Bank Loans

It would be tedious of me here to set out every method of
borrowing money from a bank. They all offer similar services
and advice, and all of them are only too happy to explain details
to you.

In effect, however, it can be summed up that one of the
cheapest ways of borrowing money is still the overdraft, at
about 2½ or three per cent above base rate, and this method is
normally recommended for 'working capital' – i.e., money to
pay bills, wages and day-to-day demands and for sudden
emergencies. The borrower's current account is 'marked' for a
certain amount of overdraft which has been agreed beforehand
with the manager, and over-stepping this amount results either
in dishonoured cheques (if your relationship with the bank is
poor) or in a slightly higher interest charge for the time the
account is over the original 'mark'. You and the bank can
quickly identify the amount of money you will need and, of
course, you pay interest only on the amount actually borrowed,
or 'overdrawn'.

For capital projects there are Business Loans or Business Term
Loans. In a Business Loan, sums as high as £100,000 are
sometimes available, and the amount of interest charges will be
agreed beforehand and will remain unchanged throughout the
loan period, which can range from six months to five years. A
Business Term Loan is normally for greater sums, repayable
over about ten years at fixed, negotiated monthly or quarterly
instalments for capital and interest.

Alternative Sources of Loans

Apart from the major clearing banks, money is sometimes available from merchant banks for certain projects, but it seems unlikely that you, as a new-comer to the whole catering trade, and possibly in a modest way, will want to enter, or be able to enter, this sort of minefield. Merchant banks are where the Big Boys play, and the Big Boys are beyond the scope of this book.

I mentioned in the previous chapter the possibility of loans through solicitors or accountants. It is a little unlikely that their clients will wish to invest money in someone without any track record, and for the most part a solicitor would advise against it anyway, as his prime duty is to protect his client. But Equity Finance can sometimes be sought this way, especially if the borrowing requirement is greater than the security.

Briefly, this involves giving the lender a 'piece of the action', as the Americans say, and is tantamount to a sleeping partnership in your enterprise, or even a partner who wants some regular involvement in what you are doing. This may be reasonable if it is a family matter – money from some relation, perhaps – but again the very fact that you are a newcomer militates against you in the 'open market'. In any event, it is not a very desirable way to raise money initially, and people's natural suspicion of the food business is sufficient to make most 'investors' very cautious. You may remember what I said at the start of this book: anyone with an agreeably large portion of money to invest should go and invest it elsewhere than the catering trade.

So, having been somewhat crushing about your chances of raising money, apart from the high street banks, what else is there, I can hear you asking? Here again we hit a snag. There are, it is true, many ideas.

The Loan Guarantee Scheme in which up to £75,000 can be borrowed from a bank which thinks you have a good idea (but is not prepared to put their own money into it) may be considered, as the loan itself is guaranteed by the Government. But the interest rate is about five per cent higher than it would be if you got the money direct from the bank which acts for you.

The Business Expansion Scheme was set up to help small companies by allowing people prepared to invest money a substantial amount of tax relief, on sums up to £40,000, providing they had no other connection with the company itself. I am probably quite wrong, but I do not imagine a new restaurant would attract interest from such a scheme.

And CoSIRA (Council for Small Industries in Rural Areas) can lend money if they think the business will help create employment in a depressed area – but would such an area actually want a restaurant? In fact, the amount of money which CoSIRA lends is small, from my enquiries, and none to restaurants – though CoSIRA is a good source for vacant premises and worth calling on locally if you are interested in certain catering opportunities, such as a fast food outlet, or a café, on an industrial estate. In fact, CoSIRA's main operation is centred on advice; only occasionally are loans available for buildings, equipment and working capital, from £250 to £75,000, with interest at a slightly lower rate than on the normal market. The amount advanced is never more than fifty per cent of the total costs involved. The Council can also help in obtaining a twenty-five per cent Development Commission Grant towards the costs of converting old buildings to a new use, but you must remember that it is employment opportunities they exist to create, and a restaurant may not exactly qualify.

There are also National Development Agencies in Wales, Scotland and Northern Ireland, and the Small Firms Service of the Department of Employment publishes helpful (free) booklets on setting up new firms. But I have to tell you, in all honesty and without trying to be cynical, that you may well be better off on your own, with your bank, solicitor and accountant, in setting up your own business, which, once it is going and looks like thriving, opens up all sorts of opportunities for expansion from a great number of agencies.

But one piece of advice I do urge is to contact your local Job Centre, which I mentioned before in this book. Their 'Action for Jobs' booklet is well set out and interesting, covering all sorts of schemes, from the Small Firms Service to Business Expansion. I do know of one or two caterers who have benefited enormously from the Enterprise Allowance Scheme, which even provides £40 a week to suitable applicants setting up a new business to help them get established. To qualify, you need at least £1,000 of your own money, and you have to have been unemployed for at least eight weeks. It is the sort of very practical help which is available, and it is a pity if people do not take advantage of it if they can – particularly if you are starting a new operation or even intending to revivify a collapsed one.

A Cash-Flow Forecast

But while your time is taken up with all these considerations and worries about raising the money, you still have work to do for your presentation. It is a task which logically seems fairly ludicrous, because it is called a cash-flow forecast. How you can actually forecast a cash flow, when no cash at all has flowed your way because you are not yet even in business, may be somewhat puzzling to you, but it is a reasonable discipline demanded and understood by bankers and other varied financiers. At best, it can be only an educated guess and at worst a curious exercise in crystal-ball gazing.

To give you an idea, I have set out what it should look like, and I have sprinkled in a few figures to make it more appealing. It is actually, you will notice, quite easy to understand. The trick lies in choosing the figures. I cannot do that for you. Only you can. You know the sort of place you want; you know the sort of trade it is doing, or hopefully will do if it is an operation newly set up by yourself.

It is not cynical, but practical, to work out all the expenses you know and guestimate the rest. The receipts section is going to be somewhere behind, but not too much, you hope. I am afraid it *will* be behind, for there is no way you are going to take more in the first few months than you are going to spend.

To be fair, and if you have honestly attempted some truth with the figures you enter, you may be pleasantly surprised at how near the mark you have got when you alter it and update it when you have some information of a definite nature – as you will once you are in business and can see how it is going. I think Table A is pretty self-explanatory but, once again, do not ask *me* what figures to put in – you are entirely on your own with this one. I have just supplied some examples.

The cash-flow forecast not only is valuable once you have started in business (for, as I said, you can alter the figures each month, updating them in line with outgoings and receipts) but also prevents any sudden panics and last-minute tearful pleas to the bank manager when you find that your overdraft limit is not enough. It is meant to be what it says it is, a forecast, allowing you to plan ahead financially and, if possible, delay or bring forward any major purchases you need, new kitchen equipment perhaps, to allow you to keep within the forecast.

For instance, in Table A I have put in for June a sum of £5,000

Table A: Cash-flow Forecast

Month	Jan	Feb	Mar	Apr	May	June	July	Aug	Sept	Oct	Nov	Dec
Bank Balance/OD	nil	6.95	4.6	3.25	1.90	.79	[5.36]	[5.66]	[5.01]	3.91	2.81	3.92
PAYMENTS												
Equipment	2.00	1.00	.40	nil	.10	5.00	nil	.25	nil	.10	nil	.05
Suppliers:												
Food	.50	1.00	.60	.80	1.01	1.10	1.20	1.00	1.00	.80	.60	1.15
Drink	1.00	.50	.50	.90	.85	1.50	.95	.80	.70	.60	.30	1.10
Wages	.75	.70	.60	.75	.75	1.00	1.00	1.00	1.00	.90	.75	1.00
Overheads	.50	.50	.50	.80	.50	.50	.60	.60	.60	.60	.60	.70
VAT										1.71		
Maximum borrowings (As required)	[4.75]	nil	nil	nil	[1.31]	[8.31]	[9.11]	[9.31]	[8.31]	[6.91]	[6.77]	[7.92]
RECEIPTS												
Own capital	10.00											
Sales:												
Food	.90	.65	.70	.85	1.15	1.60	1.90	2.10	2.30	2.10	1.55	2.85
Drink	.80	.50	.55	.90	.95	1.35	1.55	1.95	2.10	2.00	1.30	2.30
VAT				.15				.25				
Closing Balance:	6.95	4.60	3.25	1.90	.79	[5.36]	[5.66]	[5.01]	[3.91]	[2.81]	[3.92]	[2.77]

Note: Figures in £s 000. Square Brackets = Deficit

which could be for dining-room alterations, a new kitchen range or major plumbing and electrical work. It increases your overdraft demands somewhat steeply. If the bank will not wear it or advises against such a large expenditure when you have been at work for only six months, at least a useful point has been made. The closing balance at the end of twelve months may be enough encouragement for any manager to help you, especially if, after six months, the actual figures are a little better than appear in the original forecast.

There are other pointers too. I have indicated, in my examples, those months when trade is notoriously slack, and others show an increase in staff costs at times when you are likely to be busy, as well as allowing for extra fixed overheads as the year progresses, when new rating demands come in, or other expenditure (perhaps electricity or gas) for which you under-budgeted. The buying of drink, too, may be a little excessive at first, a common error but one which nevertheless leads to your tying up in your stocks quite large sums of money.

As I said, these are only guide-lines – they do not take any account of inflation at the time of writing (1988), and the VAT figures are a little arbitrary, as much depends on what is actually spent or earned. We shall take a closer look at VAT in Chapter 14.

The second exercise in the fairground's Gipsy Rose Lee Tent is Table B – a profit and loss forecast for the year ahead. Again, I can hear you saying, how do I know what figures to put in even before I have earned a penny or lost it? Quite so. But it is only a forecast to help you get a better understanding of what money your restaurant needs to take in order to cover your outgoings. It is not difficult. Once again I have put in example figures only – just to give you an idea of the layout.

Whereas VAT is included (somewhat inaccurately perhaps) in the cash-flow forecast, because it is money you actually get back or have to pay out, you should not take any account of VAT in your profit and loss forecast, but to make it simpler for you (I hope) I have put into Table B the exact figures as they appeared in Table A, including those for monthly sales. In fact, your sales figure for January (1.70) should be reduced by fifteen per cent (to 1.44), a similar reduction being applicable for all the other months. You can see, therefore, that, if you do not exclude VAT, your monthly profit (or loss) will be misleading. In this forecast

Table B: Profit and Loss Forecast

Month	Jan	Feb	Mar	Apr	May	June	July	Aug	Sept	Oct	Nov	Dec
SALES	1.70	1.15	1.25	1.75	2.10	2.95	3.45	4.05	4.40	4.10	1.85	5.15
less COSTS												
Food	.50	.80	.60	.80	1.01	1.10	1.20	1.00	1.00	.80	.60	1.15
Drink	1.00	.50	.50	.90	.85	1.50	.95	.80	.70	.60	.30	1.10
Wages	.75	.70	.60	.75	.75	1.00	1.00	1.00	1.00	.90	.75	1.00
Gross profit/loss	[.55]	[.85]	[.45]	[.70]	[.51]	[.65]	.30	1.25	2.70	1.80	.20	1.90
Overheads	.50	.50	.50	.80	.50	.50	.60	.60	.60	.60	.60	.70
Net profit	[1.05]	[1.35]	[.95]	[1.50]	[1.01]	[1.15]	[.30]	.65	1.10	1.20	[.58]	1.20

Note: Figures in £s 000. Square Brackets = Deficit

you can also divide your overheads into twelve equal parts – there is no need to split them up as in Table A, though once again I have left them as they were originally.

You can also work out from Table B what your break-even point needs to be to cover all your month-to-month costs, which will have a bearing on what sort of prices you are going to have to charge your customers – a subject we shall deal with in Chapter 14.

But once break-even is achieved, you have moved into profit – and the knowledge that your business is going to make a profit is not only going to reassure you but will also persuade the bank manager that his overdraft facility is in good hands.

Neither Table A nor Table B, however, makes any provision for your own living-costs, and they also ignore interest on any loans. But they can forecast reasonably accurately when those loans might be repayable, which the banker or any other lender will like to see.

Neither am I suggesting that the 'sketchiness' of the two tables will be sufficient for your presentation – more work may have to be done on them, and that would certainly need a proper accountant. They are, however, good enough as a sound basis for a proper approach to a banker, or other source of finance, to show how well you understand the need for forecasts and to interest them sufficiently to ask for greater detail.

Later, again in Chapter 14, we shall take a look at the necessary accounting tasks needed to help you stay in business, what books to keep and so on. But that is enough figures for now.

9   Legal Complexities

To eat is human, to digest, divine.

Copeland

The legal complexities of buying a new business are not necessarily very different from those involved in buying your own home, although the raising of the money is somewhat different from the ordinary mortgage procedure, as we have seen. And it is worth bearing in mind, unless you are buying 'lock-up' premises, that, all being well, your new home is part of that business – a fact that will be an advantage if and when you come to sell it, for your accountant will have established with the Inland Revenue which part of the premises count, for Capital Gains Tax purposes, as a private house. Normally about one-third of the sale price will be 'free' of CGT, though this will naturally depend on the type of property.

Your solicitor will cope with all the necessary procedures, and there is little you can do yourself, so there is no point on dwelling upon them here.

Leasing
Leasing a property is however, somewhat different, for there will be certain things you must decide upon for which your solicitor will need your 'instructions'. In particular the length of the lease, the rent and its reviews and clauses regarding repairs and so on.

All the advantages and disadvantages will be pointed out to you and fully explained (unless your solicitor is not doing his job very well) but bear in mind that there is no such thing in the world as a 'good landlord'. However reasonable they may appear, and whatever their reputation locally or nationally, there will always be many tenants who complain, often with justification. And there will be just as many landlords who complain about their tenants. This may sound somewhat sweeping but it is by far the best attitude to take, for there can be no mistakes, or disappointments, if it is accepted as a major precept.

Remember that any landlord will be quite ruthless in insisting upon his own legal rights, and it is incumbent upon you to make sure that your own position is just as water-tight. So, whatever the landlord might promise in the way of repairs, or 'putting things right', before you move in, you must insist that the agreements are properly made and that nothing is left to chance or the 'old boy' attitude. In this way there can be no misunderstanding which will mar future relationships. Believe me, who pays for which repairs etc is among the first bones of contention to arise between landlords and tenants unless it has been agreed beforehand and made legally binding.

Whether the lease is 'full-repairing' or not, and all the many complexities thereof, will be fully explained and the problems pointed out to you by the solicitor, and he will also be alert for that infamous clause which some landlords try to swing on unsuspecting leaseholders which allows the lease to revert to the landlord if the leaseholder wishes to leave the property at any time: i.e., the leaseholder surrenders his right of selling the lease to someone else, even though all other terms of the lease have been strictly observed. I have actually seen leases with this clause in them – attempts by landlords, and often their 'reputable' solicitors, to 'pull a fast one'. Under no circumstances consider signing a lease with such a 'non-alienation' clause in it, however attractive the other terms may be.

But to go back to the repairs question, I am merely trying to point out quite strongly that you must be careful, when taking a building over, not to take over as well problems which strictly should not be yours. For instance, you will doubtless have a surveyor look the place over or, if not, you will go over it carefully with the landlord's surveyor. You will see many things wrong with it, especially if it is old and in one of those quaint country towns we have been considering. Just what is your responsibility and what is the landlord's – *exactly* what?

This becomes even more important if the building is already operating as a catering outlet, for in this instance local building control, environmental health and even the fire safety officers will all want their say – and their say not only may be extremely expensive to carry out but also has the weight of law behind it if you fail to do as they tell you. We shall consider the roles these people will play in your life at a later stage in this book but, as I mentioned earlier, take on no property without first obtaining a report on it from the environmental health department. They will either have the place 'on file' or make a special visit to the property and give you a written report. It is their duty to do so when asked, and the service is, of course, free. Environmental health officers will also discuss with you what should be done and when. On the whole they are reasonable people (even if their demands are not), and you will have adequate time to carry out any work suggested, but it is no good signing a lease (or even buying a property) and then discovering, too late, that it has been under threat of closure for failing to comply with various health regulations. Yet people have done that, and then complain they did not know or that no one told them.

Why am I sounding such a cautionary note?

Well, it is for a very simple reason. We started this book by discussing the enormous problems of finding a suitable place, doing all the research as to position, catchment and so on. Having found the property of your dreams, it is understandably human (but very unwise) to rush in to secure it at more or less whatever the cost. Enthusiasm often blinkers the most careful thinker. Your solicitor will not be very enthusiastic about anything, nor will your accountant. But they are trained for the eternal gloom of human frailty – to them, *everything* is girt about with suspicion, and what seems to you to be a most reasonable proposition fills them with dark forebodings as to what is wrong with it. And quite rightly too. Alas, there is so often something wrong with it, and you are paying good money for good advice, or should be. Only you can decide at the end of the day to take whatever chances you may – but it is the job of your advisers to point out to you what the chances are.

Now, I hope that you will find, as I have always been lucky to, the sort of solicitor and accountant who will become friends. But, remember, they are professional people and make their living by advising others. So do not be too much on 'old boy' terms when it comes to using their services, otherwise it can be very expensive.

Many problems can be thought out on your own. Reliance

overmuch on advisers quickly becomes a crutch and inhibits your own power of thought. Too much advice can also become debilitating. You will never run a restaurant if you spend your time running for advice once you have started off.

Legal Status

Another thing you will have to make up your mind about is the type of business, legally, you are going to become. As a 'sole trader', you alone will be responsible for all the debts you incur, although the Income Tax position will be somewhat simple – in fact, it will be no different from that of any other self-employed person. There is no obligation on you, either, to keep audited accounts, although obviously accounts will help you not only to prove your position to the taxman but also in everyday business and when you come to sell.

Partnerships too are responsible for all debts, even though a debt might have been incurred by the incompetence or stupidity of one of the partners without the knowledge of the other. But partnerships can be very tricky. It is alright if, say, you and your spouse are going to be the partners, but if you are thinking of someone else, a friend or relation, perhaps someone who has money which you could do with, it needs very considerable thought beforehand.

Your first reaction to such a thought should be a resounding 'No!' You may remember what I said in Chapter 2 about partnerships between two married couples, or friends – they never work. It is only a matter of time before they break up. They will break up, never fear. I daresay someone is going to prove me wrong by pointing out a dozen establishments which have been running successfully for years and years and years with just such partnerships. Well, so be it. They must indeed be very special but, however many such places you can produce, I still say 'Don't!'

And even if you and your spouse are going to be the partners, make sure your solicitor draws up a proper deed which will set out the terms of dissolution and the division of profits and responsibilities. Cynicism again? Not at all. Just practical. And if you need such a deed with your spouse, it becomes fairly obvious that a partnership with other people has got to have cast-iron agreements. If you lived happily side by side for a dozen years, you are still one day going to thank your lucky stars that you insisted on such a course.

The third type of business is the limited company. It has some advantages but it also requires a lot more formal structure and is governed much more tightly by the law.

It is very rare in your early days, with a small restaurant along the lines we have envisaged, that you will be advised to form a limited company, though you may well grow into one with your continued success. Let us hope so.

Very briefly, a limited company, which any solicitor can set up for you at a cost of about £200, is a legally bound entity which limits the shareholders (of which there must be at least two) as regards their liability if the company should fail. They are liable for the debts of their company only to the extent of the face value of their shares. But such a company has to prepare proper accounts, it has to have an annual audit, and it has to disclose its activities to the public if so required. Should you grow and prosper into a large operation, your accountant will advise you on the possibility of setting up a limited company, not just to limit your own liability should something go wrong but also to alert you to some tax advantages which may help.

The complexities of limited companies are not within the scope of this book, and it is essential that professional advice be obtained should you wish to consider such a move. It is not within your capabilities unless you are legally or financially trained. And, if I may say so, you are meant to be a restaurateur. Concentrate on that.

The only problem that may confront you, and again on which you will need professional advice, is whether you are, perhaps, buying an already-existing company. This is quite different from buying a business from a sole trader or a partnership, for in that case any past problems, to do with taxation, debts, claims and so on which arise subsequently, are still the seller's problems and cannot affect you, the new owner. If, on the other hand, you have bought a company, that company is liable for all past and present matters, and this is certainly not to your advantage. The company, as I said, exists whoever the directors are, and it is the company which owns the business, warts and all, and not you. It may take a lot of time and money to charm away those warts.

So, if you are faced with a company, you must insist on buying the business and not the company itself, which will be retained by the seller to do as he wishes. If the seller refuses to sell the business without selling the company as well, it could, sadly, be a very hot potato indeed, and you are best advised to drop your plans and look elsewhere.

However, there are some other things you must now do if you are certain you will be opening your own doors to the public within a short while.

Registration for VAT

Having assured yourself not only that the property is to be yours but that any possible problems are either overcome already or capable of smooth solution once you have the keys, so to speak, let the local office of the Inland Revenue know what you are intending to do, if only to ensure that you keep on the right side of them, and above all you will almost certainly have to register for VAT with the local office of HM Customs and Excise. There is no escaping this obligation and the concomitant exasperation and irritation at becoming an unpaid tax-collector whether you like it or not. Indeed, among the draconian powers which the VAT inspectors have is that of imposing fines for late registration – and that is only one of the many sweeping measures available to them.

At present, any business with a turnover in excess of £23,000 has to register for VAT. This may seem a lot of money but in fact it is very little – there is hardly any business in the country which actually *turns over* less money than that in a year. VAT is actually not a tax on earnings or profits or anything like that; it is a tax on the amount of money you take in and pay out, even though you may make not a penny piece profit on any of it.

The rules and regulations surrounding the VAT imposition are enormous. We shall consider them later.

'Change of Use' Permission

There are two further points that should be mentioned here, one of which I have already touched upon, but I feel it important to put it into your mind again.

I mentioned in Chapter 4 that you will need 'change of use' permission from the local authority Planning Department if the premises you intend to buy or lease have not been used for catering purposes hitherto. To be fair, planning officers know how difficult it is for a business scheme to go ahead without the necessary permission, and they also know that not many people can wait around for too long a time. So they are more than understanding, usually, to get through such permission as quickly as possible. It is quite normal for 'provisional' permission to be given in certain designated areas where there is almost a blanket cover for business operations. The 'strings' attached to such provisional permission are almost always dependent upon other factors, such as environmental health and so on. In more tricky areas – residential or rural, for instance, the process may be a little more complicated, but even then, as I said earlier, you will get some very good idea, if not a definite 'go ahead', as to whether permission will be easy to obtain.

Licensing Laws
The second point concerns the question of whether you intend applying for a licence to sell alchohol.

Now, you do not need me to tell you that the licensing laws in Britain are a veritable quagmire. Although England and Wales are lumped together officially, Wales frowns on Sunday drinking, Northern Ireland has its own set of regulations and the Isle of Man and the Channel Islands are different again. Only in Scotland are these things better ordered – their law is absolutely cut and dried and standardized. But wherever you are setting up a business it is essential that a local solicitor advises you, and he will also be able to tell you what your chances of success are should you wish to apply for a liquor licence for the first time, especially in England, where personal attitudes by magistrates and the local police are allowed free rein.

Before dealing with this, however, let me reassure you that, in the case of your buying an existing restaurant with a licence under Part 4 of the relevant Act, which allows you to sell alcohol with meals, you need apply only for a protection order which will allow you to take over the licence temporarily until such time as the annual meeting of the licensing magistrates, which will then confirm the issue of a full licence for one year. Licences are issued annually, and most licensing courts sit early in the year at which application is made for a renewal. In practice, in most areas, there is one firm of solicitors which handles all types of annual renewals, but your own solicitor will advise on this. It is your first application which concerns us here.

Leaving aside for the moment what happens in Scotland, the local bench has to decide whether you are a fit and proper person to hold a licence and whether the premises are suitable. In the case of a new conversion, it will mean the submission of plans for the layout of your restaurant, and the premises which include it, as well as the 'improvements' demanded by the environmental health officer, fire safety officer and so on. In fact, you must make no structural alteration to any building which is subject to a liquor licence without first submitting the plans to the licensing court. In practice, if you are seeking a provisional order which will allow you to apply eventually for a full 'on' licence, you merely have to promise to do all the things needed. The grant of a provisional licence does not, however, mean you can serve liquor on the day you open. It is provisional until various tasks have been carried out and certified as satisfactory by the relevant officials and serves merely as a reassurance that you will be granted a licence in due course. It saves you a lot of time and money in the long run, because regulations are strict as regards premises and their suitability, and you obviously do not want to carry out vast works only to be told at the end that you are not going to get a licence at all, meaning your starting all over again in another place.

Your own suitability to hold a licence seems less of a hassle. You have to be over eighteen but preferably over twenty-one, without a criminal record, and it helps if you have had some experience in the licensed trade, even if it was a temporary barworker in a local pub. Women can be licensees now, though at one time the whole idea was frowned upon, and if you are a foreigner, especially from outside the EEC, you may have difficulty. But, remember, the law is administered by the local magistrates, and whatever the Lord Chancellor's department may say, this is definitely their territory, or so they believe, and both they and the police can put up all sorts of objections which only time and money can overcome. Once again, a good local solicitor can work wonders. He or she will know what local practices are, and local prejudices too, which are often more important.

In the case of new premises, you have to face the problems of objectors, who can range from other licensees to some old woman who lives next door and for whom the Demon Drink is the incarnation of Old Nick himself on earth. There are many instances of applicants for a licence having to gather signatures of approval from customers to present to the bench showing that they need a licence in order to go on visiting your establishment. This is difficult if you have no customers to start with.

So if a licence is important to your operation, get a provisional one first, otherwise you could be in big trouble. It is often very difficult to obtain one later and may take two or three years. In the meantime you will have to allow customers to bring their own bottles and, although many restaurants have operated successfully in this way, it is a frightful bore, apart from meaning the loss of some very useful profit. (As a matter of interest, even though you can charge what is called 'corkage' on wines brought into your unlicensed premises, if a customer wants a bottle of wine from your local off-licence and asks you to get it for him, he actually has to give you the money in advance – you are not allowed, under these antiquated laws, to go out and buy a bottle and put the cost of it on his bill.)

There may be all sorts of objections to a licence, perhaps the unfairest of which is the one of 'too many places' in any one area. This is still being listened to, and debated about, by local benches. These objectors are normally members of the local Licensed Victuallers Association, to which most publicans belong. It is a restrictive and for the most part obstructive association, and very few restaurateurs should dignify such an organization with their own subscriptions.

Remember, the LVAs are against *competition* from 'outsiders'. They are not *for* relaxation of out-dated liquor laws unless it concerns them directly. Few LVA branches are able to understand that freedom to sell liquor will help everyone eventually and even, one day, perhaps, get rid of entrenched attitudes and prejudices about the whole question for ever.

Objections of 'too many' licences are still common, even though most supermarkets now have off-licences and the big chains of liquor shops have outlets in most towns, virtually side by side. It is true that you are not likely to get objections from these sources – they are far too commercially wise, but certainly local pubs, various religious groupings and in many areas the police themselves find indignant morality and not the law sufficient cause to intervene and plead with a bench against the granting of a licence for someone like yourself. No one has yet been able to explain why a local police superintendent should have the 'right' to stand up in court and object to anyone selling liquor just because a number of other people do, though the very cynical among us might have one or two ideas of our own.

On the other hand, it is certainly true to say that in some areas the police and the magistrates take a much broader and more reasonable view altogether.

The position regarding licences in Scotland is much more sensible. For a start, there are only four 'statutory objectors' – those who can appear in court and argue against your having a licence. The first is the police, and the second is the Kirk. For all practical purposes the Kirk can be disregarded, as the courts pay no heed to it any longer – so much so that the Church authorities hardly ever bother to take any interest in the subject, apart from their sermons in pulpits and the 'fire and brimstone' element which still exists in some areas. The other two 'objectors' can be the community council in the area where you want your restaurant, or any person owning a property adjacent to your premises.

Normally there is little to worry about from these sources, but there are certain 'dry' areas in Scotland, and it is unlikely you will get a licence in such places. They are well known and preserved almost for their curiosity value more than for anything else. They are, however, geographically small and few and far between, being mainly slightly 'upswept' areas of social standing but of no ancient tradition, and they need not concern us here.

Perhaps the main difference between Scotland and the rest of Britain is its attitude towards the whole question of drink which permeates right down from the courts.

Among the properties which my wife and I once looked at and which we thought suitable for conversion into a hotel was a former manse which had a restrictive covenant, as almost all former Church properties do, against the sale of liquor in any form. Our solicitor told us to ignore the question. No Scottish court would uphold such a restriction, we were told, and the Kirk would not object to the necessary easement because they knew they would lose any case they brought. Although we did not buy that particular property for other reasons, we did eventually buy a property which had a similar covenant against liquor sales, though this time imposed more than a century ago by the local duke who sold the land. Once again we were told not to worry – Scottish judges did not approve of the restriction of the individual any more than absolutely necessary, and any attempt to enforce the covenant would fail. We were advised to buy an easement from the present duke, so we did. It cost £25, and our solicitor paid it 'on the nail', in cash!

The liberality of the Scottish system means, in theory, that you could have every shop in every high street selling liquor – just as every shop could sell a bar of soap if it so wished. Contrary to the sorry-heads' woeful predictions that the whole nation would soon be awash with alcohol in which small children would drown in the city gutters, no such thing happened.

The law of supply and demand, and commercial sense, operated as it does in everything else.

I do not wish to get into any argument about the relaxation of liquor laws and its effect on drunkenness, but I do know that the marvellous city, Glasgow, is now a very different place to walk about in compared with many years ago, and I am sure the same goes for most other cities north of the Border.

I mentioned earlier that licences have to be renewed in England and Wales every year but this is not so in Scotland, where licences for restaurants and hotels are granted for every three years. But, as in England and Wales, no 'reminders' are sent out. This led to a very amusing incident with our own licence in Scotland which had run out without realizing it some two years before we decided to sell the hotel. A prospective buyer had made the necessary enquiries and been told that we were not, in fact, licensed at all. I have to admit that a very worried 'former' licensee telephoned the proper authorities at once to apologize and see what could be done to stave off almost certain prosecution – only to be told by a most amused woman court clerk, 'Not to worry, Mr Pitt – it's my fault. I don't think I could have told you that the law was altered a few years back and no reminders are sent out any more. Leave it all to me.' The renewal of our licence arrived by next post.

I am not at all sure that such would be the treatment of a similar offender down in England, certainly not with the magistrates on my local bench. But, as I said, they order these things better in Scotland.

Toilets

In any catering establishment the law, in the shape of the Sanitary Conveniences Regulations, 1964, inevitably governs, in a most complex way, the whole question of toilet facilities, both for the public and your staff. The environmental health officer will be obsessed with this subject and will very often be at variance in his views with those of the building control inspector. So it may be best to summarize, as briefly as possible, the overall legal situation and leave the details to be discussed with your own EHO.

In smaller establishments where few staff are employed you need toilet and personal washing facilities easily available. These can even be next door in an adjacent premises, but not if such facilities are the local public convenience. In other words, they must be more or less your own or over which you have some control. In the majority of all instances, these toilets must have flush lavatories and a basin with hot and cold water, soap, towels or driers. Only in larger operations (those employing more than five men and women) are separate male and female toilets demanded. So much, then, for staff – what about the public who come to your establishment?

Well, once again, it depends on the type of operation and how big it is. But, in principle, if you employ more than ten people, and/or the public has access to the same toilets as the staff, you will need separate sanitary facilities for men and women.

Public access is the crux of the problem.

As an example, if you have a sandwich bar, or a take-away operation which is small and which does not cater for eating on the premises, then you only need ordinary single toilet facilities for you and your staff, even if members of the public can use the toilet now and again. And in such places which do have a limited 'eat-in' provision, a single toilet may well suffice for everyone. But when it comes to what is termed a 'restaurant' operation or a pub, or anything on a similar scale, the EHO will probably insist that male and female facilities are provided, with proper ventilation and a 'dead' area between the closet space and any other room in which you can fit basins and suchlike. As all such plumbing and drainage work is very costly, it is essential that the EHO is consulted before you commit yourself to anything. On the other hand, make sure that the EHO is not riding some mysterious hobby-horse of his (or her) own and that what he (or she) lays down as being the regulations are, in fact, exactly that.

10 The Kitchen

Born in the garret, in the kitchen bred.

Lord Byron

The quote from Lord Bryon, who died in 1824, seems to sum up a whole slice of opinion towards work in the kitchen, which, in Britain, alas, persists to this day. Very few want to work in a kitchen, even in the catering trade, and although today's mantle of sanctity surrounding the more publicity-minded chefs should do much to diminish this feeling of servitude, it has not, in reality, done any such thing to the public at large. I find it curious, but after many years in a kitchen I have come to accept it not just with a wry smile and a shrug but with some smugness. I *like* the kitchen. I am unable to understand others who do not, even though they may call themselves chefs.

Our many travels in France, as well as many other European countries, naturally make public attitudes towards cooking in Britain all the more odd. When I say I am a chef, I am immediately accepted. I am not questioned as to why, as to whether the work is hardly suitable for a man, as to whether I find it menial. Such questions simply do not occur abroad. A chef is a distinguished practitioner of a great art. That suits me just fine.

The Greasy Spoon

I started with that little moan because it is time now to consider that engine-room of any restaurant, the kitchen. It is the kitchen which dictates everything about any eating-place. It dictates the size of its dining-room and the number of 'covers' which can be served. It dictates the style and type of restaurant you are going to run, and it dictates the type of customer you are going to welcome. Everything about your kitchen is going to tell

93

everyone else what exactly it is that makes you attractive to some and repellent to others. Perhaps that is why, in Britain, I have seen such awful kitchens. It seems to me that, because the kitchen is 'behind the green baize door' in most people's minds, it is also a place where no human being would wish to tread. Most odd.

Take the average fast food outlet – and, why be coy, what about a Little Chef? Now, to say there is any element of the cooking of great food in such a place would be straining credulity overmuch. Yet the kitchen is in full sight of every customer, it is invariably clean, the staff are invariably clean as well, there is no smell of greasy chips, old fat, unclean hot plates, spilled and congealing gravy, long burned-on food.

I do not have shares in my local Little Chef (it is a franchise operation anyway) and I do not regard them as the embodiment of the *Encyclopédie Gastronomique*, but I do regard them with considerable favour, because I cannot see why, if they seem to be able to do it up and down the country, the rest of the country's caterers seem perpetually to get things so wrong. I am sorry to have to say this but it happens for the most part to be true. The Greasy Spoon is alive and well and going great guns throughout Britain. And for the most part it starts in the kitchen and, unfortunately, does not remain there. The Greasy Spoon does have one advantage, however. It is egalitarian. However much you pay, or however little, the state of restaurant kitchens is not only an eye-sore but a nose-sore too.

And this in a country crawling with environmental health officers armed with manuals of regulations needing fork-lift trucks. But perhaps that may be the problem – no health officer has ever been a chef. If he had, or was, perhaps our kitchens would get better and our food attain a general level of acceptability.

But I am not, actually, talking about cleanliness alone. I am talking about general *attitudes*. I am talking about what makes great kitchens and what makes frightful ones.

The Open Kitchen Door
The truth of the matter is that great kitchens come from men and women who know about and understand food, or from organizations which have so cleverly targeted their market that they are able to insist on certain standards being observed by all

who work for them. And in this context I put the vast majority of the fast food outlets. I am sure they have problems with cleanliness, with staff, sometimes with supplies or disagreeable customers, but those problems rarely seem to rub off on me, as a customer travelling the country on business or pleasure.

Ah, I hear you say, but we started off about kitchens and now we are into a diatribe about cooking. No, we are not. We are on about a great many so-called restaurateurs who seem to feel that what is out of sight is also out of mind and has nothing anyway to do with their customers. They could not be further from the truth. Although I am by no means an apostle for the 'open-plan kitchen on view to all' school of thought, I am an exponent of the belief that a kitchen, your kitchen, *should* be open to all if necessary and not just to the environmental health officer once you have shoved the dog-bowl under the sink and the dishcloths into a cold oven. It is, yet again, an attitude of mind. A closed kitchen is a closed view of the catering trade.

One of our great happinesses, when we had a hotel and restaurant in Scotland, and again in southern England, was that a great many of our better guests always seemed to end up in the kitchen – as my wife and I do when we are in France. And inability to pay the bill is not the reason in either case. Our guests, customers, felt somehow at home, at ease, and it was a measure of our success that we were able to convey this to them.

Now I am not suggesting in any way that every restaurant should open its kitchen doors to every customer (though that is just what a Little Chef, Wimpy or what-have-you actually does). And I am not suggesting that every customer actually wants to finish his evening sitting around in a kitchen after his meal instead of talking to his companions in a pleasant dining-room. But what I do very often feel in Britain is the extraordinary *division* between the kitchen and the dining-room, and it all goes back to that quote from Lord Byron at the head of this chapter. Kitchens are for working wretches, scullions no less, and those who work in them are a form of sub-order of the human species.

Some years back I was haughtily informed by a hotel 'manager' who was fresh out of catering college that, even though I might be the chef, I had no part in anything that went on in the dining-room – the customers were no concern of mine. He was somewhat taken aback when I told him peremptorily to get out of my kitchen and that the guests were in his dining-room only because of my cooking. I regarded the diners as *my* diners, and he had better remember it.

Perhaps it is because of that attitude on the part of a young manager that so few people want to work in kitchens in Britain, and why the food which comes out of so many is so bad and unimaginative. Why the British public put up with it is another thing.

Planning the Kitchen

The first thing to do with the kitchen in your new premises is – nothing at all. To avoid expensive mistakes, you are going to need a long, hard look at your new operation and the sort of place you intend to run. It is no good, for instance, calling in a plumber (at about £12.50 an hour) or, for that matter, an electrician at about the same price, to do just the 'odd job or two', and then about a year later calling them both back to undo what they first did and do something else. Please do not yield to that temptation, however inconvenient it might be one day in the future because you have got busier and more successful.

Once again: research, reconnaissance, planning is the way to start, as it is the way to go on.

Now I am not assuming you are opening a great restaurant with marvellous 'classic' cuisine and delicate patisserie right from the start. For that you would have to go to a great restaurant in Britain, or a fairly good one in France, to see how they order such things. And unless you are made of money, I am not suggesting either that you call in a specialist kitchen-designer who is an expert in commercial kitchens. I am suggesting that the first thing you have to do is study and plan the work-flow.

To show what I mean, I have attached a small and very simple diagram of what a basic kitchen should be like in an ideal world. But none of us lives in an ideal world. Your kitchen is the wrong shape, for a start, and it is far too small or too big. In any event, none of the 'services', such as water, gas, electricity, is anywhere near where you want them. Exactly. But how do you know where you want them until you have discovered exactly what your problems are? Apart from the specialized 'fast food' operations I have already mentioned, the average kitchen starts as being a mess and goes on getting worse.

For the most part, if you have taken over an existing business,

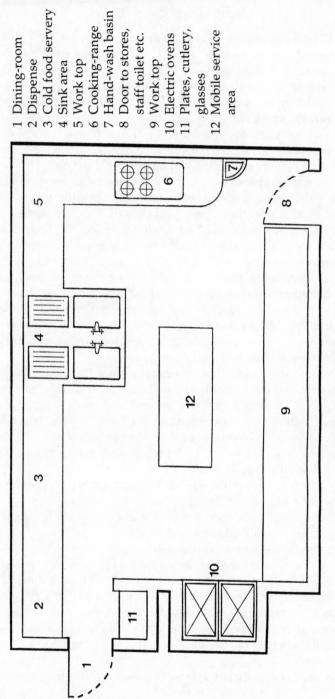

1 Dining-room
2 Dispense
3 Cold food servery
4 Sink area
5 Work top
6 Cooking-range
7 Hand-wash basin
8 Door to stores,
   staff toilet etc.
9 Work top
10 Electric ovens
11 Plates, cutlery,
   glasses
12 Mobile service
   area

Hugh Pitt's Kitchen in Scotland

it will be inconvenient if not downright grubby, and if you are starting up anew, it will be sadly lacking in everything you feel you must have. (Bad thought. 'Must have' is not something you can know about until you have put at least a toe into the water.)

Of course you can go to one of the many very good kitchen equipment suppliers who also offer a kitchen planning and advisory service, for the most part free if you order their equipment. And, remember, you do not always have to buy such equipment: leasing it could be a better proposition for you. On the whole, I have nothing but praise for such companies but they must know in detail what you are intending to do. It is obvious, is it not, that a fast food operation needs equipment very different from that of a traditional restaurant, apart from certain basic items, and certainly the suggested layout may be different? Yet the work flow will remain much the same: preparation, cooking, serving and keeping warm, collection for the dining-room, clearance from the dining-room, an area for plate-cleaning and stacking, along with cutlery and glasses, washing-up of such items and racking for storage after washing-up, or for redistribution again for further customers, and a pot-wash for the larger cooking utensils.

The law also states that you must have a handwash facility with soap and clean towels in the kitchen, as well as at least two sinks, for vegetable preparation and for other uses. Quite simple, really. The trick is getting it all in, because you need work surface, a cooker or two, storage areas, waste bins and a lot more besides. And where is the refrigerator going to go – and what about the deep-freeze?

Yet chefs like me often say that too big a kitchen is worse than too small a one – it merely increases the leg work.

I hope I will not depress you overmuch by including now a plan of how a really great kitchen looks.

So somewhere in between is yours.

I am not going to waste time on the sort of pots and pans you need, what glasses and plates and so on. I think such things are trivial, and you have more than enough sense to decide for yourself rather than read about *coupe* dishes and so on. (I thought they had gone out years ago!) It is the 'grand plan', the 'overall scheme of things' that must be considered and discussed.

There are basically two types of kitchen layout – that in which

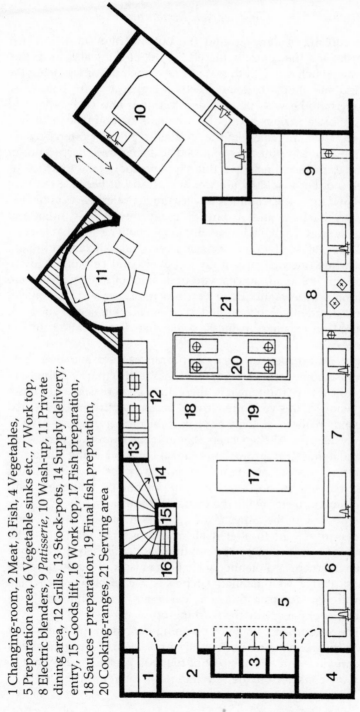

1 Changing-room, 2 Meat, 3 Fish, 4 Vegetables, 5 Preparation area, 6 Vegetable sinks etc., 7 Work top, 8 Electric blenders, 9 *Patisserie*, 10 Wash-up, 11 Private dining area, 12 Grills, 13 Stock-pots, 14 Supply delivery; entry, 15 Goods lift, 16 Work top, 17 Fish preparation, 18 Sauces – preparation, 19 Final fish preparation, 20 Cooking-ranges, 21 Serving area

The Troisgros Brothers' Kitchen, Roanne

the cooking is done around the outside (the walls, in other words) and the centrally placed 'island' cooking site, or 'piano' as the French call it. Both systems have their advantages, but the island site almost certainly needs a bigger area for it to work properly, otherwise people tend to bump into each other and might cause serious accidents. Accidents are endemic to kitchen work. They are mainly of the 'cutting' type (very often because knives are too blunt, as opposed to being too sharp) and, of course, the scalding type. But slippery floors take their toll as well, not because they are wet and clean but because they are wet and greasy. Cleanliness is very much preferable to godliness in any kitchen, and, I daresay many, many holy nuns and monks would agree with me. But more about cleanliness later.

I have, alas, all too rarely seen a very good kitchen in Britain, but when one does it is a joy to behold and certainly a joy to work in. It is going to cost you quite a lot of money, if you are setting up anew, and if you have any intelligence at all, you will almost certainly find your first 'ready-made' kitchen, if you have bought an existing business, somewhat disappointing, to say the least.

But do not be put off by appearances, and above all, just because some item of equipment is already 'there', do not fall into the trap of thinking it is 'there' for a good reason and cannot be changed. It is very often 'there' because at the time it seemed the only place for it. Only rarely is it the proper place for it. Only rarely has the kitchen been thought out from the start. Very often it has just grown piece-meal, one bit being added to another, without any real idea as to why or questions being asked about it. So, even if your kitchen is crammed with equipment, never make the mistake of not seeing the wood for the trees. On the other hand, as I said earlier, you do not necessarily want to alter it all round right at the start. Who knows, even the most apparently chaotic kitchen might have been planned, and planned well. Being biased, I would hazard a guess that a well-planned kitchen is a chef-planned kitchen. Beware of domestic kitchen 'designers' or architects. They hardly ever have to do the washing-up.

The second advantage of planning your own kitchen is that from early on you can decide the sort of cooking-equipment you eventually want and the sort of fuel you prefer. And try not to buy, or consider buying, anything, unless you have seen it in action first, in a commercial kitchen.

For instance, I once worked as a relief chef at a very prestigious country hotel. On my first Sunday lunch I was faced with a number of joints, including beef, which were easy enough, but the gas oven which I had to use to cook the Yorkshire puddings in had 'tricks' of which I was ignorant. I burned at least thirty-six individual ones so black that they had to be thrown away, and my wife had to come in from 'front of house' to make quantities more batter for me.

But I had always hated gas ovens, so perhaps I was allergic to that particular one. I much prefer gas hobs and electric ovens, but other people have different views, and you must decide for yourself.

Choosing Equipment

Do not decide for yourself until you have seen the incredible equipment now on offer. Even if you cannot, regretfully, afford it from the start, just to look and learn is a joyful experience.

And that takes us to the next point. Where do I go to get an idea of what I might need or would dearly like to have? The easy answer, indeed the only answer, in my opinion, is to go to the catering exhibitions which are held alternately in London, Olympia, and Glasgow, Kelvin Hall, early each year. The dates of these main exhibitions are well heralded in such trade magazines as the *Caterer and Hotel Keeper*. There are many other exhibitions too, both in the major cities and in smaller provincial towns, at which a considerable range of equipment and food products are displayed. They are without question Wonderlands of ideas, both established and innovative, and for the most part the demonstration staff on every stand are knowledgeable, helpful and courteous.

When my wife and I first started our own operation, we spent long hours in the Kelvin Hall, and we have to say quite honestly that, novices as we were, we learned a vast amount and gained information and help we simply could not have obtained elsewhere.

These exhibitions will give you a basic idea, but perhaps you cannot afford everything you see. Then, as I mentioned before, discuss the possibility of leasing certain items, which will free what money you have for those other, essential cash items which will always crop up. And if leasing is not possible, try the second-hand dealers. In practice, we found that very little good second-hand equipment was available, but there are one or two specialist firms in London which have quite large selections, and some do exist in major provincial towns.

Main tourist centres, such as Bournemouth, often have such outlets and, of course, there are auctions in various parts of the country which are advertised in the trade press. The only problem with auctions is that you want to know very definitely what you are looking out for, and roughly how much it should be worth, so they should be approached with caution.

But in any event, once again, you must know the sort of operation you are going to run. Write down the main requirements for such an operation and if necessary contact the Catering Equipment Distributors Association, who will be pleased to help about your local suppliers.

Another source of help – and one much to be admired – is a first-class catering suppliers. Once again there are two or three in London, certainly a very fine firm in Glasgow and others dotted about the country. But you will be better off if you concentrate on your nearest provincial city – Birmingham or Manchester, for example, if you are not near Glasgow or London.

These shops sell everything from vast commercial equipment, suitable for hospitals or institutions, to smaller pieces of equipment which you might even find in your own domestic kitchen. Once again I have found their staff enormously helpful.

It is a good thing to try to deal regularly with one major supplier and become known to them – even in the Highlands of Scotland a representative of our Glasgow suppliers called on us regularly, and we could also ring up and order items we required urgently, which would be delivered very quickly – items ranging from glassware and table napkins to heavy cookware and knives.

Above all, do not be afraid to ask questions wherever you go – newcomers to the trade always seem especially welcome and ignorance explained away. When my wife and I first went into the trade, we were totally ignorant and always pleasantly surprised at the help offered to us. Which was just as well, as in those days there were no books of advice, no 'dos' and 'don'ts' written down for us to study.

Air Cleaning
There is one item of equipment which I have mentioned in

passing but not dwelt upon – it is almost always forgotten in average kitchens, it is always an afterthought, if it is considered in the first place, and yet it is, to me, jolly nearly as important as a sink or a cooker.

It is ventilation or air-cleaning equipment.

Now, I am conscious that this is a bit of a hobbyhorse of mine. But I make no apology for it. I find old, stale cooking-smells – and especially that of the ubiquitous chip or fried fish – utterly revolting. In fact, neither my wife nor I will stay in a place which smells as so many do.

How often have you got out of your car in a pub car-park, say, and been assailed by that awful stench of chip oil? How often have you gone into a restaurant to be greeted first of all by that smell? I can think, alas, of more times than not, which is why I mentioned Little Chef earlier. The franchise agreements for such places are very strict about cooking-smells, and I always feel that, if they can get rid of them efficiently (when most of their operation is frying or grilling), why cannot other establishments? Quite honestly, the answer is simply that the owners of such places do not, themselves, notice how frightful their property smells.

An inn and restaurant we know not far from where we live used to have owners who were very strict about how their place smelled and even went so far as never to serve chips, because their extraction equipment was fairly non-existent. Most customers commented, as we did on entering, that the hallway always smelled so good, of enticing food being cooked, and the dining-area so good, of polish, fresh flowers and wood fires. The important point about the smell of that place was the word 'enticing' – it made you hungry just to go in there. Now the same place has new owners who do not seem to worry about it. One of our friends said she was not going back there any more – she had hung her coat in the hallway and, when she collected it on leaving, it stank of old chip oil and had to go to the cleaners before she could wear it again. We thought it very sad, but very typical.

There are a number of systems on the market, and firms which specialize in 'tailoring' ventilation of a kitchen to your own requirements. The filters have to be kept clean, of course, and the whole thing must be regularly serviced, which is normally done under contract with the suppliers or engineers.

But remember that 'extraction' means what it says – the warm air goes out as well as the smell, and places can get quite chilly if the extractor is not well regulated.

An alternative is the air-cleaning system, which we have found very effective, though they tend to sound a little noisy at those times when your restaurant is none too full.

Air-cleaners recirculate the atmosphere by sucking in stale air at the bottom and pushing it through a system of filters designed to eradicate various types of smell, including tobacco smoke. The air at the top has thus been 'cleaned' but none of the natural warmth of the room has been lost. There is also a rheostat which controls the speed of the fans inside. My own experience has shown that even people smoking cigars go undetected and that, where such equipment is fitted, the increasing number of 'No Smoking' areas you find in eating-places are unnecessary. For the most part, the owners of such establishments prefer 'banning orders' to save them the trouble of finding an alternative. This is a shame, especially when air-cleaning equipment works out at about £30 per month, which includes a servicing contract if you are dealing with a reputable firm. Yet very few establishments use them. I often wonder if it is just sheer ignorance.

In practice I have found that an ordinary extraction fan, in a window, say, coupled with an air-cleaner, is very often efficient both in a kitchen and in a dining-room, but very busy kitchens, especially those serving quantities of fried food, must, repeat *must*, have proper extraction systems. It is better for all concerned, staff and customers combined. But I shall remind you about keeping the dining-room comfortable when we get to Chapter 11.

From Floor to Ceiling

Let us, finally, take a quick look at the various items of equipment you may need and set your mind at rest about some of the 'technical' terms you may come across.

For all work surfaces, stainless steel is the most practical and easiest to keep clean. It is also the most expensive. Most catering suppliers have 'ready-mades', either with racking underneath or with drawers or cupboards, or a combination to suit your own requirements. There are also firms which specialize in 'tailor-made' work units.

Laminates tend to 'lift' if not very carefully fitted, and the inevitable joins also harbour dirt which does much to upset the visiting environmental health officer. They often look nicer, however, and with care and professional joinery there is no reason to dismiss them out of hand.

Floors should be easy to clean but non-slip. Tiles are very hard on the working feet – just heed what I say – but they are practical, as are most of the surfaces recommended by the dozens of specialist suppliers. In an ideal world, floors would be laid with a 1 in 120 slope to suitable drain-aways, making washing down extremely easy, and where floor and wall meet there should be curved coving for ease of cleaning and protection against bugs and dirt.

Ceilings too should be washable. Wood is frowned on unless very smooth and well coated with high gloss paint, but ordinary plaster is perfectly acceptable, again with gloss paint, as it is on walls, although in areas of heavy wear, such as around a stove, concrete walls with gloss paint are often used. One or two proprietary wall claddings are available which can be acceptable to the health officers and make for a very nice, often decorative finish, in cases where existing walls are in very poor shape or have to be done away with completely. This cladding saves a lot of time, as it comes in easy-to-cut sections, is fixed to battens on the original wall and can save a lot of mess. It is not cheap, however, and the services of an old-fashioned plasterer still go a long way in acceptability and suitable finish.

Cooking-Equipment

Ranges, or 'boiling-tables', to use the catering terms for the domestic cooking-hob, can be had in a number of sizes of four, six and eight 'rings'. Choice of fuel is up to you. Either they are free-standing, with storage space below, or ovens are fitted beneath, again of various sizes, although you will increasingly hear the word 'gastronorm' being used in connection with all ovens and steamers – a belated attempt to standardize sizes so that oven trays etc will fit any item of equipment.

There are certain objections to having ovens below boiling-tables, access being high on my list anyway. Nothing is more annoying than having to move aside from a stove just because someone else wants to get something into or out of the oven. I prefer separate ovens, preferably at waist height, with drop-down doors upon which pans can be rested if required, but space and personal attitudes can make this debatable.

One word on fuel: if you do not have town gas or natural gas, do bear in mind the liquid petroleum gases which are available, normally Propane, which has a much higher BthU rating than Butane and also a lower freezing temperature, which makes quite a difference, believe you me, if you have to cook in places like the Scottish Highlands in wintertime. The cylinders come in various sizes, or a larger vessel is filled regularly by a visiting tanker, similar to that for oil heating. Automatic change-over valves are a normal fitting so that the gas does not 'die' on you in the middle of service.

Various 'package' deals are available with LPG suppliers, so discuss these in detail with their local representatives before you make up your mind, especially as not all existing gas equipment can be converted from ordinary gas to LPG.

Britain has been slow to accept the advantages of LPG, possibly because of supply problems in the past, the proliferation of strictly 'local' gasworks and the fact that not many restaurants existed outside towns and major villages, but its use is becoming much more widespread now, especially in the catering trade, and there is a choice of equipment – at one time only the French (inevitably) made gas hobs which came with all three different jets as standard.

As regards electricity, there are new boiling tables available now which use halogen lamps. They heat almost immediately – very much faster than normal electric rings – and can be controlled with all the delicacy of gas. There is no surrounding heat either, the hob surface outside the lamp area remaining quite cool to the touch. Although I have not cooked on these hobs (they only really 'arrived' towards the end of 1987), I can see quite a bright future for them, despite their expense (between £2,000 and £3,000), for they are easy to keep clean and appear extremely efficient.

Another development has been that of magnetic-field hobs which work on the induction principle, so that, when a pan is placed on the surface, a current is generated which boils the water or cooks the food. The moment the pan is removed, the field ceases to work.

There is no ambient surface heat at all on the hob surface or surround, which makes them very safe.

So far I have received conflicting reports about these magnetic-field cookers but I daresay they will eventually overcome any problems they might be experiencing now. The whole electricity industry has been aware for years of many disadvantages (mainly cost and slowness of response) of cooking on the old-fashioned 'rings', and I can see some very positive work appearing in the future.

Ovens are too well known to dwell upon. There is little difference between domestic and commercial apart from size, but I do favour the convection or 'fan' ovens now available as they cut cooking-time by as much as thirty or forty per cent and are marvellous for baked products. But I would not advise the fan oven unless you have space for a conventional oven as well – a fan oven can play hell by drying out certain dishes before they are properly cooked.

Microwave ovens are a different matter. They are still being sold as a primary cooking-tool, and the catering industry, always quick to jump on an easy bandwagon, took them to their hearts, often with disastrous results. They are not, in my very definite opinion and experience, a primary cooking-tool but they are good for defrosting and for the reheating of certain foods. I think they are much over-rated, and a microwave oven would be very far down any list of mine for kitchen equipment.

The ubiquitous deep-fryer, considered a 'must' for so many kitchens, comes in a great many varieties, free-standing or as part of a range. It is important they conform to British Standards, as most do nowadays, and that they are easily drainable. Fryers are one of the prime sources of foul smells, as I have stressed, so the essential and regular changing of the oil is made all the more tedious by not being able to get rid of the used oil quickly and easily. If you must have this often odious piece of equipment, two smaller fryers side by side are better than one big one – their recovery time is quicker and they can be used at the same time for different things. In general, as a rough guide, a fryer should hold about 1½ times as much food as oil or fat: five pounds of cooking-agent to seven or eight pounds of food at any one time, say. Thermostats should hold temperatures steady for anything between 150°C and 200°C, and they take up to thirty minutes to heat. Oddly enough, unless you are getting through a vast amount of chips, they are very expensive to run, so be warned.

Steamers are good for the cooking or 'holding' of certain items, especially vegetables, even though they are designed primarily for the larger, institutional type of demand. Once again, new types are always coming onto the market. Make quite sure, however, that you really do need one before committing yourself.

Grills are another much-debated item. If the heat source is above the food-tray, it is technically a salamander; if below, it is a grill. The widespread availability now of the very heavy, often cast-iron griddle, which is an electrically heated 'hot plate' upon which the food is directly placed, has meant the need for old-fashioned grills has lessened. You can see these working in any fast food outlet, and they are very acceptable to all chefs, although cleanliness once again is the watchword.

The *bain-marie* is merely a method of keeping food and sauces gently warm, usually by putting the article into one pot which is in turn put into another holding hot water – not dissimilar to the old-fashioned double boiler used for porridge. More often than not in British kitchens, the *bain-marie* is abused by being made to keep items hot for long periods at a time, such as vegetables or potatoes which eventually mush down or taste revoltingly stale. This is not the fault of the *bain-marie*, however; it is the fault of bad chefs or cooks who are not capable of planning menus and items to be cooked so that prolonged 'holding' is unnecessary. Laziness and ignorance are two of the most common reasons for poor food in restaurants; it is rarely lack of quality or freshness of product, or the lack of proper equipment which is to blame. Hot cupboards are abused in a similar way. Use them for plates, not food.

Storage

Storage is a problem in most kitchens. Very rarely is there enough of it. A good old-fashioned walk-in larder is ideal. Perforated zinc, or a similar small-mesh screen, at the windows, rodent proof, well-fitting doors and good ventilation are all you need, along with stout shelving to take heavy items. Most Victorian houses had such places, and jolly good they were. All too often nowadays food is stored in unsuitable areas just because there is not enough room for a proper 'larder'.

The health officers will want to know about where you store foods of all kinds, so make sure any area is kept spotlessly clean.

They object to stuff on the floor – at least eight inches above ground is required. There are specialist suppliers now of very good wire racking which can be bought and built up on a modular system. Once again, a catering exhibition will have many such examples. The same goes for wine 'bins' which can be built from 'kits'. Do not keep even red wine in too hot a place – I once went to a restaurant where the owner actually boasted of his red wine storage system; it turned out to be exactly on top of a radiator. The bottles were hot to the touch, and he did not take kindly to my remark that he would be better to stuff them into the cabbage water when needed rather than keep them where they were.

A steady temperature, about 14°C, is better for all wines, whatever their colour, if you do not have specialized, separate storage areas or wine cabinets. A lot of nonsense is talked about wine, as we shall see in Chapter 16. It is better to have one main storage area from which you take red wines into the restaurant, and put some white in a cooler each day.

Water and Washing-Up

Hot drinks need hot water, and small boilers are available for these. They are sold on their hot water output per hour, fifty, a hundred or 150 pints, but they are also quoted in cups or gallons. There are eighteen cups to a gallon. Choose a boiler which is reasonable to your projected need.

And while we are on the subject of hot water, your kitchen is going to need a vast quantity, so make sure your hot water system is able to cope adequately. Nothing is worse than 'running out' of hot water just when you need it most. And it will happen, never fear, unless you have a proper supply. Remember, every meal served needs between one and four gallons of hot water.

Dish-washing machines are not always necessary, providing you have a *plongeur* coping with the dirty plates and cutlery. And you should always try to have a special 'pot wash' area reserved for saucepans, which are extremely unwieldy.

Basically, dish-washers are of two types – and the type distinguishes their price ticket. The cheapest to buy are of the domestic type. They are 'stacked' with the dirty plates and cutlery and then left to get on with it. This process takes an hour or more, depending on the make of machine. They are comparatively cheap, however – less than £500. The second, or commercial type, has sets of trays or racks which are stacked with utensils and put into the machine, which then washes and dries them in a matter of minutes. These are going to cost at least £800, possibly more.

There is a third type which will probably not concern you at this stage: it consists of a 'conveyor belt' system onto which the utensils are placed, the 'belt' taking them through the washing process in one continuous movement until they emerge at the other end, clean and ready for storage. These machines are used in very large restaurants, hospitals and so on.

As I say, forget the third type. But consider the difference between the other two. The most common commercial type, which washes in a very short cycle, has a knock-on effect in that your stocks of crockery and cutlery need not be too enormous, as it copes with up to 200 items an hour, allowing for five items per meal. If you use the 'domestic' type, you 'lock up' great amounts of your eating utensils for long periods, which means you will have to carry very much greater stocks of every item.

Shelves

May I make a plea for shelves, and not cupboards, in kitchens. You have probably seen those depressing, glossy photographs of 'designer' kitchens in the Sunday magazines and elsewhere: all neatly planned with masses of cupboard doors and work surfaces empty except for the obligatory bowls of aubergines and lemons. That is nothing like a commercial kitchen. Indeed, it is nothing like my own kitchen at home.

It is the cupboard door which amuses me, for I bet that within that cupboard are shelves on which bowls are stacked, one inside the other.

Just imagine that situation in a busy kitchen. In the first place, whenever you want something you are bound to be carrying something else in one hand. You have to put it down, having opened the cupboard door, and then use two hands to get what you want, not forgetting to close the door afterwards. If you do not close that door, someone else will come along and walk into it. Yet time and again I see doors on cupboards even in restaurant kitchens. Forget it all. Go for shelves, open shelves, and, above all, hooks under them and on the ceiling. Hooks to hang every cooking-utensil you can imagine: sieves, spoons, choppers, colanders, saucepans, jugs and the 101 items which make a kitchen so enjoyable to work in. Keep cupboards for foodstuffs, not cooking-tools.

Gadgets

I do not see the need here for a 'checklist' of smaller items in your new kitchen. If you need something, go out and buy it. You do not know what you will need before you need it. Any proper kitchen collects all sorts of odds and ends, few of which last the course of actually being used. Chuck those out. Over the years I have been given dozens of items, and bought a lot too, which I thought, or other people thought, 'would come in useful'. Some have, most have not.

I will even admit to a bit of heresy here. A kind friend (and a very good chef) gave me a food-processor years ago. It stood under its cover for more than four months, unused. It was an expensive present but somehow I just could not get used to the idea of it, despite being shown many times how versatile and useful it could be. Then one day I thought I would 'have a go'. Unbelievable. A whole new world opened up to me. It became a constant companion. Yet not to this day have I once used the slicing discs. Perhaps I am a very old-fashioned chef, or perhaps I can slice the things I want quicker by hand, without making the machine dirty. I do not know. But what I do know is to not follow fashion slavishly and buy things just because everyone else has them. Make up your own mind.

I even use regularly a wooden-bowled *hachoir* for chopping up herbs very finely, which I bought in Paris nearly thirty years ago. It cost me about 5 shillings. I have found nothing to touch it for speed, and I would not be without it.

Any decent catering supplier will have everything you could need (but not the *hachoir*, I'll be bound, not one like mine with an off-centre handle) and I do not see any point here in dealing with the minutiae of environmental-health-approved chopping-boards and so on.

Domestic equipment is generally not suitable for a commercial kitchen where staff are less careful than you are, but, before discarding the idea altogether, you would do well to compare costs of certain items and make quite sure that the use to which any item of equipment will be put does in truth necessitate the extra expenditure on 'heavy duty' bits and pieces. Some domestic equipment nowadays is very robust, especially the more expensive electric ovens. In the case of cooking-hobs, however, there is rarely enough space between cooking-rings for large saucepans, or enough power to boil their contents quickly.

Refrigeration
The only other item worth mentioning is refrigeration equipment. A decent-sized refrigerator in the kitchen is a must and, if you have the space, at least a small deep-freeze to hold items you regularly need, such as stocks, sauces and so on, to be topped up every day as necessary. There should be room for a larger deep-freeze outside somewhere, if you do not have room in the kitchen.

Cabinet, or up-right, freezers with pull out drawers are less caring about electricity but quick to rummage around in. Chest freezers are economical, but whatever it is you need will always be at the bottom. They are, however, better for large joints of meat and so on.

Some of this equipment may well be offered to you for free if your operation requires large quantities of frozen foods. Ask about such concessions when you have become established with a large supplier but do not tie yourself unnecessarily to that supplier alone. It never pays in the long run.

It has always been said that no kitchen has enough refrigeration equipment. As you expand, you will probably want a 'walk-in' cold store. They are made in sections and fitted quite quickly by specialist suppliers. You can sometimes get one secondhand, by keeping an eye on the classified advertisement section of the local paper.

Finally, remember that a deep-freeze can also supply you with ice if your operation does not warrant an ice-making machine. I remember once going out to dinner one very hot evening at a local restaurant where the staff were almost proud to tell you that the ice-machine had broken down the previous weekend and the engineer had still not called. They were less than amused when I asked them why they had not thought of making ice in their deep-freezers, which I knew they must have, because of the quantity of 'bought-in' dishes on their 'extensive' menu. A little forethought, and a proper routine, which we shall consider in Chapter 16, would have ensured that at least one deep-freeze held a large plastic bag of ice-cubes, kept topped up after every service from normal ice-trays.

11   The Dining-Room

Gourmets, if they are not seated comfortably and have no elbow room, count both the wines and the food for nothing.
Lucien Tendret

Lucien Tendret was the great-nephew of Brillat-Savarin and wrote a book about him and his work. As you may already have gathered, I am somewhat fond of the whole background to cooking and eating, and the stories which have been created therefrom. A sense of history is often sadly lacking among many people who regard themselves as chefs or restaurateurs, and I find it strange. The world of food is full of good things, and a sense or knowledge of the past adds to the pleasures of the table, both for yourself and for your guests.

So, with the above quote in mind, we turn now to the dining-room and the sort of image you wish to create. It is an important image. From the moment your customers walk into your establishment, you proclaim to them exactly what sort of food they are likely to be offered. This condition is, I believe, peculiar to Britain. Most of your customers may seem to care more for the setting than for the food, perhaps, but it is the restaurateur who, over the years, has to be blamed, for it is he who has created the idea that the two go hand in hand, as if by Holy Writ.

Much as I would like to say to you: ignore this whole idea that décor is more important than food, to many, if not most, customers, the fact remains that many very successful restaurants have been founded, and thrive, on this whole idea. It is no good my saying that in France, for instance, I have far more regularly eaten very well indeed in places with paintwork peeling off the walls outside, and wallpaper peeling off the walls inside, than in the 'smarter' establishments which are designed largely to lure the unsuspecting within their webs. It is no good my saying that for centuries, so far as I know, the French have ignored paintwork to concentrate on the food and drink. It might well be that paint and paper were too expensive in that country until the arrival of the ubiquitous DIY shops a few years ago. The fact must remain that in Britain the 'face' is more important than the food and that you can get away with culinary murder providing the decorations are presentable.

Themes and Beams

I am assuming that you are not made of money and cannot afford the specialist restaurant interior designers who nowadays abound and often make their living out of what are known, today, as 'themed' restaurants. Both the designers and the 'themes' cost a great deal of money. I do not necessarily think that all designers are a waste of money (for those with success already achieved) but I do think 'themes' very definitely are.

But you must get used to the technical, modern jargon. A 'themed' restaurant is very often a sure sign of previous design failure among the big chains or, anyway, lack of sufficient profit for the money invested. You have certainly come across what I mean: those places with the odd fishing-net and glass float strung across the ceiling, an oar or two and an old sail artfully draped on a wall. That is, crudely, a 'theme'. It is designed to give the customer a feeling that he is in a place where sea food is of the best. The fact that it is frozen fish and chips, same as you would get in dozens of other places, and more honestly (and probably better too) in a local fish-and-chip shop, is immaterial.

A vast amount is spent on 'themed' restaurants, and it is not too cynical of me to say that it is all a great cod on the general public. I can think of at least a dozen restaurants, each of which has been 're-themed' in the past ten years and still serves the same old food (badly) as before.

Because they have a great amount of money, the larger chains of outlets constantly do this, and change their brand name too. The big brewers are high on the list, spending thousands of pounds on new décor and ideas while leaving the food sold in their pubs in the same old, soggy state.

Not surprisingly, the change of interior décor often results in floods of 'new' customers, who then suddenly realize what a 'con' it all is and start staying away in similar quantities. So it is back to the drawing-board for the invention of yet another 'theme'. In the trade papers there will never be any mention of the real reasons behind failure – poor food. There will be just another announcement that the marketing division of the brewery, or whatever, has had a newer, more fashionable idea with its invention of a new theme. The food remains markedly the same, of course. That is the real reason the places do not make as much money as their owners wish: a question of kidding all of the customers some of the time etc.

Sometimes these fashions come and go with extreme rapidity; sometimes they take ages. You may yourself remember the craze many years back for the destruction of genuine Victorian interiors in pubs and restaurants, particularly by one brewery chain in the Midlands and north of England, which owned a very large number of outlets. After ten years or so, they discovered they had made a mistake – and set about re-creating the self-same Victorian interiors they had wantonly destroyed, but at enormous cost. And serve them right. Unfortunately, as always, it was the customer who paid the bill, along with the shareholders.

These warnings serve merely to put the dangers into your mind. If, say, you want to run a restaurant specializing in fish of all types, by all means think in terms of making the sea part of your décor. But remember the money it is going to cost. You may be better off keeping your décor pretty ordinary, though attractive, and being content with its lasting for years until success has been achieved. I think that would be a better course; certainly it will be more prudent.

Our restaurant in the south of England, for instance, was late seventeenth- to early eighteenth-century and had its fair share of 'beams'. When we were thinking of some minor alterations, and being comparative strangers to the area at that time, a drinks-supplier kindly put us in touch with a local builder who specialized in such properties. Neither my wife nor I was very keen on this chap when we met him but he sent us some ideas and plans, among which was the need for a number of extra 'beams' – all in fibreglass. Our horrified protests brought only the reassurance that 'no one would know the difference'. I am afraid we had to point out to him very strongly indeed that *our* sort of customers certainly would know the difference, and did he really want us to display a large notice saying 'THESE

BEAMS ARE IMITATIONS' – a thing we would certainly feel obliged to do with our lot!

Not unnaturally, that builder and ourselves parted company. Yet he was an 'expert', or considered so, in the trade. I suspect he had something to do with the 'theming' of another place in a village not far away, where they actually removed some sixteenth-century beams which were considered not old enough, replacing them entirely with fibre-glass, all running the 'wrong' way for a building of that age. It was very sad, but I wonder whether it increased trade dramatically just because customers got the feeling they were in a genuinely old building rather than one a mere 400 years old?

Comfort and Convenience

So much, then, for 'themes'. But there are a number of established 'rules' on interior design with which you should be acquainted.

The first is probably the old adage that harsh lighting and hard seats make for quick turnover of customers and that subdued lighting and soft seats make for fewer numbers staying longer and being charged more for the privilege. Once again, you must decide in essence right from the start into which category your restaurant is going to fall, which category you, yourself, wish to adopt. The adage demonstrates the extremes.

There are qualifications, obviously, within this statement.

For instance, low tables and chairs, even if very comfortable, make for a quicker turnover of customers, which is particularly suited to a coffee- or tea-shop or something similar. After a time, customers feel psychologically awkward, and they hasten away, leaving the table for someone else. This is not true, however, if you have a bar area where customers can order their drinks and discuss what they are going to eat before going into the dining-room proper. Chairs and tables which are too hard and uncomfortable in those circumstances tend to focus attention on how long customers are waiting for their food. A judicial blend is necessary.

Similarly, seats facing a wall, even an attractive alcove, will not remain filled for long. People are too curious about knowing who is behind them for such arrangements to be popular. A local coffee-bar in my area has just such an arrangement, and in the centre of each room is a long communal table. The turnover in customers is very quick, as neither type of seating is conducive to long-stay trade. Whether the owner planned it deliberately that way I do not know – I suspect not, but he certainly achieves an aim of increasing his through-put by not encouraging his customers to tarry long over their coffees, salads and so on.

A visit to your catering suppliers will show you a range of furniture suitable for a dining-room. It should be sturdy, able to cope with the constant use which often rough-handed customers will give it, and of correct height for the operation you are planning. It will be expensive, and in my opinion the design often leaves much to be desired. In our first restaurant I became so exasperated at not being able to get exactly what I wanted in the way of tables that I made all of them myself – but I was lucky in having my own workshop and an interest in, and knowledge of, woodworking and cabinet-making. Because of long periods in France, I also knew more than most caterers about how dining-rooms should be planned for optimum versatility as regards parties of people. This is particularly important and, I think, worthwhile explaining more fully.

In an ideal world, an area of two square feet is needed for each customer seated at a table. Round tables, especially if old or antique, often look nice, but they are impractical as a general rule – and those with centre pedestals are often rocky or unsafe as well. If you use square tables, however, it would seem to follow that for four people you would require a table four feet by four feet. But this is not necessarily accurate – you can get away with less.

By making the tables rectangular, and ensuring that customers sit opposite in pairs, your table, to give plenty of comfort and room, can measure four feet long but only about twenty inches deep. The saving of those few inches can make quite a lot of difference to the apparent 'size' of a dining-room. With such a table, two customers can use it, either side by side or facing each other or three, as well as four.

I think there is a better way. I made tables which were about two feet four inches square. Some had drop-leaves on one or two edges, about ten inches by two foot four, which allowed a table which was generously comfortable for two being usable for three or four people, again with plenty of room. For larger parties we could also join up tables, normally end to end, with leaves either up or down, depending on the numbers. In this way T-shapes were also possible, and even a squared-off horseshoe. The design gave us enormous manoeuvrability as well as pleasing our customers, who never felt cramped.

As I say, I had to make such tables because I never found a similar design in Britain. We also gained an insight into the truth of the saying, 'Your table will be ready in a moment, sir,' one lunchtime when that was, literally, the case. Whenever we hear this said in any restaurant, we all tend to collapse with laughter but, alas, the explanation never quite rings true.

In France, similar tables are often placed in front of a *banquette* running round the walls. If your dining-room is suitable, this is an extremely good and versatile design, leaving space in the centre for displays or other dining-tables. Couples will normally sit side by side facing outwards into the room, or, if preferred, they can sit facing each other, as can four people dining together.

Apart from the seating, a form of cosiness can be achieved by room-dividers, if you so wish. These divisions can be achieved by plants in long troughs, open-work screens or, as we saw once in a famous restaurant in Limoges, blinds of thin bamboo cane, which hung from the ceiling and could be unrolled at will to divide off, as required, groups of diners at various seating configurations.

I am not, however, trying to write a treatise on interior design – I am merely trying to put into your mind a number of ideas which may appeal to you and may be adapted for what you desire. Once again, if you remember our dear old notebook, you will have jotted many ideas down while doing your researches – those that appealed to you and those that did not.

The important thing throughout is to fashion your own restaurant design to that of your type of trade – your market, in other words. If you are going for the fast food operation, fixed seating of some discomfort to those built like myself will suffice. But not if you are planning an up-market operation, obviously. And above all, if you are not interested in fast food and quick turnover of customers, make sure, I beseech you, that there is plenty of room around each table, as well as on it. Lack of elbow-room is not just a matter of comfort for the customer, it is essential for the staff who have to wait at table. I know of one, now very successful restaurant in a southern town which started off by crowding in too many tables. The atmosphere was stifling for the diners, and impossible for the waitresses – both in heat generated and in terms of service. The food was excellent, and I regretted that I would never visit the place again because of this over-crowding. The restaurant has now learned its lesson, I understand, and is much more comfortable for everyone. It deserved to do well but took years to recover from an initial, and near-fatal, mistake.

Which brings us to air-cleaners again.

I promised you, in the chapter on the kitchen, to return to this subject and, true to my word, I am. Space also means room to breathe.

In a country town near where I live there are, as I said, a number of eating-places, and I realized a little while back that in only one of them was there an area in which a customer could smoke.

Now, you are perfectly entitled to run your business exactly as you wish, but as a customer I am entitled not to use it if you forbid my friends or me to smoke. It is actually immaterial whether I, personally, smoke or not. I simply am not going to enter any restaurant which makes restrictions on reasonable enjoyment without going to the trouble of installing air-cleaning equipment. The business of smoking, harmful or enjoyable, is not at issue. Restriction is. And, moreover, a restriction which is unnecessary. I see no difference in principle between a No Smoking rule and a refusal in some of those ultra-precious establishments to put salt and pepper on the table or provide a jug of cold water and some glasses. If you want a customer's money, within reason that customer should be indulged.

Of course, if you wish there to be a non-smoking *area*, that is a different matter. Many chains of fast food restaurants have such areas. On the whole they work well. But I notice that virtually all of them have some form of air-cleaning or extraction. In such places I have never found any trace of stale tobacco, nor indeed detected any smell of tobacco being smoked.

I find it odd that it is the fast food outlets which take steps for everyone to enjoy their meal in airy, clean and fumeless conditions, yet still allow smoking. After all, to the most seasoned smoker there can be little inconvenience in a ban which lasts, in effect, for such a short while, for the smoker, along with other customers, is in the premises for only a minimal amount of time. Such places go to enormous trouble to try to please as many people as they can, whereas you have the ludicrous situation that many very expensive restaurants do not take any trouble at all – a blanket ban is all they can manage. There is no excuse for this, but, as I say, you must make up your mind as to how you are going to run your business, and if you wish from the start to alienate many customers, so be it. Remember, thirty-seven per cent of the male population in Britain still smoke. That is still quite a lot of potential customers.

I hope, however, that, if you do decide to ban smoking altogether, you will not give as an excuse the reason given to me some years back – that smoking plays havoc with the decorations and furnishings. That is your problem, not that of your guests.

In furnishings, be very careful that they are not too heavy or dark, otherwise a 'suffocating' air can be unwittingly created. A not dissimilar precept also arises with heating.

Dining-rooms are a very difficult balance between cosy invitation and simplicity. I am not, let me hasten to say, in any way an expert on interior design, but I have had to redecorate my own hotel dining-room no fewer than three times within a month simply because I got the 'mix' wrong. In actual fact, I always mixed my own paints, and what had seemed very nice on a small area turned out to be disastrous on a larger one. So I reckon I have a small knowledge of the problem.

As a very broad guide-line, dining-rooms should be 'cool' to look at, as opposed to 'hot'. Therefore try to avoid the red end of the spectrum. Greens are excellent but virtually impossible to get right first time, as they always seem to turn out too wishy-washy or too harsh. I also know many people who have a positive dislike of green, for psychological reasons I have never managed to discover, but it exists nonetheless. And with all colours, remember it is the overall effect that is important. How does the room, as a whole, look? Cool and inviting, warm and inviting, cold and functionally distant?

Dining-rooms should, if possible, have a temperature lower than that of the rest of the building. They tend to heat up quickly once full of people and get very uncomfortable. So, although they should be pleasantly warm, but not hot early in the service session, try if you can to control the temperature downwards the busier you get, or as the session goes on. This is not impossible; it just takes care and forethought. Most people find their appetite sharpened by a room slightly cooler-looking, and cooler-feeling, than their immediately previous surroundings, which might even be a small bar area inside the entrance. If you have no such area or perhaps do not want a bar, some form of division, say with a screen or two, should be designed to separate, however subliminally, the entrance from the restaurant itself. This is not, of course, necessary in certain operations but it does help to put the customer at ease, except in fast food or the 'bistro' type of outlet, though even many of these do, in fact, have such an area, however notional.

If I have sounded somewhat disparaging of interior design consultants, I have given the wrong impression. Not all of them are bad, by any means, but all of them are expensive, and I have just tried to point one or two helpful fingers of advice in your direction.

At its best, interior design is excellent. I remember some years ago reading about a newly opened local restaurant which seemed to make more of its design than its food. It sounded quite frightful, heavy brown tablecloths, brown candles, rich furnishings and drapes in reds and so on. In fact, it sounded so appalling that my wife and I just had to go. It was quite marvellous, and the work of David Hicks. But only a Hicks could have done with those colours what was achieved. He seemed to have broken every rule, but it worked wonderfully. Such is true expertise. Curiously, perhaps, the food too was excellent, and we became regular customers. Alas, it was a short-lived triumph, for it changed hands within a few years and soon became tawdry, while its prices mounted and quality went down. Such a happening is endemic in the catering trade in Britain. I shall have something to say about greed and pricing policy in later chapters.

Stations and Still-Rooms

We have considered the overall look and effect of the dining-room, but what of the practicalities? Well, I do not intend to go into great detail about knives and forks, plates, salt and pepper-mills and glasses. I would have thought that you do not need me to remind you that such things are necessary – but they are going to cost a lot more money than you thought, so be careful to make provision for such items if yours is a new operation.

What is often forgotten are the service 'stations'. These are quite simply storage cabinets, for want of a better word, from which cutlery, glasses etc can be drawn for laying-up tables in the immediate area, and they should contain everything that may be needed by a waiter or waitress (even ash-trays!). As far as possible, the top should be kept clear and be large enough to take a decent-sized tray, carrying food from the kitchen as well as for loading with dirty plates and cutlery before being taken to the wash-up. Such stations make the work of your staff much easier, as they have to do less walking. It also helps customers, because anything they might want is nigh at hand and no time is lost in fetching it.

Unless your restaurant is very large and with a great number of tables, it is not likely you will need many of these stations. Indeed, just one will often do, somewhere near the kitchen doors, providing it is large enough to do the job by holding everything the dining-room may require.

In the great restaurants of the world there are many such stations, jealously guarded over by a *chef de rang*, who is responsible for all aspects of service to the tables under his station, and perhaps one or two *commis* waiters who do most of the fetching and carrying.

In fact, to someone like me, the atmosphere and skilled attention of a great dining-room are absorbing, but in lesser places, with ideas, as they used to say, 'above their station', ill-discipline, lack of skill and inattention become irksome to the customer, and restaurants quickly lose their popularity. Do not attempt too 'smart' an operation at first, unless you are extremely skilled and can afford to pay extremely skilled staff. But more of that in Chapter 12.

Apart from one or two stations, it is also a good idea to have the equivalent of what used to be a 'still-room', where hot and cold drinks are prepared and where cold first courses, as well as sweets or cold puddings, can be kept for service. This saves time and the weary feet of staff and takes some of the load off the kitchen. Years ago, every restaurant worth its name had a still-room, but the fashion has largely died, owing to the 'wasted' space being needed to earn money or just because there is not enough room. If that is the case, a sort of 'mini still-room' can be set up on your work station, perhaps for a coffee-making machine. Even that alone will save time and tempers in the long run.

The object of the exercise, however, is to make your customers as comfortable as possible and help your staff to be as efficient as possible. Neither your diners nor your waiters will want too much rushing around, fetching and carrying, weaving in and out of tables with heavy trays. A well-laid-out dining-room means a well-ordered system of service, satisfactory to everyone. Pay a visit to one or two very good restaurants and see how they do it, if you are unsure. The experience will be well worth the pleasure of the investment.

Restaurant Licensing
We have already considered the position regarding a liquor licence, but if you decide to apply for one, you will need to satisfy the licensing justices about its service, as well as supplying plans of the bar and surrounding area. If there is no room for a bar as such, you will need a dispense area where you keep drink and 'dispense' it; hence the name. In Scotland there are, to many minds, curious laws relating to actual bars, which in restaurants have to be no bigger than a certain size, to prevent, it is said, customers leaning on them and thus using a restaurant as they would an ordinary pub. These regulations are not irksome, however, and for the most part it is better for you to have a dispense area, rather than going to all the trouble of applying for a proper bar, for which permission is still hard to obtain.

To comply with the liquor laws, whether you have a proper bar or not, remember that you must display a list of prices and a notice stating what size measures are used for spirits. In England and Wales the common size is one-sixth of a gill, in Scotland it is at least one-fifth, but one-third gill measures are quite common – they do not believe in anything less than a decent drink! You may even be asked for a 'wee half' in Scotland, which is no less than a half-gill, though this tends to happen in pubs rather than in restaurants.

The whole question of liquor sales in restaurants was made somewhat simpler by the Licensing Act, 1964, as it specifically defined eating-places rather than just 'lumping' them in with other premises where alcohol was sold. Regulations since then have allowed alcohol to be sold throughout most of the trading day rather than just within the old 'permitted hours', as they were called, and restaurateurs wishing to obtain such a licence should have no difficulty. One no longer need face the ludicrous situation which obtained previously, whereby a person eating, because of his job or personal preference, outside pub licensing hours could not have a drink with his meal or was forbidden another glass of wine, say, just because the clock said half past two when he was eating his cheese.

There is, at the moment, no regulation governing sizes of wineglasses – a contentious subject in the trade and among various consumer groups. Personally, I think the size of wineglass used by restaurants, bars and so on should be notified to customers, as recommended by most reasonable pressure groups, and set out in a code of practice. I see nothing other than dishonesty in refusal to display such a sign voluntarily, which accounts for considerable irritation in customers who believe they are getting a decent-sized glass only to have one of the smallest possible put in front of them. (I shall deal with that, and other 'tricks of the trade', in Chapter 18.) But if you sell wine in a carafe or other 'open' container, you must specify the amount being offered – either 10 or 20 fluid ounces, or 25 centilitres, 50cls, 75cls, or one litre.

Restrictions regarding the age at which young people can be supplied with liquor are the same in restaurants as in other licensed premises: eighteen, but youngsters over the age of sixteen can drink beer, cider, porter or perry with their meal; although wine is not specifically mentioned, it would, I believe, take a special sort of policeman, or magistrate, to do anything about it.

Remember, too, that you need to display a notice outside your restaurant listing menus and prices. It is a good idea if you were also to list, on the same notice, the sizes of your wine measures, and the cost if sold in carafes or by the glass. Honesty of this sort not only helps create a decent image for yourself and your establishment but obviously helps the customer too.

Performing Rights
Finally a word about 'piped music'.

This, like smoking, is a decision for you alone. Some places seem to feel that piped music is a 'must', others that they can do without it. Customers, too, vary in their demands. But most people seem to agree that music which is too loud and intrusive is a very definite 'turn-off'.

Whatever your own feelings, you will have to decide if it is right for your sort of restaurant, but if you are going to have music, you will need the appropriate licence from the Performing Rights Society. Do not think you can 'get away' without one; do not be tempted into thinking no one will discover it. The Performing Rights Society have inspectors in every area of Britain, and they are very efficient. Do not break the law unnecessarily.

12 Staff

We may live without friends; we may live without books;
But civilised man can not live without cooks.
                                    Robert Bulwer Lytton

Whenever and wherever restaurateurs and hoteliers meet
together, the talk will inevitably turn to problems of staff. How
to get them, how to keep them, how to get rid of them, how to
find, above all, reliable, good and efficient employees. For most
employers in the catering trade there seem to be times when
little else crosses their minds or concerns them. Whole mornings
or afternoons at various trade conferences are taken up by
discussions, lectures, advice and question-and-answer sessions
on the topic.

But one factor is shiningly and singularly clear: the ones who
complain the most are, without question, the worst employers.
It is a fact you must learn from the start, and you must ask
yourself whether you are going to join the grumblers or whether
you are going to have a fair, just and generous policy towards
those upon whom you must often rely and without whom your
business would almost certainly fall apart.

I can see many of my colleagues in the industry, and perhaps
you yourself, seizing on one word I have just used: generous.
No – it does not mean money alone: more importantly, it means
in attitude of mind. For I cannot think of one other single great
industry which has such a poor record in pay, standards set and
demanded and general attitudes as catering. And I do not think
there is another industry which so ruthlessly exploits the
'Sixteen-Hour Rule', and therefore exploits the people within it.

What I have said so far has without doubt infuriated vast
numbers of employers. Good. It was intended to do just that,
and about time too. And there is yet more to come.

The Sixteen-Hour Rule

But first let me explain what, to so many, alas, is a golden rule, the one about the sixteen hours.

Throughout industry the myriad regulations and conditions relating to employing people do not apply to those working fewer than sixteen hours a week. There is thus an exploited minority who receive no protection of any kind, and it is onto this minority that the major portion of the catering trade battens – for catering is uniquely suited to 'casual' labour which can thus be manipulated without fear of the law.

Coupled with this is the fact that the catering trade is not 'unionized'. Although the TGWU does have a catering section and does try to recruit as many members as it can, the numbers of card-carrying union members is but a tiny drop in an otherwise vast pool of labour.

Now, I am not in any way criticizing the many large hotel and restaurant chains which not only have good union agreements, with proper rates of pay, which they apply to all staff, regardless of whether they are permanent or 'casual' workers, but also treat them with essential and befitting dignity whatever their position in the hierarchy. I am speaking of that other section of the industry, and huge it is when added together: the smaller restaurants, hotels, pubs, tea-shops, coffee-bars and so on. The record for this section is extremely poor and quite inexcusable.

I said earlier that the sixteen-hour-rule deprives most workers of any rights under the law. This is not quite true. Even a casual worker, if employed for between eight and sixteen hours per week over a period of five years is entitled after three months further work to receive a written statement as to his or her hours, pay and terms of employment as well as a job description.

In all honesty, I have to say that it is unfortunately rare for 'small' employers to regard this Statement of Employment regulation as anything other than irrelevant. I dare say some employers do, in fact, observe it, and I have just been unlucky, or lacking in diligence, in not having found any, but for the most part the question is either simply ignored or the employers do not even know about it. After all, five years is an unconscionably long time for any 'casual' to be around.

There is, of course, nothing to force anyone to work in the catering trade – if he or she cannot stand the heat of the kitchen, as they say, they should get out of it – but I find that attitude in this case cynical. The fact is that the trade does suit some people, and it suits a great many of them who are interested in the work, enjoy it and are of value to the industry as a whole, apart from being good 'ambassadors' for it. This pool of 'casual' labour for the most part consists of women, many with children, for whom full-time jobs are out of the question. Casual working suits such people, as it certainly suits the employers. But there is no need to exploit them just because the law does not cover them and they hold no union tickets.

It is this casual indifference to casual labour on the part of employers to which I am objecting. It leads to bitterness, lack of loyalty and any form of pride or job satisfaction, which, when coupled with poor pay, as it always is, causes a bad reputation in a good industry.

'Dignity and Fairness'

At the National Restaurateurs Conference in London in November 1987, I heard a number of speakers complain interminably about shortage of staff and about keeping them once you have got them. Not a single speaker ever for a moment gave me the impression that they, as employers, should ask themselves any questions at all about their own behaviour, ask themselves if, perhaps, they should not put their own house in order before complaining about the work-force – lack of it, laziness of it, incompetence of it and, above all, the way it constantly moved around or demanded a living wage.

But at the end of the session there came one single exception, the tone that of weariness at hearing yet again all the familiar complaints from so many people. This man, owner of a large and successful country restaurant, merely said that he never had any trouble with staff. They never seemed to change around much. One of them had been in his employ for nineteen years and another for twenty-three years. He did not understand the complaints he had been listening to.

His short speech was met by a stunned silence of disbelief.

I found that man enlightening. I had never met him, nor visited his establishment, although I had heard well of it. I wondered why there were only two of us there with apparently similar views.

Another speaker, at this same conference, highlighted

another facet of employment in the catering trade. Although now the owner of a well-known restaurant in the Home Counties, he had always worked as a waiter. He was proud of his job and thought it a noble one, yet he was constantly being asked if it was merely interim employment until he 'got something better'. Not even his chosen industry seemed to have much time for him as a waiter.

This was echoed, sadly, in the Young Waiter of the Year competition early in 1988. None of the three finalists confessed to any future interest in waiting at table, however famous the restaurant. They all wanted to be 'managers' of some sort. The thought of perhaps one day being the head waiter of a first-class restaurant simply had never occurred to them, it seemed. Such a job was obviously beneath their dignity. I wondered why.

I think it was Nubar Gulbenkian, that enchanting millionaire, who, when asked the perfect number for dinner, replied, 'Two – myself and a damned good head waiter.' But I doubt if the young men in question had even heard of Gulbenkian, and the romance of having a great restaurant under your charge had passed them by – if they had ever come across one. Which is yet another facet with staff in Britain, as we shall see.

I have mentioned these incidents in order to demonstrate the extent of the problems which will certainly face you. On the one hand, you will have the problem of getting staff – and it is by no means easy in the first instance, I have to admit – and in the second place you will have the problem of instilling into them a sense of doing a decent job. You will neither get staff nor keep them unless you are prepared to treat them with dignity and with fairness.

Your Team

So the first thing you must do is sit down (yet again) and work out exactly what staff you will need. Bear in mind that a *plongeur* may be more important to you than a 'greeter and seater'. And to this you must add your own position in the scheme of things. I have already stressed the need for you to work this out, to work out your own speciality, your own skills which will contribute to the success of your new restaurant.

I am assuming, of course, that, because you are not made of money, you will be working hard throughout, doing what you know best. It may be that you are, like myself, interested in

cooking and that your spouse or partner is interested in administration or 'front of house'. So be it – you have already saved
money on two jobs. But if you are not a chef or do not feel you can
cope in a kitchen, you must start with the old 'engine-room'.
Getting a good chef is not going to be easy.

Naturally you will probably think of the local catering college.
But here you must remember that they are training-establish-
ments for a vast variety of skills and that none of the skills they
teach can possibly be perfected while still in college. Experience is
the name of the game, and no student will have anything like
what you need. Remember too that, although a student may
leave college with City and Guilds diplomas (706/1 & 2) as long as
your arm and may well claim the name of chef, he or she would
not even get a job as a *commis chef* in France – simply because the
training has not encompassed the necessary range required.
Certainly he or she is unlikely to have had any sort of experience
of eating out other than in a local burger bar. Appreciation and
knowledge of good food is not one of those subjects easy to
inculcate in the native Briton, even in one from a catering college.

On the other hand, if your new operation is to be a fast food
outlet, you will probably find students from the local college only
too eager to join you, and they will certainly possess those basic
skills which such a business needs, though 'skill' is not the word I
would choose as being particularly apt. In any event, if you are
opting for fast food, staff will not be quite the same problem as it
would be in a different sort of restaurant. And in a franchise
operation the necessary work patterns and methods will be
taught to staff and insisted upon rigidly. Some franchise outlets I
know have kept good staff for quite a long time, compared with
other food operations, and I cannot help thinking that this is
because standards are set out beforehand and maintained all the
time, and terms of work and contract laid down, along with a
not-unreasonable rate of pay for local conditions. There is a
lesson to be learned in that for everyone new (and experienced) in
catering.

But, you will be saying, if I cannot get a good chef from a
catering college, where do I find one? Well, you can always try
advertising in the trade press or even in your local weekly paper
or 'freebie'. This may work on occasion but it is often expensive
and the result disappointing. So I am going to be very unpopular
here. Poach one from someone else.

It sounds very unprincipled perhaps, but you are in a business which is just as competitive for staff as it is for customers, and it seems to me to be illogical to deny one and admit the other. In the upper echelons of business, of course, they use euphemisms. They call it 'head-hunting'. But it is still the same thing.

During your researches and travels you will surely have come across a restaurant similar to the one you intended to run and which pleased you as regards food and service. Well, perhaps they may have a *commis chef*, or a second chef, there who is just itching to 'do his own thing' and who will be amenable to a courteous approach. No one objects to being approached, providing it is done in a pleasant way and there are definite prospects that the worker can improve his pay and position. And, incidentally, I think it is very wrong if employers object to such a practice. Good employers should (and I know many who do) feel somewhat flattered when their own staff are sought-after. It gives them a good image, and their natural disappointment at losing a valuable member of staff should not turn into one of irrational irritation.

The same could be said for any other member of staff you may need – a good waiter or waitress, perhaps. But for most purposes, starting in a small way, it will be the casual worker you will wish to attract, probably locally from among those looking for some 'pin money' or an interest outside their own homes.

There is one possible other source which you may bear in mind – and that is the Youth Training Scheme, details of which you can get from your nearest Job Centre.

About 10,000 youngsters a year join training schemes in the catering industry, supervised by the Hotel and Catering Training Board, and the courses are for one or two years. In return for a payment of £20 to the HCTB from the employer (1988), the trainee is paid £28.50 a week during the first year and £35 in the second year. The scheme is seen as a new source of labour for the catering trade, which traditionally drew on students from the catering colleges. You may even be able to take on a youngster or two yourself, sending them to day courses at a local college if they show promise and have the interest.

However, there is one very important precept to remember:

begin as you mean to go on. Not only, as I said earlier, in your style and type of business but also in your employment of staff. That, in my opinion, is why it is important to set out terms and conditions before you take anyone on, not just because the law requires it after three months anyway but because it is the proper way to conduct your affairs. It helps you and it helps your staff to know exactly where each stands. And it is going to avoid the possibility of a lot of trouble later on.

Let me give you an example.

Because of the type of restaurant my wife and I ran, we made it clear to all staff when we first saw them that they had to be clean and neat at all times, and under no circumstances were female employees allowed to wear trousers. Very anti-feminist, very unmodern, very much an attack on the supposed freedom of the individual. So be it. We still insisted, and we never had the slightest objection to such rules. Why? Because we stated at the outset that such was one of the essential terms of employment. You see, it would have been no good at all to have taken someone on and have them arrive in scruffy jeans, scuffed boots and a T-shirt, work for some time and then tell them to change their ways and clothing. Pretty obvious, you might remark. Well, you may think so, but it is not at all obvious to a great many employers I know of.

In the kitchen, whether you are the chef or you employ one, insist that 'whites' are worn. They are not only smart and the correct wear, they are also exceedingly practical and comfortable. And your washer-up, or *plongeur*, if not wearing whites, should at least look decent in a garment suitable for the work, and not be allowed to dress in any old clobber. Remember that he or she too may have to fetch or carry something 'front of house' one day, and all your staff should reflect the clean, decent image you have of yourself and your new business.

Pride in one's work often goes hand-in-hand with pride in one's appearance, and a slovenly dressed man or woman, even behind the bar of your local pub, does not instil great confidence in their attitude to the quality or cleanliness of the food and drink a customer is being offered.

Casual Staff
Your new operation is going to require casual staff. What could be easier (instead of making promises you cannot, or have no

intention of, keeping) than working out beforehand what those hours are likely to be and how much you are going to pay for them? Ah, but so many employers say, how do we know in advance when we shall need such staff? Wednesdays, for instance, may turn out to be slack, and I do not require them on that day. Well, that should be your problem, not the problem of some poor, willing casual worker whose hours and days on or off are constantly being changed, even at a moment's notice. This is simply not the way to behave towards anyone; just because someone is paid by you does not entitle you to chop and change their work hours because it suits you. Such employers are the first to grumble if any of their staff treat them the same way.

In a country town near me there is a coffee-lounge-cum-tea-shop. In the window is a more or less permanent notice appealing for staff. Every time anyone goes in there, the waitresses are different – only the owner remains a constant factor. Customers find it unsettling, certainly, but what must it do to the owner's nerves and peace of mind? All this because the owner's treatment of staff is notoriously bad – those contracted to work, say, on a Tuesday, from 10a.m. to 5p.m., are more often than not telephoned the previous evening either to be told they are not wanted after all or to have their hours shortened or changed completely. Yet from this person come the loudest and longest complaints locally about difficulties with obtaining staff in the first place, and then keeping them.

The catering trade is notoriously fickle. One disastrous Monday can be followed by a Monday which breaks all till records. There is no way anyone can foresee what is likely to happen from one day to the next. This does, of course, make it difficult for employers, but surely the easiest thing to do is to explain to a prospective 'casual' what the problems are and then guarantee a certain amount of work and a certain amount of 'shortfall' pay. There is nothing illegal or wrong in this.

When we found ourselves in a similar position, we experienced no difficulties, because our own problems had been explained to the members of staff in advance. We guaranteed such people a certain amount of money per week. If they did not work the required hours which that money covered, they would still get paid that amount. If they worked more hours than the guaranteed minimum, they were, obviously, paid extra. And because of judicious organization, no 'casual' lost money by being sent home on a 'quiet' day rather earlier than they expected. And they were never 'sent home'. They were simply told that, if they wished to go, they could. They regarded it rather like being let out early from school, because they knew they would not lose money. And it 'paid' us in the long run too: we never felt bad about ringing them up or asking them to come in for an extra stint. Because we played fair with them, they played fair with us. Staff loyalty cannot be bought by money, but it can be 'bought' by a generous understanding of their problems and an agreement in advance about the terms of employment.

There was one extra thing: when staff were on duty, they were fed – and fed properly, as near to normal meal-times as the catering trade can manage.

This sounds proper and reasonable, yet is it not the practice among a great many catering establishments. In one restaurant I know, staff are given half an hour for their own lunch-break but they are not paid for that half hour and they are not allowed to eat anything except a bowl of soup and a sandwich or filled roll without paying for it. Staff problems again? You have guessed it. Yet that particular owner complains all the time about the way she is constantly looking for staff because they constantly leave for other jobs.

If you are working for a very large organization with a great chain of hotels and restaurants, the hours you work, the meal-breaks you get and the food and payment therefor are laid down and written into the terms of employment. It is usually more than fair and reasonable. Staff know where they stand. But in smaller establishments, such as your own is going to be when you start off, you may not be able to employ many full-time staff, and 'casuals' will suit you excellently. They *will* suit you excellently – but only if you treat them as human beings from the start, with homes, lives and problems of their own. Especially those upon whom you can really rely, the older man or woman with a sense of responsibility gained from years of experience, not necessarily in catering.

I have deliberately mentioned older people here because I think that, if you can persuade them to work with you (and we always feel that people work *with* you, not *for* you, in any employment contract), they are a much better bargain and much better ambassadors for you and your restaurant than younger people. Indeed, the very best people we have ever found to work with are those who never even knew they needed a job or wanted one with us. Perhaps we sort of lured them into it, baited a hook. We were never disappointed, for they were people who ran their own homes, knew about responsibility and, left to get on with things, were utterly sensible and reliable.

There is today an accent on youth, and perhaps many good reasons for it. The young often make malleable employees and are quick to accept new ideas without questioning whether they are good or bad. Large hotel groups insist on them – straight from college – and build up 'teams' which they invite other youngsters to join. There is nothing wrong with this: the young are not paid as much as more experienced staff, they can be made to think their employer's way instead of their own, and the appointment of only slightly older 'managers' or 'under-managers' ensures that the juniors are kept very much in line.

But what is right for large organizations is not really right for a smaller one. An older man or woman is actually more likely to put in more work for similar money and will not be so inclined to be a clock-watcher. They will often do the work of two juniors and will almost certainly be better with your customers, as they will be used to the idea of service and not servility, and will see nothing demeaning in waiting at table or helping in the kitchen. Indeed, for my part, I have been lucky in having marvellous, cheerful people to work with me – and, I like to think, so have my guests and customers.

But whatever staff you employ, make sure they know exactly what you want done and how you want it done. Do not leave anything to chance. It is not fair on them, and it may damage you. But having shown them, leave them alone, let them get on with it. And do not be worried about what are called 'service staff' – e.g., those who work front-of-house, in the dining-room or bar. Unless you are going in for 'silver service,' the skills on waiting at table, with dishes plated in the kitchen, are minimal and easily taught and assimilated, especially by older people. They are, after all, common sense. And mature staff will make up for any lack by being very much better with your customers.

In every department in which you employ staff – and I think the best small restaurants are those with no demarcation, where everyone 'mucks in' and attends to whatever job needs doing at any one time – make sure you remember the old Navy adage: if one man does not do his job properly, you are not one man short, you are two men short – one to do his own job and then do the other one. And bearing in mind the tea-shop I wrote about earlier in this chapter, if you employ casual staff, do not have so many that you have to juggle with them all the time. One good member of staff is worth at least two poor ones – even if the sixteen-hour rule comes perilously close to being broken. Indeed, you never know, you might find it easier to employ staff properly!

Inheriting Staff

If you are taking over an existing business, it is not a good idea, in my opinion, to take over existing staff as well, unless you are absolutely sure of their loyalty to you as the new owner, their efficiency at the job you (and not the previous owner) intend them to do, and their enthusiasm for your new project. Nothing is more depressing than to be told, or to have it implied, that somehow you are not as good as the previous employer, or that what you are doing is somehow meeting with their disapproval.

Neither do you want to be saddled with the previous proprietor's contracts. Taking over staff (and I am not saying *never* do such a thing, for you may be perfectly satisfied with them and glad to have them with you, if only to avoid the problems of finding replacements) means that you must ensure you are able to replace their old contracts with a new contract of your own, otherwise it will be very expensive in things like redundancy payments and so on should you decide to get rid of them. It is better for you to start with a 'clean sheet'.

Having said that, however, the law says something quite different, I am afraid. In May 1982 the Transfer of Undertakings Regulations came into force and states quite clearly that a new owner in effect 'inherits' all the previous owner's staff and contracts. These regulations make no differentiation between sizes of business. It can be an operation employing a thousand people or merely a small country pub or garage. So perhaps now you can see why the catering trade is so keen on casual workers – they work very definitely to an employer's advantage.

In reality, however, you, the reader of this book, will in all probability not be taking over such a large and thriving business as to inherit even a few permanent staff, and perhaps what few there are will not relish the idea of working for you. So problems may be spared all round. On the other hand, keep this legislation very firmly in mind: redundancy payments, or compensation for unfair dismissal, are not things you want around your neck at a time when you have all sorts of other financial burdens on your back. And it makes no difference whether you are buying a 'private' operation or a company as we mentioned in Chapter 9. So just make sure exactly what you are buying when you agree to that place of your dreams – it is not just bricks and mortar, equipment and furnishings; it could be a whole load of trouble with employees who are 'wrong' for you and your intended style.

At the end of this chapter there is a brief review of employment conditions, which should help.

Foreign Staff

Quite a number of restaurateurs employ foreign staff – either because they want to create a particular ambience in their restaurant or just because they cannot get local people – and quite a number of employers and staff are breaking the law. It is a tangled field but in principle nationals from EEC countries (with the exception of Greece, Portugal and Spain which have not yet completed the seven-year 'probation' necessary for full EEC membership) are entitled to work in Britain on the same terms and conditions applicable to those born here, but they must have a residence permit, obtainable from the Home Office, if they stay for more than six months. As an employer you should therefore make sure any EEC workers understand these rules, for you will both be guilty of an offence if the residence requirement is ignored.

For Commonwealth citizens and foreign nationals a work permit is required, obtainable from the Department of Employment. These are not always easy to get, for you will have to prove that the incomer speaks English reasonably well, is here to fill a key post which cannot be filled by anyone resident in Britain and that you have first tried (and can show you have tried) to employ a British resident.

On top of this, you have to assure the Department that your terms of employment are the same for the foreigner as for a national and that he (or she) is aged between twenty-three and fifty-four. Certain exceptions apply to students from abroad who are here for up to five years, but in all cases you would do well to ask at your local Job Centre for the up-to-date rules and regulations. To complicate matters there are special conditions attached to the catering industry, which for too long tried to get away with a particularly unpleasant form of 'sweated labour': foreigners were being employed regardless of qualifications, for low wages and long hours. The question of foreign catering staff is now very much focused on their suitability for the job, coupled with experience and recognized qualifications. I know a great many people in the catering trade who will laugh at the above strictures. I advise you not to. There seems to me to be little point in breaking the law gratuitously.

Finally, a word on employing children. Be careful. Always contact your local education authority to find out the exact terms and conditions if you want to give work to anyone aged between thirteen (the minimum) and sixteen. And in some circumstances the rules even apply to your own children.

Tip and Tronc

Finally a word on the tipping system. Whether you like the idea or not, the British feel under an obligation to tip, often, alas, when they have had poor and rude service. But do make up your own mind first – and I hope you will make it up by deciding that there will be no 'extras' on your bills such as VAT, service charge, cover charge and so on. All such considerations should be included in the price of the meal, and your menu should clearly state that VAT etc are included. Nothing irritates a customer more than having to fork out more money than he had expected by bits and pieces being added on. And all too often the so-called 'service charge' is merely a hidden source of profit for the owner, never actually being passed on to the staff at all.

Whether you add a note to your menu, or your bill, saying that gratuities are left entirely to the discretion of the customer, is again up to you – at least it is more honest than stating 'Service not included', as though it was some peremptory 'or else' threat. Personally I think the matter is best left entirely to the customer, without any form of prompting, but the whole catering industry is divided on the topic, and many employers are even against the *tronc* system by which all gratuities are put into a common pool and shared either equally or on a percentage basis by all staff. Personally, I prefer this system and can see nothing against it.

An Outline of the Law on Employment of Staff

All employees who work for at least sixteen hours a week are entitled, after thirteen weeks, to a written statement setting out the main terms of their employment. The statement has to say quite clearly between whom the contract is made, the hours of work and the pay, and whether it is to be paid monthly or weekly. It includes such items as holidays, pensions, length of notice, disciplinary rules and job title, and a host of other things which are usually too numerous to mention in any individual contract, in which case there must be a notice to which the employee's attention is drawn, and to which he can refer at any time, setting out those terms not actually stated in his contract.

The world of employment is, without question, a jungle, but over recent years the Department of Employment has taken its head from the sand and published excellent and clear pamphlets on every aspect. The pamphlets are called 'Employment Legislation', numbered 1 to 17, and they cover every single facet concerning your rights as an employer and your employees' rights. There is another booklet, called 'Employment Acts, 1980 and 1982', also available from the Job Centre, which lucidly outlines the whole morass of current legislation. They are readily available at any Job Centre, and I do not see the point of including in this book what could only be a re-hash of publications which cost nothing except a visit locally.

Wages councils will also enter your ken, along with the wages inspector. Regulations on basic pay, or recommended agreements, change, it seems, every few months, and anything written now will be out of date by the time this book is published. These councils operate in industries which do not have powers of collective bargaining, by unions for example, and they can enforce the payment of minimum rates for all employees over twenty-one. Minimum rates of pay vary by a small amount between licensed and unlicensed premises and whether they are residential or not, but in 1987, just as an example, the minimum was £1.85 an hour for a maximum of thirty-nine hours in any week. The rules also govern resident staff and what can be deducted for accommodation, as well as general deductions for meals and so on.

It would be foolish, however, to pay less than what is customary locally, and a quick look at the Jobs Vacant columns in your local newspaper (or a call at the Job Centre) will provide the information you need. But do try, if you possibly can, to pay more than the 'going rate'. Believe me, it will be well worth your while.

13   Food

Good cookery is the food of a clear conscience.

Des Essarts

We saw, much earlier in this book, that cooking for a restaurant is quite different from cooking at home. But it is not merely a matter of quantity. It is a matter of careful planning – as though you were giving a huge dinner party day after day, week after week, at which on occasion no guests turned up and at other times more than you had asked. It is enough to give any housewife a nightmare – as a restaurateur, you will just have to learn to cope with it.

Wastage

Perhaps the biggest enemy in any commercial kitchen is wastage. It is, literally, money down the drain. But do not confuse wastage with lack of what today is called 'portion control' (which so often merely ensures that no customers get more than the owner wants them to). 'Portion control' should be an aid to better profit; it is not a method of cutting down wastage.

To revert to the domestic scene, the eating on a Monday night, cold, of the roast Sunday joint is an obvious example of culinary wisdom and economy. It is a simple piece of practical planning. Remember it.

It may be that your restaurant will be using pre-portioned, packaged meals exclusively. In that case wastage will concern you only if plates come back with food uneaten. The reason for that will be either that the food is dreadful, which it probably will be if everything comes out of a packet, or that you are giving your customers too much. Over-generous portions are as bad as under-generous ones. In the first you lose money, and in the second you lose customers. The 'mix' has got to be right – right for you wanting to make a profit and right for the customer wanting to eat wisely and well.

The correct amount of food to serve is not always easy to judge without experience, but if you take very careful notes, you will quickly find what is correct.

Obviously, there are rough-and-ready guidelines. Six ounces of meat, uncooked, is average and is a reasonable calculation when buying meat at the butchers. But it may be quite unreasonable – either side of too much or too little – when the other things served with it are taken into account. Good stews, casseroles and so on are an example of this, so are very rich sauces, for they 'bulk up' a meal, and large portions are unnecessary and wasteful. But be careful not to cheat your customer in any of the ways we shall consider in Chapter 18.

Wastage occurs where too much food is served or when too much food is cooked for any one service. Vegetables are a prime example.

While doing the research for this book I visited a kitchen not far from where I live. At 2.45p.m. there were at least five or six pounds of potatoes still lying in the water in which they had been cooked, having been kept hot for nearly two hours. It was not my duty to criticize as I watched them thrown away – more to reassure me as to the owner's good intentions than anything else. Alongside that saucepan was another containing at least two pounds of frozen peas, also 'held' for nearly two hours. These were carefully drained to be saved for the service that evening, after re-heating.

Now, it struck me that two cardinal sins were on offer in that kitchen: too many potatoes had been cooked too early for customers who did not materialize, and too many peas (the whole saucepan-load, in fact) had been cooked and kept to make them anything other than awful when served 'next time round'. Not surprisingly, that particular eating place changed hands a few months later.

Now it must be obvious to you, the reader, that if the potatoes had been cooked in smaller batches and the frozen peas just 'on demand', the wastage would not have occurred.

When expressed quite simply like that it seems somewhat obvious. But if it is so obvious, why do not more caterers observe such very simple rules? They do not observe *any* rules, actually, because they have not thought the problem out and planned away the possibility of wastage.

It struck me, in that particular restaurant, that if such wastage of ordinary vegetables occurred, then much else must also be subject to the same rule. Meat and fish are very much more expensive, as we all know, but I wondered how much of that was thrown away.

Lack of planning, lack of knowledge, lack of understanding and lack of intelligence all contribute to waste. Suppose a smaller amount of potatoes had been put on to cook so that they would be ready, say, at 12.30p.m. And then suppose that if it looked as though those potatoes were going to be eaten another batch was put on, similar in weight to the first. This is not as difficult as you might think; it just needs a bit of forethought and, I admit, educated guesses at your probable work-load on any day. OK, but supposing you put the second lot on and no customers turned up? Or only one or two. The trick is to understand that by trying to keep them hot you are not preventing wastage, you are creating it. Take them off, cool and *sauté* them to order, or mash them with butter and cream and perhaps a little *sauté*'d onion or grated cheese, to turn them into potato cakes. Whatever method you choose, you will be able to sell the result to later customers, that evening or the following day, without any deterioration to the original vegetable at all.

Now, this is not a cookery book, I know, but I have tried to put into your mind that there is an awful lot you can do to prevent wastage and please your customers at the same time. It just needs a bit of thought, and a bit of action too, when you realize that food is likely to go a bit 'over the top' and become useless. But unless there is in your mind, or in the mind of your chef, that sort of planning, that sort of rule, you are going to lose money, and probably customers.

The peas, too, had not been thought about. Would it not have been better, if you must use frozen peas, to have had a very large pan of boiling water ready for batch cooking as and when required? After all, they take only a few minutes straight from the freezer, providing there is a lot of boiling water ready for them. And if you have cooked too many, what is wrong with taking them out while still before their 'peak', stopping any further cooking by refreshing them under cold water, and using them with mayonnaise in a salad, or heating them gently again, swirled in butter – as you can do with virtually every other vegetable known to man. Not only would it be good-bye to your soggy sprouts and limp yellow cabbage, it would be good-bye to wastage, and certainly hello to a lot more satisfied customers.

No, this is not a cookery book, but it is a book about how to run a (better) restaurant, and the more knowledge you have on how to please those people who come in through your front door, the more money you are going to make and the happier all of you are going to be.

Of course, these are only pointers in what I hope is the right direction for you. The ideas are obvious, glaringly so, yet I have been into dozens and dozens of kitchens and in most the obvious is ignored.

Menu-Planning
Menu-planning is essential. But what do we mean by menu-planning?

It is certainly not those vast, printed, plastic-bound 'books' which some restaurants present with such a flourish. Always remember, the longer the menu, the more frozen, packaged, boil-in-the-bag, bought-in, pre-portioned and often old food is lying somewhere in the deep freeze. It does, it is true, impress some types of customer; why, I do not know. And it may well be that you have set your heart on that type of restaurant, with a lengthy menu that a chemist and not a chef would be better employed in producing for the unfortunate customers.

There is nothing, I suppose, wrong in such an ambition, and the customer you attract will be very much the type who feels at home with his 'extensive menu', from which, whatever its extent, he will almost certainly choose the prawn cocktail, the steak and chips and the Black Forest gâteau. That may sound cynical, and it is. But, before setting up such an operation, you must make sure that your catchment area includes enough customers of that particular bent, so that you will not be competing too fiercely with other outlets serving similar things.

On the other hand, these long menus should preclude food wastage, as everything comes from the deep-freeze and into the microwave or fryer the moment it is ordered. Coupled with an Iceberg lettuce, a few tomatoes, the odd slice of cucumber, wrapped butter pats and vacuum-sealed cheese portions, the only danger of wasting money may well be that too much coffee has been kept hot for so long that even to the customer it has begun to taste like stale buns and he thus leaves it.

But this book is not about that sort of place, the sort of place run, doubtless, by Derek Cooper's famous character Ray Gunge. No, this book is about running a real restaurant where people can eat well and where food is cooked for them.

It does not matter whether it is one of a franchise chain (where food wastage is absolutely minimal) or a very much 'up-market' operation special to yourself, for at both ends of the scale there is a proper need and a rightful place in the scheme of things. But I am making a plea for some attempt at being a real restaurateur, and in this I include all honest men and women who want to serve in the best way food they are best equipped, by either training or inclination, to present.

Thus, menu-planning. For a start, try to keep menus short until you, your chef if you have one, and your staff have got used to the whole business on which you have now embarked. Good food, decently served, is going to please more customers more of the time than any attempt at chi-chi presentation of elaborate dishes. And with a short menu goes simplicity, too. Your work will be made easier, your wastage will be virtually non-existent, your customers will be happier, and your reputation will build of its own accord.

Let us take a look, then, at the experts on the other side of the Channel, in France. And, for the most part, they really are the acknowledged experts.

I know that there is an enormous resentment and even, God knows why, a feeling of superiority among British restaurateurs (and some of their customers) at any mention of French cooking. It is, for a start, 'foreign', whatever that means. It is filled with garlic. The only things ever served are snails and frogs' legs. They are no good at puddings. Their beer is dreadful. Their wine is either very cheap or very expensive. The chef always has a dog-end in his mouth and a dog on the floor. There is no health officer to ensure cleanliness and no rules about segregation when it comes to Ladies' and Gents' toilets, and, above all, you do not know what the names of the dishes mean.

All those tired old prejudices, and many more, are trotted out by huge numbers of people in the British catering trade and even mouthed at trade conferences and so on.

But your job, if you are reading this book, is to be a better restaurateur and to take the best from whatever source you can. You are not reading this book to be prejudiced but, I hope, to learn from someone with experience in what is a fascinating trade. Preconceptions and ignorance are not in your nature, even if they are deeply embedded in others. An open mind is a lot less wasteful than a shut one.

It may surprise many to know that the French are among the greatest exponents of the 'fast food' concept ever known – and were so long before it ever got its modern title. Good, fresh food, quickly cooked to order, is exactly what they specialize in. Yet when I say this to other caterers, they look at me in blank astonishment and disbelief.

For a moment I am excepting, you may think, the top end of the scale, the great restaurants with their *brigade de cuisine* of dozens and elaborate dishes. Actually, I am not. The same principles apply to all of them: speed and expertise with the materials they have. You may not, it is true, think you have that sort of speed or expertise. Possibly, but not necessarily. The expertise is something you will have to learn, which is why I have said you should stick to simple menus within your capability, but the speed comes naturally once you know your own limitations and practise within them. One of the central practices of any kitchen – essential in France but still, somehow, thought little of in Britain – is the *mise en place*. It is the preparation of the ingredients, the collecting together of everything you need for the service prior to the cooking. In this way there is no last-minute hunting for the sage, the butter or the slices of lemon. Again, if you like, it is forward planning. Just as the forward planning of your menu, or the Dish of the Day, if you have one, will not be short of an essential ingredient. All will have been thought out beforehand. The ordering of food (and ensuring its regular supply) is a nightmare which we shall discuss in Chapter 16, so it is absolutely necessary that forward thinking is rigidly insisted upon. It is one thing to nip out and get an orange round the corner at 11a.m., quite another at 8p.m. when some customer is waiting in the dining room for a particular dish.

If you have a short menu, try to balance it. I know it is sometimes difficult. I know that in the event you will never dissuade at least one customer from starting with a vol-au-vent stuffed with fish in a cream sauce, continuing with steak and kidney pudding and ending his meal with baked jam roll and custard. I know that it is not your responsibility to ensure that your customer does not get up from table feeling like the *Queen Mary* run aground. But try to help him.

They say any fool can invent a menu, only a professional can balance it. You will not be able to balance your customers' choices (though in my opinion you should have a jolly good try), but you can, by careful planning, seek a judicious mix of dishes. That does take a lot more trouble, however, which is perhaps why so many British menus are printed out once a year and hardly ever changed. It is easier that way. I remember reading some columnist in a trade paper, who wrote a weekly 'diary' of what went on in her restaurant, saying she had come across a new dish and was seriously thinking of using the idea when she had her new menu printed in a few months' time. I wondered why she could not put the new dish on then and there – it might give her customers a renewed interest in what she was serving, and perhaps her chef a new interest in what he was preparing.

Do not, therefore, let your menu dictate what you are going to serve, just because it is a typographical *tour de force*. That sort of thing may be all right in a vast hotel with a prestigious restaurant where the chef changes his menu every three months to give an idea of the seasons. You do not eat a menu; you eat food, and you should use what is good and best, and use it with flair and imagination. Printed menus are the curse of the small restaurant.

I mentioned just now the word 'seasons'. I would like to think that you will bear the seasons in mind. Try to serve broad beans when they are in season, or preferably a little earlier by insisting on small ones. The same with sprouts and other vegetables. The ubiquitous peas you see on so many menus are easy and accept-able, I suppose, but it always seems to me that the owners of restaurants who take no account of the season of the year are blissfully unconcerned about what their customers eat and more concerned about what they have in the deep freeze.

A restaurant whose menu reflects the changing pattern of the year is always a delight to eat in.

Show and Sell
Take trouble in 'selling' your food to the customer. Chains such as the Little Chef do this with all those colour photographs on the wall. You can do it in other ways.

I reckoned to be able to 'sell' anything I wanted to my customers just by displaying it properly. There is nothing wrong in trying to get rid of good, fresh food by trying to 'push' it a little. When I was lucky enough, for instance, to get hold of marvellous red mullet, I would pile it high on a clean metal tray and show it to my customers, asking them to choose which fish they would like. In that way I had no wastage, because the diner knew that what he or she was being offered really was fresh. It is commonplace in France, Italy and Spain to have a selection of foods beautifully laid out somewhere near the entrance of restaurants to tempt their customers – and tempt them it does. I can never resist choosing my own fish, or my own piece of meat, from such a display.

On Sunday lunches in my last restaurant I would carry the ribs of beef into the dining-room, fresh from the oven. No one could resist them. Yes, I wanted to 'push' the beef, but there was nothing wrong in that, from either my customers' point of view or mine.

And if some of the meat was left over, there was nothing more tempting the following day than a meat-flat laid out with great slices of cold, rare beef. It always sold; I could guarantee it.

As a further example: we always served our soups in large, pottery tureens – not those frightful pot-bellied electric imitation contraptions you see standing on the service tables in so many 'chain eateries'. The tureen remained for customers to take another helping, if they liked it, which, flatteringly, they very often did. This may seem like portion control run riot, but it is no such thing – first-class soup is a by-product of any good kitchen which uses all wastage, bones of meat and fish and the discarded leaves of vegetables and so on for stocks. In effect, this wastage has already been paid for, so a good soup is virtually free. By serving it in tureens, we were able to charge slightly more for it than other establishments do, thus making more profit than we would have done otherwise.

Similarly, our pâtés and mousselines were served in large dishes, to which customers could help themselves if they wished. Once again we were able to charge more for what they had, as it looked (and, we hoped, tasted) very much better than the ordinary slab of manufactured pâté, piece of toast and 'No Entry' wrapped butter pat offered by our competitors.

There are dozens of ways in which you can sell things to your customers if you keep your eyes open and observe how the professionals do it. Yet how many times do you go into a restaurant and see no trace of any fresh food on display, apart from a tired, old 'buffet' of limp salads and coleslaw from a bucket bought in from a mass catering supplier, along with grey, wafer-thin slices of meats? That is not the way to sell food. It is not, actually, the way to run a better restaurant. If you want to run it that way, the same as so many others do, you will find yourself in good company but you will not get me as a customer.

I know that some of you may say that this sort of 'selling' is not right for every restaurant. Of course not. But if chains like Little Chef try to 'sell' their food, they must think it worth while going to all the trouble and expense of those photographs, and if the French and Italians have lovely display tables, they too must find it worthwhile. In reality, of course, there is no restaurant which cannot 'sell' its food in some way, however humbly. And by trying to 'sell' your food you are, in effect, ensuring there will be very little wastage.

The now-common blackboard you see in so many eating-places is actually designed to give customers the feeling that the food on offer is not mass-produced but fresh, and freshly cooked, compared with the printed menu with its feeling of staleness and lack of imagination. There is nothing wrong in this, although much of what is on offer I happen to know has been bought in, as you will too once you have been in the trade a little while.

A nicely laid-out cheese-board (without those awful portion-controlled wrapped wedges) will always sell itself, especially if something like a sliced apple is added, and butter in decent bowls and not pre-wrapped. Few people can resist such 'salesmanship', as with the soup being carried to a table in a tureen, from which they can help themselves. It actually does not cost very much to do such things, and it almost certainly generates more profit and more customer loyalty. Yet how many times are such simple niceties ignored?

The smallest country pub serving food could sell it more easily by taking trouble with its presentation. There is a large range of cold cabinets of varying sizes in which to display it, yet so many have still to get round to the whole idea.

There is one curious facet of the way in which food appeals to customers worth mentioning here: for no apparent reason, you suddenly get several orders for a dish which you have perhaps tried on your menu many times in the past and yet no one seemed then to want. It is a subject often discussed by all restaurant owners and chefs. Whether there is a 'collective customer consciousness' that we have not yet managed to recognize and control, I do not know.

I was given a good example of this by a chef the other day. He had bought a box of extremely good salmon trout, laid them out nicely on display and reckoned they would sell themselves. No such luck. There they sat, glistening freshly in the cabinet, until he despaired and wrapped them individually for the freezer. Two days later, a customer came in for lunch and asked him if he had any of those excellent trout left. He confessed he had but, as they were not on that day's menu, the dish would take a little time to prepare. At that single lunch service, he sold the whole lot. The one thing that may cause this sort of 'rush' is other customers seeing the dish go to one table and suddenly wanting it themselves. Both that chef and I are not at all certain. And no one else is.

Fads and Fashions

A further point worth making is not to be a slave to fashion, especially if the fashion is one of convenience to other restaurateurs and otherwise quite useless. The main bogey-man of this is the 'garnish'. Why on earth dishes like steak and chips have to come to the table with two quarters of tomato, three slices of cucumber, two small, tired lettuce leaves and a round of raw onion and be sprinkled with watercress or mustard-and-cress is quite beyond my comprehension. It is laziness and ignorance on the part of the chef or owner, who does it just because everyone else in the trade does it. It adds nothing to the dish. Although 'fashions' like those silly garnishes are ludicrous, there are other fashions for which you should keep an eye open. Some are as useless as the garnish syndrome, some are sources of customer pleasure and therefore worth bearing in mind.

I shall take two examples. First the laughable.

It is (no! – at long last one can actually, I think, write the word 'was') the *cuisine minceur* craze. This began as a perfectly reasonable mode of cooking, lighter than the strictly classic methods, which was worked on by Michel Guerard at his restaurant in Eugénie-les-Bains from the mid '70s onwards. The man is a superb chef, and his ideas were adopted, and adapted, in many great restaurants and by many other great chefs. When it came to Britain, inevitably it was seized upon by less knowledgeable, less skilful and certainly less reputable restaurateurs as a quick and easy way of 'cashing in' on a fashion and exploiting it to the full for their own profit. Like wildfire, the little plates of barely cooked vegetables, more often than not two mange-tout, a stick of carrot and a slim stalk of broccoli, began appearing beside meat plates bearing a tiny medallion of cheap veal, placed on a sauce which seemed to consist mainly of water and raspberry vinegar. The price for such offerings rose in inverse proportion to the size of the helpings.

The British public were kidded into believing that this was the new cooking, the healthier way to lose weight along with the money in their wallets. Many restaurateurs became skilled operators at this rip-off, and their cause was assisted by the awesome praise lavished on them by the majority of the food critics, who were, and still are, probably even more ignorant than their readers. Nothing blinkers a critic more than a very large expense account, his or her taste and common sense apparently disappearing along with their employer's money.

It was good while it lasted; at least, it was for the restaurateur.

Curiously, I believe it probably had something to do with creating the other fashion I am now going to mention: the re-introduction of what many like to call 'nursery food'. Good, old-fashioned, nourishing traditional food swept back – a backlash against so much previous chi-chi nonsense. Quite suddenly, steak-and-kidney puddings were back, as opposed to that effete pie, and good nosh like milk puddings made a re-appearance. A great chef even swept the board with a special bread-and-butter pudding, and excellent it is too.

It was a public rebellion not against the original idea of *cuisine minceur* but against the way in which it was 'translated' by the unscrupulous restaurateur, out for a fast buck, and promoted by the now discredited 'foodie' movement and the media.

By keeping a close eye on the trade press and the ordinary newspapers and, above all, by listening to what the representatives say, you will quickly get an 'ear' for new trends, and experience will tell you what is wrong and what is right.

The Language of Eating

There is one further pre-occupation of the catering trade which crops up at regular intervals, at all conferences, and even spills over on occasion into the daily newspapers or magazines: it is the question of 'French' menus.

This arouses intemperate words and passions, and it never ceases to amuse me. On the one hand you have those who scream from the roof-tops that in Britain you should never, ever use any French words in any menu. These are in the vituperative ascendancy, like so many minorities which endeavour to persuade themselves they are the majority by sheer volume of noise and by the hectoring tactics of the bully.

On the other hand there are those who defend the use of French, but in a much quieter way.

Somewhere in between are people who are vilified by both the other sections: those who use French in their menus and get criticized (possibly quite rightly) for using it incorrectly.

You may possibly believe that none of this concerns you. It does. You are coming into a trade which is passionate about the ludicrous. It is just as well you know what you are letting yourself in for. The catering trade in Britain may not be passionate about food, but it is jolly well passionate about the use of French words describing it.

Perhaps you may judge me a little harsh by using the word 'ludicrous'. I shall explain.

It is not my intention, nor my brief, to criticize other authors of books about the catering trade, few though they are. But one of them seems almost to foam at the mouth for more than two pages criticizing a mixture of French and English on menus, which, he writes, is to be deplored as pretentious and bad. He even argues that the use of French in any extensive way necessitates the waiter's knowing what the dishes are and how they are prepared – one of the prime requirements, I would have thought, of any person who serves in any dining-room.

However, to continue with this author who seems to me to encapsulate the argument: he gives a number of exemplary menus and sets out some phrases used in menus which he considers should be translated from the French. I am sure he is right. But why, I wonder, do the 'exemplary' menus, which he avers are all in English, contain so many definitely 'foreign' words? Mayonnaise (French), bolognaise (French), vol-au-vent

(French), Vichy (French), vacherin (French), gâteau (French), vinaigrette (French). I can see the difficulty, but I do not think he, and his followers, can.

The world of cooking is inextricably tied up with France and Italy, perhaps neatly demonstrated by the dish spaghetti (Italian) bolognaise (French), so often seen, incorrectly, on menus but which seems to escape even the attention of the purists. To endeavour to translate everything or fly in the face of common usage, as such people insist, is ludicrous. Far better a judicious blend of correct words and, above all, a solid, unwavering determination to ban that awful descriptive word 'style' – as in that author's rendering of *boulangère* as 'bakehouse style'. What, I wonder, would such people suggest as a translation for that famous Italian dish of cooked meat known as *in calzoni*? Would they really have me translate it as 'cooked in a pair of trousers'?

No, a judicious use of *correct* terms and phrases, whether German, French, Italian or what-have-you, is without question, in my opinion, essential, providing they are necessary and, so far as possible, explained either by the dining-room staff or in the menu.

I do not understand why so many restaurateurs (French again) get their *calzoni* in a twist over the matter. I do not even see why a blend of two languages is considered to be in poor taste – after all, the author I was using as my example, while castigating the practice on the one hand, happily uses 'peach *vacherin*' and 'avocado pear with *vinaigrette* sauce' – the last very odd, as *vinaigrette* is a sort of sauce anyway. This is a bit like using the words 'Gâteaux cake', which my wife has actually seen on a menu in central London (but not so bad as another menu in north London, which a friend saw offering 'gateaux's', just to make the plural doubly sure, perhaps).

Your Own Standards
You must decide what you are going to do when it comes to menus, but whatever happens, do not copy slavishly what other people do. Be your own guide: do away with the garnish, and substitute something which enhances the actual dish; eschew those awful pats of butter in a wrapper which you need a jemmy to open; use fresh flowers on tables, not plastic; make sure your restaurant smells clean – of polish, not cooking-oil; make sure

that your kitchen cooks food properly and not slovenly; that wastage is eradicated by sensible menus. And, above all else, try to go to France every year to pick French brains, to find out how they do things, to look at the smaller touches – all of which you can pass on to your customer to make him or her more welcome and better fed than anywhere else in your own neighbourhood.

And finally, do not debase the art of cooking by calling a dish by one name yet using ingredients or a method of cooking totally foreign to it. We all have our favourite examples: a 'Spanish omelette' sprinkled with mixed vegetables from a tin just before serving, a 'moussaka' topped with mashed potato instead of aubergine, a 'Welsh rarebit' which is simply toasted cheese. If a recipe calls for certain ingredients and you do not have those ingredients, do not do the recipe. It is as simple as that. Many great dishes are simple to do, many much more complicated. But do not dress mutton as lamb; do not try to pull the wool over your customers' eyes.

As a nation we traduce cooking. We are stingy about cream, mean about eggs, miserly with good olive oil, butter and herbs. We put bottles of cheap wine, which arrived in bulk on a British dockside in a vast railway tank-wagon having sloshed its way from all over Europe, into baskets, on their sides, in order to impress the customer, and we then offend him further by filling the dining-room with fumes from a spirit or gas lamp while we *flambé* some extraordinary concoction at his table – a process best left to the kitchen, where cooking actually belongs. And as a last straw we decry 'un'healthy ingredients and force our customers to eat thick, soggy pastry made with brown flour.

Healthy eating is one thing, but trumped-up dishes using 'natural' ingredients quite another when used to cover up poor cooking and a dearth of knowledge.

Once again, I plead that, if you put a dish on your menu and call it by its proper name, it should contain the proper ingredients and be cooked the proper way. Alas, how few, how very few restaurateurs actually do just that. It is so easy, perhaps, to mislead the public – but it is just as easy to be honest with them. And in the long run a lot more profitable.

14 Loss, Break-Even and Profit

Business? It's quite simple. It's other people's money.
Alexandre Dumas the Younger

So now that your doors are open and you survey the wreckage of your bank balance, you have to look forward actually to earning your first money and keeping some of it as profit. This involves, in the first place, the simple (or tricky) question of what you are going to charge your customers.

Estimates

For a start, you will know by now, or be pretty certain of, your estimated overheads. These must include rent, rates (an ever-increasing burden to most businesses), insurances, a provision for wages and possibly National Insurance, and an estimate of energy costs, even though some of these may be variable (e.g. the place must be heated and lighted even when you are not busy, although the kitchen will be using less power). It is essential that nothing is left out and that the figures you compile are as accurate as they possibly can be. It may, at this stage, be comforting to bear in mind the happy fact that, as you become more successful (busier, that is), the proportion of these fixed overheads against earnings will decline. But that is some way ahead yet. The thing to stress here is that you must include everything, even costs like telephone and stationery.

As a very rough rule – and this can be only a merest guide, because such 'rules' will vary between one type of place and another – your fixed overhead should eventually work out at about twenty per cent of your turnover, staff costs up to forty per cent of turnover (much less if you do a lot of the work yourself) and materials, food and drink about thirty-five per cent of turnover, but this depends very much on whether you are

156

buying in most of your food or preparing fresh food from the start. However, that is still in the future.

You need accurate costs because the trade works on gross profit, from which your net profit can be deduced. And at no time include VAT in any calculations. At the end of this chapter I have gathered together some calculation tables for working out various profit, mark-up percentages and VAT-inclusive selling-prices which you will find useful, as well as self-explanatory.

The prime aim when you first open your doors should be to cover your variable costs by the prices you are going to charge. Obviously you are going to have to cover all your costs eventually, but if you see a reasonable return just on the variables – food, staff and so on, you are also contributing towards your fixed overheads.

But there is a danger here of underpricing your business.

This is a very real danger for the newcomer for, although it would be silly to price yourself out of the market at the outset, you have already decided the sort of operation you are going to run, the sort of clientele you hope to attract and the sort of prices for similar businesses locally, and it is a mistake to try to undercut all and sundry. If you undercut overmuch, you will be forced to increase your charges at a later stage, and customers do not like this one bit, for they rarely understand – and why should they? – the complexity of restaurant charges. Once again, begin as you mean to go on.

A restaurant not far from our own business made the mistake of too-low prices when it first opened. It did, indeed, attract customers, including some of mine, but all of them said that no place could stay in business too long on those prices in this day and age. It actually became a bit of a joke but, alas, the joke was on the owner, who soon had to shut his doors as the enormous hoist in prices which he was eventually forced to make lost him most of his hard-earned reputation. It is a warning all should heed.

Next fact: the greater your overheads, the greater your mark-up must be to cover them.

This is easier said than done. The mark-up – the price you are going to charge for your meals – depends on local factors as well as costs. And the mark-up is not necessarily the same on all foods sold. It is just not practical to establish a rule for your gross profit margin applicable to everything you sell. You are bound to have to vary the charge depending on whether it is a first, a main or a sweet course, otherwise customers will find themselves paying ludicrously low or unacceptably high prices on dishes which are simply not worth either. So once again your common sense will have to do battle with your fiscal policy.

Thus your overheads may well dictate your mark-up policy, but your customers alone have the say in whether they stay away or come regularly.

In fact, mark-ups tend to be thirty-three, forty or fifty per cent throughout the trade. It may be easier here if we look for a fifty per cent gross profit as our example.

At this figure, if you spent, say, £500 a week on food and drink, you would have to sell it for £1,000. Your overheads for that week must then be deducted, preferably both the fixed and the variable, which, again let us say, comes to £300. A simple sum gives you your **net profit**:

Sales		£1,000
Food/drink cost	£500	
Overheads etc	£300	
Total	£800	£800
Net profit		£200

This is all well and good, but advice on, or examples of, sums tends to go wrong when you are dealing with the fickle public. The sales figure is merely notional, because you will have no idea that you can attain such sales until you have been in business for quite a time. So at the start you are going to be groping in the dark with your mark-up, which may have to be very much greater if you are not achieving the sales target, in order to cover the overheads. What on earth do you do?

You grin and persevere; that is what you do. And providing the amount you charge for your meals and drinks seems to be right to you, taking into account all local restaurant charges on which you have done research, as well as your style of service, the setting and so on, you will not go far wrong. If you are successful, and you have got the sums right, you may even be able to reduce charges slightly to give you an edge over the competition. But you must be careful – customers like 'special offers' but they abhor very large swings in prices, especially upwards.

So your pricing, or sales, policy has to be reasonable for what you are offering, taking into account all your overheads.

Fair Dealing

Above all, I would urge you at this point to ensure that your pricing policy is fair and honest. So I will tell you a perfectly true story of what happened to my wife and me when we started our research before we opened our first restaurant.

We went to see a very successful restaurant-owner in Glasgow, who was flattered that we had asked his advice. During the course of the conversation we told him we thought it best to start with a 'set menu' in which everything, except coffee, was included, whatever choice they made. He was absolutely horrified.

'The punters won't thank you for that,' he told us flatly. 'Price everything individually. I'll give you an example. Are you going to have a speciality cheese, say?'

We were puzzled. 'What do you mean by a speciality cheese?' asked my wife humbly.

The man sighed patiently. 'You know,' he said, 'something like Camembert, Stilton, that sort of thing.'

'But they're all cheeses,' replied my wife, who actually has a vast knowledge and expertise in cheeses. 'There doesn't seem anything special about those two.'

'Not to you, perhaps,' said the restaurateur, 'but they are to the average punter. You can charge more for them; 50p a go for the ordinary ones, you know, Cheddar, that sort of thing, 75p for the specialities. And don't forget vegetables.'

'What vegetables are special?' I asked him, not without a trace of irony, which he ignored.

He sighed. 'Courgettes for one, but there are a lot of others. Charge for each vegetable the punters have. Forget the nonsense about a fixed price, and if you want a fixed price as a 'come-on', pitch it low and don't offer much for it. The trick is to get 'em through the doors, doesn't matter how, then hit 'em with the bill before they leave.'

'Don't you think that's a bit dishonest?' I asked mildly.

He frowned at me. 'Dishonest? Dishonest?' he echoed. 'You're in this business to make money. No punter ever queries a bill, and no punter likes paying too little, not in this country, he doesn't. You'll get no thanks for being reasonable or cheap.

Unless it's expensive, the punter'll think it wasn't any good. The more you charge, the more they'll enjoy it.'

It was, to us, a sad lesson, and we set out to prove him wrong. I am not sure we succeeded.

Some months later a former colleague of mine and his friends took me to lunch at that man's restaurant. The menu was very long, intricately formed and ingeniously priced. The only item on the fixed price menu was kidneys, of which I am inordinately fond. They were absolutely disgusting, having been cooked some days previously and then reheated again and again. I do not remember what the others in the party had, although their own choices looked particularly unappetizing to me, but I did catch sight of the bill. It was enormous. All of them said they enjoyed their meal, and the whole restaurant was packed. So who is right – that restaurateur or me?

You will make up your own mind. All I can say in my own defence is that a great many of our customers have commented pleasingly on our bills, which come to exactly what they reckon they will be, and we based a reputation on it – no hidden extras is, I think, fair and honest, and the system of charging for every single thing (whether it be butter with bread – a common practice in my part of the world – or extra for courgettes in place of, say, fresh broccoli) is something which I find unpleasant. I also think it is unnecessary and shows that the restaurateur is not doing his job properly.

Spend-per-Head
This brings us to the need to estimate in advance the amount per head that you expect your customers to spend. This is an essential estimate.

It is no good saying you are going to take £1,000 a week just because you need to take that amount of money in order to stay afloat. Such a figure depends not only on 'getting 'em through the doors' but on a sensible appraisal of the service and food you are providing. Only you can estimate that. 'Spend-per-head' is very important indeed, and yet I have come across a great many people who run restaurants who have never actually estimated that and have no idea what the figure is.

In our own restaurant we knew exactly what the average was: at the end of each week I divided the takings by the number of 'covers' we served. I strongly advise you to do the same. It is an easy but instructive exercise. And remember: exclude the VAT.

Some restaurants charge for set meals on the basis of the main dish. This practice, which is common and quite fair, has the slight disadvantage in that customers who want just one dish resent paying for others they do not wish to eat. Our own way round this problem was to offer all dishes priced individually, from starters to pudding, and with the main course inclusive of vegetables. But we also offered a three-course meal, taken from the main menu, at a price slightly less than the three dishes added together. We found this was very popular, especially at lunchtime.

There is nothing original about this idea, but it came about because of a close study of our market. It is a typical example of what I mean about a reasonable pricing policy coupled with flexibility and maximization of profits.

It so happened, that in our country restaurant in the south, we became known not only for the quality of our food but for the reasonableness of our lunches, which attracted the retired 'gentry' and (we liked to think) the professional man with a little more time to spare than his junior colleagues. That was the market we aimed at, and it was a market in which we were totally successful.

For most of the retired, older customers, it quickly became apparent to us that lunch was the main meal of their day, but for the most part they seemed content with just the one dish, although many of them always had a pudding if it appealed to them. Hence, in our place, the three-course menu was born as an experiment. It became enormously popular – it was balanced, well cooked and presented and at an acceptable price. As a result we moved, almost unconsciously, into the situation of selling three dishes when before we had sold only one. Our lunch 'spend-per-head' moved from an average of £5 to £8 almost overnight. Our costs remained virtually the same.

Back to Our Sums
The complexity of book-keeping, whether double or single entry, and the need for various 'ledgers' to go with them are quite often beyond the capability of the ordinary, smaller restaurateur, especially when he starts up in business and there do not seem enough hours in the day. I would therefore urge you to ask your accountant to set out, plainly and simply,

exactly what he would like to see and how you should keep the necessary records. This will not in the long run cost anything more than his normal fees, because, as we pointed out before, it will save him time at the end of the year, and therefore you money, if everything he wants is neatly documented in the way he finds acceptable for his own method of working.

The first 'book', in my opinion, is something akin to the Kalamazoo or Lamson Paragon VAT ledger, which actually does, a number of things, by no means all of them to do with VAT. Into this book you can enter every cash or cheque transaction made: on the left-hand pages are columns into which you can put all takings, and on the right hand are columns in which to record all payments. This is so blindingly obvious, and so easy, that, if the worst came to the worst, you would need very little else.

It is a good idea to make time – say, every week – in which to enter all these items. They do not, in the case of receipts, obviously have to be itemized bill by bill – totals will do, either for the whole day or for the morning and evening services. By splitting the service, for instance, you have a record for yourself of any differences between lunches and dinners. It is of no interest to the tax people, the VAT officers or even your accountant, but it does form a record for yourself, takes no extra trouble and allows you to see more clearly where you are going.

On the right-hand pages you must record all your outgoings and to whom they were paid. Include everything. In this way you will have an absolute record, and it will be useful not only to you and the authorities but to your accountant and the bank. It is a daily record of the business, and from it you can take any information you subsequently require.

You can use the various columns you will find in the book for purposes designated by you: perhaps a column for cash and another for cheques paid to you, perhaps a column for food costs and another for drinks. Be guided by your accountant: he is the expert, you are not. But the use of each column is simplicity itself. And in any event, this is the book that the VAT inspectors will want to see, and they truly *are* experts.

But what this general ledger does not contain is any information regarding money owed to you or money you are going to have to pay out in the future. It is merely a record of what has happened, not what is going to happen. Neither does it contain any standing orders which you have authorized your bank to pay on your behalf, perhaps for rates, hire purchase, equipment on lease and so on. Nor does it contain depreciation figures which will be needed to work out your annual accounts, or any assets in terms of stock, buildings, equipment and so on.

On the other hand, you are asking, what more must I do?

The man or woman who is a fiend at figures will be keeping many more 'books': petty cash, a bought ledger, a non-bought ledger, a cashbook, a sundry debtors ledger, a takings book, a wages book. There is no end to the paperwork. You must call a halt, otherwise you will be swamped. Most of these records are for larger businesses, where, perhaps, the owner has plenty of time to do the bookwork while employing staff to look after his customers. This is a curious state of affairs, you may imagine. Surely, I hope you will say, I should be the person who is looking after the staff and the customers? I cannot look after both and still remain sane. Very true. Well said. Get someone else to do it, someone who knows, understands and enjoys it.

Early on in this book I mentioned this point. The world is actually full of people who understand figures – retired accountants or their 'moonlight' clerks, bank managers or their 'moonlighting' tellers or assistants, men and women who have worked in accounts offices in local firms and other businesses, and many quite reliable people who advertise in the local papers, perhaps mothers of schoolchildlren who have had experience of book-keeping, who cannot work full time but need a little pin money and an interest outside the home. The service they can provide will be well worth the money and, above all, it will free you to work where you are most needed – earning money by attracting customers, not by keeping records.

But, having said that, I must urge you to get *regular* help. The odd occasion is no good. Once a week is ideal, as the work may then take about an hour, or, say, three or four hours a month. But do not get too far behind. That is a certain way to muddle. It can also be dangerous. And if you cannot get help, set aside a very definite time each week in which to do the books; make it sacrosanct, and it will very quickly become a habit. Leave it too long, skip a week, say, 'The end of the month will do', and it won't. By that time you will be in despair at the work you have to catch up.

However, whether you do all your own accounts, or whether

someone else does, it is essential that every bit of paper be kept. Your office will quickly resemble some vast waste-paper bin, I know, but you must be able to prove, if required, where the money has gone and on what it has been spent.

So keep, preferably in separate files, the following:

1. All suppliers' delivery notes, invoices and receipts.
2. All bank statements relating to the business (keep your own money in a separate bank account).
3. Bank paying-in books. (Try not to use single paying-in slips.)
4. Cheque-book stubs.
5. Cancelled cheques. (Ask the bank to return them to you with each statement.)
6. Receipts for all cash purchases. (Always remember to ask for a receipt, however small the amount.)
7. Copies of your own bills, whether for customers paying cash or for invoices you have perhaps sent to company clients.

The mountain of paper may depress you, but it will impress accountants, tax and VAT inspectors.

Taking Stock

The idea of all these records is not, however, just to please those three people, and all the others who will take an interest in your business. They are to help *you*. The net profit figure at the end of every month is all-important. It will show you how your business is progressing. From the records you have kept, you can draw up a monthly trading account and a profit-and-loss account. And to do this properly you must try, at least for the first few months or even a year or more, to do a stock-take on a certain day.

This is not as complicated as it sounds. In a small business it should take no time at all, and you will very soon get used to it.

Basically you need to know, on that certain day, the value of everything you hold by way of food, drink and so on. You must estimate what is left in bottles, of course, but cases of beer, wines and spirits are easy enough, as you can refer quickly to your invoices from your suppliers. Do not forget food in the deep-freeze or in the storage cupboards and larders. In practice, these should be comparatively similar each month, unless you have been drastically over-buying, in which case the monthly stock-take is going to be helpful in another direction too. Over-buying is in reality a waste of money. Your stock-take should reveal a more or less constant figure, certainly when averaged out over a year.

A Monthly Balance Sheet

You take this stock-take value as your starting-off point at the beginning of a monthly period, and to it you add all your purchases during the new month, along with all your other expenses, such as wages, phone bills and so on. You then enter the value of your stock at the end of that monthly period. This will give you a *gross profit* (or loss, probably, in your first few months). As an example, it may look something like this:

Value of stock	£1,500
Payments	£850
Wages	£500
	£2,850
Less closing stock	£1,350
	£1,500

Against this figure of £1,500 you can then set your sales figure for the month. So if your total sales for the month are, say, £3,000, you have a gross profit of £1,500.

To get a *net profit* (or loss), you now have to add in your overheads. The balance sheet will look like this:

	£		£
Value of opening stock	1,500	Sales	3,000
Payments	850		
Wages	500		
	2,850		
Less closing stock	1,350		
	1,500		
Balance (gross profit)	1,500		
	3,000		3,000
Overheads	1,000	Gross profit	1,500
Balance (net profit)	500		
	1,500		1,500

Of course, this is pretty basic stuff, and by making it more complex, i.e. adding in more information or breaking down the payments and overheads, you can make it more informative, perhaps even including the money you pay yourself, thus making your income tax easy to calculate at the end of the year. There are no hard-and-fast rules, but remember to exclude VAT from *all* figures, as it forms no part of your personal or business income. It is essential that VAT be kept separate from all calculations; you should pay it directly to HM Customs and Excise, less your own deductions as allowed under VAT regulations.

The disadvantage is that, although this monthly balance sheet seems to be a pretty healthy one, it does not necessarily include, say, the actual cash you have received in your sales figure. This could lead to an unbalanced view of things. You may well have paid out cash for certain items, or because some suppliers want cash in advance or on delivery. Some of your customers may be business clients who pay late the following month, but your sales figure has included them for ease of calculation. So even, if on paper, your business seems to be doing quite well, you could still run out of actual cash at the bank sometime in the future.

That is where a cash-flow forecast comes in. Only this time it is going to be a lot more accurate than the first one you did. So an update is required and, if necessary, a visit to the bank manager to ask for a future overdraft to cover any shortages which loom on the horizon. So go back to the cash-flow table in Chapter 8. You will now have definite figures to put in at least for your first month's trading. If you do that regularly, you can foresee any trouble ahead and help yourself as well as pleasing your bank manager.

Breaking Even
Important to you at all times is the break-even point, and you should calculate this in advance. It is at least something you can do in your early days, or even before you open, as the figures can be based on a fair and reasonable knowledge or guess.

The break-even point, fairly obviously, is when your sales are yielding just enough money to cover the cost. Before this is reached, you are trading at a loss; when it is exceeded, you are making a profit. Simple as that.

In the restaurant trade your projected sales should be based on the number of meals you need to serve multiplied by the average spend per head, a question we have dealt with earlier, in order to cover all your fixed and variable costs. The costs are almost certainly known to you, certainly the fixed ones, and, as I said above, you should be able to guess the variables until your trading pattern is established and you have evidence for them. The only problem is the sales.

But it is also fairly obvious when calculating your break-even point that, if your total costs are going to be, say, £2,350 a month, to use the example on p.165, you must sell 1,000 meals at a price of £2.35, 500 meals at a price of £4.70 or 250 meals at £9.40.

This, once again, is where your market study comes in – just what is the price band (and therefore the type of person) at which you are aiming? You know you cannot guarantee to get all those customers in that first month, or even in subsequent months, but at least with an idea of a break-even point you can see what you need to achieve in terms of sales, and by how much you are either topping the figure and making a profit or dropping below it and making a loss. If you are clever enough, you can even draw a neat graph and update it every month on the known figures of your costs and your sales.

VAT

Now, what you have been waiting for all this time – a word about VAT.

I have already mentioned the need to do your books regularly, and nowhere in this more important than in keeping your VAT records. VAT returns are due every quarter, and if you leave them until the end of three months, you are creating for yourself a whole load of trouble.

The VAT officers' powers are draconian and, although most VAT inspectors I have met are courteous and helpful when they call to inspect your books, the enforcement officer, should he have to call, is anything but.

VAT regulations seem to change regularly and by the time this book is published will almost certainly have changed yet again, probably more than once, as eager Customs and Excise officials invent new rules or bring within their grasp more ways in which they can impose their dreaded fifteen per cent.

Basically, everything you sell as a restaurateur has a fifteen per cent tax on it, even though some of the foods you buy do not. This is not a treatise on VAT – that would take a whole library to house – but, broadly speaking, unless you are in the business of selling cold food as 'take-aways' (but not drinks or ice-cream or confectionery), you are subject to that fifteen per cent. This can make life difficult for delicatessen/coffee-bar operations which might sell a range of items, some VAT-free, some not.

The other problem is the fact that most food outlets deal mainly in cash, and the VAT inspectors are especially attuned to such a situation, which offers plenty of scope to cheat them out of their money. The teams of inspectors specialize in certain trades and industries and can spot attempts to cheat a mile away if the books somehow do not 'add up', not in a fiscal sense but in comparison with other businesses.

On the other hand, it should be said, and said fairly, that you are not actually cheating the VAT system, you are cheating the public at large who have paid you their fifteen per cent share, willingly or unwillingly, in the knowledge, they presume, that it will be passed on automatically to HM Customs and Excise. There is an important principle here: it is not your money, in effect; it is money taken from someone else under false pretences if you do not pay it over to Customs and Excise, which is why the regulations are so strict. In any event, the VAT inspectors are sadly lacking in any tendency to argue the point – they want their money, and if they do not get it promptly and correctly, they have the power to penalize you heavily, as well as putting in the bailiffs without further ado.

It is no bad thing, then, to stay on the right side of HM Customs and Excise and call on them whenever you want a point clarified. They are usually very keen to ensure that traders do not get into any trouble, and most are reasonably understanding of genuine errors or omissions, providing it does not happen too often.

On one visit by the usual two inspectors I was chided for my poor book-keeping and my ignorance about claims I had incorrectly made and which they disallowed. But they then pointed out that I had failed to claim on some other items, and within a few days a substantial cheque arrived from the VAT office in settlement of my own errors.

Some years later the boot was on the other foot, and the two inspectors found a shortfall of £1,200 in their favour, which I had to pay within thirty days. It was very bad news and not something I would like to happen to anyone else, even though both inspectors recognized a genuine error and told me as kindly as possible that no one trying to cheat with their VAT would have been foolish enough to do what I had done. There is no argument worth making against any decision they make, as they always have the whip hand, and the corruption commensurate with such absolute power means that 'awkward customers' are not likely to be forgotten but marked forever in their files.

As background to the extraordinary jargon you will have to face (jargon which only a Civil Servant allowed to run riot with the English language could have invented), the VAT you pay on the goods and services you buy for your business is called 'input tax', and the VAT charged on the goods and services you supply to your customers is called 'output tax'. You claim relief on the input tax by deducting it from the output tax, paying over the difference within twenty-eight days of the end of the quarter's accounting period.

If, however, the input tax claim is greater than the output tax debt, as sometimes happens, for understandable reasons, that money is paid to you by the VAT office once you have filled in the quarterly form. There are penalties for late return of forms, as there are for virtually every infringement, honest or otherwise, of the regulations.

There are three classes of goods and services: exempt, on which no VAT is payable such as insurance; zero-rated, on which VAT is payable in theory but not in practice, such as books, food and so on: standard-rated, on which VAT is charged at fifteen per cent. It is unlikely that the nuances of these differences will affect your own business, but they are of importance to, for instance, exporters.

It is an offence not to register for VAT, as it is for registering late, so once again, ask their help if at all in doubt. Mistakes can be very expensive. If you buy a ready-made business but intend to trade it down below the level at which VAT becomes compulsory, you must first de-register for VAT, and until you have done that, you must continue to charge, and pay, VAT.

This can be particularly applicable in 'seasonal' businesses if, for instance, you are going to operate in a tourist area and may be open for only part of the year. There are regulations (inevitably) which may mean you should have registered for VAT because your quarterly turnover has exceeded £8,000, even though your annual turnover may be less than the £23,000 'floor' at present (1988) in force. The VAT inspector has to be convinced that it is not increasing success on your part but that the business really is 'seasonal' and not open all the year, or, if open, is trading down very considerably during the other quarters.

Many business people make a point of paying the money due for VAT into a special deposit account at their bank, where it earns interest before it has to be paid to HM Customs and Excise in one lump sum. Other people say the money is better off helping their own cash-flow situation. The policy you adopt is entirely up to you, but if it is the second, please make sure you actually do have the money every quarter to pay over, and have not spent it on something else.

Now, I know that this chapter has been far from exhaustive, and I hope that the quantity of paperwork will not depress you, but some personal understanding of the complexities of simple book-keeping is absolutely essential.

A Note on Insurance:
Earlier in this chapter I made a passing reference to the need to include insurance costs in your overheads. What particular insurance do you need?

Obviously you must be covered against the normal disasters which could threaten your business: burglary, flood, fire and so on. Remember, your business is your only source of income, and insurance should be effected to cover loss of any income in the event of a disaster, as well as re-building costs etc. You will also have a quantity of expensive equipment, furnishings and fittings – do not under-estimate the *replacement* costs of such items. You can also insure against loss of profits if something terrible happens. But perhaps most important of all, you must have public liability insurance, which will cover you against claims made by staff or the public who, say, trip over a carelessly placed carpet or slip on the proverbial banana-skin or perhaps get burned by having very hot soup poured over them accidentally.

The best course is also the simplest: find a reliable insurance broker and take his advice. He is an expert, and he is also highly unlikely to urge you into unnecessary expenditure, especially if he is a member of the British Insurance Brokers' Association.

The following tables and calculations are used by kind permission of Croner's Catering.

Some gross profit guidelines

Type of business	Gross profit	
	Liquor	Food
Public house	40–50%	40–60%
Restaurants	45–60%	50–65%
Wine bars	45–55%	40–50%
Self service	55%	60–70%
School meals	N/A	30–50%
Members' clubs	25–45%	30–60%
Outdoor catering	50–60%	50–70%
Fast food	N/A	55–70%
Kiosks	N/A	30%

Table C: Gross Profit
Selling prices for percentage gross profit on sales

COST	10%	20%	30%	40%	50%	60%	70%	80%	90%
10p	.11	.13	.14	.17	.20	.25	.33	.50	1.00
20p	.22	.25	.29	.33	.40	.50	.67	1.00	2.00
30p	.33	.38	.43	.50	.60	.75	1.00	1.50	3.00
40p	.44	.50	.57	.67	.80	1.00	1.33	2.00	4.00
50p	.56	.63	.71	.83	1.00	1.25	1.67	2.50	5.00
60p	.67	.75	.86	1.00	1.20	1.50	2.00	3.00	6.00
70p	.78	.88	1.00	1.17	1.40	1.75	2.33	3.50	7.00
80p	.89	1.00	1.14	1.33	1.60	2.00	2.67	4.00	8.00
90p	1.00	1.13	1.29	1.50	1.80	2.25	3.00	4.50	9.00
1.00	1.11	1.25	1.43	1.67	2.00	2.50	3.33	5.00	10.00
2.00	2.22	2.50	2.86	3.33	4.00	5.00	6.67	10.00	20.00
3.00	3.33	3.75	4.29	5.00	6.00	7.50	10.00	15.00	30.00
4.00	4.44	5.00	5.71	6.67	8.00	10.00	13.33	20.00	40.00
5.00	5.56	6.25	7.14	8.33	10.00	12.50	16.67	25.00	50.00
6.00	6.67	7.50	8.57	10.00	12.00	15.00	20.00	30.00	60.00
7.00	7.78	8.75	10.00	11.67	14.00	17.50	23.33	35.00	70.00
8.00	8.89	10.00	11.43	13.33	16.00	20.00	26.67	40.00	80.00
9.00	10.00	11.25	12.86	15.00	18.00	22.50	30.00	45.00	90.00
10.00	11.11	12.50	14.29	16.67	20.00	25.00	33.33	50.00	

Table of selling prices for various levels of profit on sales
1. Look up pounds in lower table
2. Look up pence in upper table
3. Add results together

Example:
If a dish costs £2.80 to produce, what should its selling price be to achieve 60% profit on sales?

£2.00 cost = £5.00 selling price
0.80 cost = £2.00 selling price

selling price	£7.00
Add VAT from table E	£1.05
	———
Final selling price	£8.05

Table D: Mark Up
Selling prices for mark up or profit on cost

COST	33%	67%	100%	133%	167%	200%	233%	267%	300%	333%	367%	400%
10p	.13	.17	.20	.23	.27	.30	.33	.37	.40	.43	.47	.50
20p	.27	.33	.40	.47	.53	.60	.67	.73	.80	.87	.93	1.00
30p	.40	.50	.60	.70	.80	.90	1.00	1.10	1.20	1.30	1.40	1.50
40p	.53	.67	.80	.93	1.07	1.20	1.33	1.47	1.60	1.73	1.87	2.00
50p	.67	.84	1.00	1.17	1.33	1.50	1.67	1.83	2.00	2.17	2.33	2.50
60p	.80	1.00	1.20	1.40	1.60	1.80	2.00	2.20	2.40	2.60	2.80	3.00
70p	.93	1.17	1.40	1.63	1.87	2.10	2.33	2.57	2.80	3.03	3.27	3.50
80p	1.06	1.34	1.60	1.86	2.13	2.40	2.67	2.93	3.20	3.47	3.73	4.00
90p	1.20	1.50	1.80	2.10	2.40	2.70	3.00	3.30	3.60	3.90	4.20	4.50
1.00	1.33	1.67	2.00	2.33	2.67	3.00	3.33	3.66	4.00	4.33	4.66	5.00
2.00	2.67	3.33	4.00	4.67	5.34	6.00	6.67	7.33	8.00	8.67	9.33	10.00
3.00	4.00	5.00	6.00	7.00	8.00	9.00	10.00	11.00	12.00	13.00	14.00	15.00
4.00	5.33	6.67	8.00	9.33	10.68	12.00	13.33	14.67	16.00	17.33	18.67	20.00
5.00	6.67	8.33	10.00	11.67	15.35	15.00	16.67	18.33	20.00	21.67	23.33	25.00

Use of this table
1. Look up pounds in lower table
2. Look up pence in upper table
3. Add results together

Table E
To find the VAT to add to a VAT exclusive selling price

£	VAT element to be added to selling price									
	0	0.01	0.02	0.03	0.04	0.05	0.06	0.07	0.08	0.09
0	0	0	0	0	0.01	0.01	0.01	0.01	0.01	0.01
0.10	0.02	0.02	0.02	0.02	0.02	0.02	0.02	0.03	0.03	0.03
0.20	0.03	0.03	0.03	0.03	0.04	0.04	0.04	0.04	0.04	0.04
0.30	0.05	0.05	0.05	0.05	0.05	0.05	0.05	0.06	0.06	0.06
0.40	0.06	0.06	0.06	0.06	0.07	0.07	0.07	0.07	0.07	0.08
0.50	0.08	0.08	0.08	0.08	0.08	0.08	0.08	0.09	0.09	0.09
0.60	0.09	0.09	0.09	0.09	0.10	0.10	0.10	0.10	0.10	0.10
0.70	0.11	0.11	0.11	0.11	0.11	0.11	0.11	0.12	0.12	0.12
0.80	0.12	0.12	0.12	0.12	0.13	0.13	0.13	0.13	0.13	0.13
0.90	0.14	0.14	0.14	0.14	0.14	0.14	0.14	0.15	0.15	0.15

£	
1.00	0.15
2.00	0.30
3.00	0.45
4.00	0.60
5.00	0.75
6.00	0.90
7.00	1.05
8.00	1.20
9.00	1.35
10.00	1.50

Example of use of this table
To find how much VAT to add to a VAT exclusive selling price
of £2.96
    1. Look up £2.00 in the lower table (answer £0.30)
    2. Look up £0.96 in upper table (answer £0.14)
    Add both results
VAT inclusive selling price will be £3.40

Using a calculator
VAT element to be added: £2.96 × 0.15 = 44p (0.444 rounded
down)
VAT inclusive price: £2.96 × 1.15 = £3.40 (£3.404 rounded
down)

Table F
To find the true income after deduction of VAT

	Table of VAT exclusive prices at 15% VAT									
£	0	0.01	0.02	0.03	0.04	0.05	0.06	0.07	0.08	0.09
0	0	0.01	0.02	0.03	0.03	0.04	0.05	0.06	0.07	0.08
0.10	0.09	0.10	0.10	0.11	0.12	0.13	0.14	0.15	0.16	0.17
0.20	0.17	0.18	0.19	0.20	0.21	0.22	0.23	0.23	0.24	0.25
0.30	0.26	0.27	0.28	0.29	0.30	0.30	0.31	0.32	0.33	0.34
0.40	0.35	0.36	0.37	0.37	0.38	0.39	0.40	0.41	0.42	0.43
0.50	0.43	0.44	0.45	0.46	0.47	0.48	0.49	0.50	0.50	0.51
0.60	0.52	0.53	0.54	0.55	0.56	0.57	0.57	0.58	0.59	0.60
0.70	0.61	0.62	0.63	0.63	0.64	0.65	0.66	0.67	0.68	0.69
0.80	0.70	0.70	0.71	0.72	0.73	0.74	0.75	0.76	0.77	0.77
0.90	0.78	0.79	0.80	0.81	0.82	0.83	0.83	0.84	0.85	0.86

£	
1.00	0.87
2.00	1.74
3.00	2.61
4.00	3.48
5.00	4.35
6.00	5.21
7.00	6.09
8.00	6.96
9.00	7.83
10.00	8.69

Example of use of this table
To find the real value of a sale of £1.34 including VAT.
    1. Look up £1.00 in the lower table (answer 0.87)
    2. Look up £0.34 in upper table (answer £0.30)
    3. Add both results
The income will be £1.17

Using a calculator
£1.34 ÷ 1.15 = £1.17 (£1.1652 rounded up)

15 Behind the Scenes and Up-Front

He who receives his friends and gives no personal attention to the meal is not worthy of having friends.

Brillat Savarin

The preparation of a meal – for one or a hundred – is like the proverbial iceberg: at least four-fifths is out of sight, and, in any proper restaurant, rightly so. It is not the concern of your guests (who, to start with at any rate, deserve to be regarded as friends) as to what goes on behind the scenes, what disasters have occurred, what triumphs of imagination or organization have been achieved by the chef and his *brigade*, or the owner, or the restaurant manager, the highest or lowest in the hierarchy. If you are charging people for the privilege of eating in your establishment, you must do them the courtesy of providing good food, drink and service all the time, and without excuses, however reasonable such excuses may appear to be to yourself.

If you think back, and assuming you have put as much research into the whole project as I have urged upon you, you will doubtless recall the pathetic apologies so very often made in Britain as to why things were not quite right. I am not on the whole surprised that so few people complain.

Excuses

The excuses are legion, are they not? Why the soup is tepid and tasteless, the meat stringy, the vegetables smashed to a soggy mush, the coffee weak. The reasons proffered are trotted out with some sort of tired pride in the apology. 'The chef has had a bad day.' (I.e. he is probably drunk). 'The waitress can be

174

forgetful, can't she?' (I.e. She has had a row with her boyfriend/husband.) 'The plumber never turned up. They never do, do they?' (I.e. 'We forgot to ask him in time'.) 'We had a hectic time last night/at lunchtime. You should have seen the place. We were packed.' (I.e. 'All of us got drunk.')

These various and manifold apologies having been made, the luckless guest is then presented with a bill which does not in any way reflect the total lack of expertise demonstrated by the restaurant. Thus the unfortunate man or woman is obliged or, at the very least, certainly expected to pay in full for mistakes not of his own making. Bad food, poor service, such establishments are saying, are all part and parcel of the jolly rough-and-tumble of life in the catering trade. It's just bad luck on you, the customer, that you lost out this time round. Better luck next time. Win one, lose one, that's what we say, eh?

This, of course, is a monstrous imposition on the customer and is quite different, I would suggest, from other facets of business life. After all, if you buy a toaster which does not toast or which burns the bread, do you put it all down to the fact that the factory manager had a 'bad day', or the assembly line went haywire, or the retailer felt off-colour? Or do you take it back, say the toaster does not work and ask for a different model or the return of your money?

Yet this sort of thing happens frequently when you are eating out, and just as frequently the restaurant regards it as part of the game, par for the course. You, as a customer, should complain – or you do other customers, and yourself as a restaurateur, a disservice. But one thing is fairly certain: you as a customer would never go there again, so why should you expect *your* customers not to vote with their feet when they are faced with similar occurrences in your own establishment?

Now we all know that it is a truism to say 'mistakes often happen' – of course they do, certainly in this trade, but I am suggesting to you that it is of no concern whatever to your customers to be burdened with excuses as to why such mistakes did happen.

Under no circumstances are any excuses acceptable. If a mistake has occurred, a profound apology is the only course – along with a greatly reduced bill, or preferably, none at all. In that way your customer might well come back, and he might well become a staunch friend of your restaurant in the future.

Friends of your restaurant are what it is all about, not mere customers.

Routine

Now, professionalism is essential in the running of any catering outlet – excuses are for amateurs. And the more professional you are, the less chance there will be of any need to make excuses. It is professionalism which runs successful restaurants, because successful restaurants have routine. A dreadful, soul-destroying routine it may be to some; a joyous, heart-lifting routine it may be to others. It does not matter – routine is what works, routine is what is important, routine is what makes life easier for you and for your customer. It is this thing routine which forms the four-fifths portion of the iceberg. So let us take a look at routine and see what it entails.

In the first place, it begins early in the day.

It begins long before service, and it ends late in the day, long after service. If you are serving lunches as well as dinner, or are open all day, the routine will be considerably extended, but there is simply no easy way round the problem, except to say that the better the routine, the more acceptable, the more comforting it becomes. It actually does make life easier, believe you me.

Cleaning

The day's routine will begin earlier in the kitchen than in the dining-room, but in both places that dreaded word 'cleaning' rears its ugly head. Before you start work in either place, is it clean? If it is not clean to start with, it will become a slum during service. Are there any old crocks or pots and pans left lying about by mistake? Were there any work-surfaces overlooked at the end of the previous service? Is a table still crumby from your own breakfast? Is the floor as clean as it should be, especially in the kitchen? Remember, grease and spills cause accidents and, in any event, what could be nicer than starting your day's work with everything in its proper place, looking spotless, ready to begin all over again?

In the restaurant, too, the day should start with normal cleaning. Vacuuming, polishing, dusting, careful checking of all plates, cutlery, glassware, ensuring the flowers are fresh, the salt and peppers topped up, mustard pots filled – all of this will not only make the place look and smell spick and span but beckon a welcome to your first customer.

Horace, the Roman lyric poet and satirist and by all accounts quite a gourmet, even in about 30 BC, was passionate about eating-places – he should be the patron of all environmental health officers. He once wrote: 'The stomach heaves when one receives a goblet bearing the greasy imprint of sauce-stained fingers ...' So just make sure your own goblets are not like that. There are plenty of latter-day Horaces around.

By making cleaning very much a part of everyday routine, it quickly ceases to become any problem. I do not make any apology for dwelling on it. I would urge a general but nonetheless thorough clean-up in the evening after last service, especially in the kitchen, and something similar in the dining-room in the morning. But that is not to say you can just abandon the dining-room at night: smouldering cigarette butts, for instance, not only cause foul air in the morning but might cause a fire as well, and lack of general care and attention after last service makes the dining-room positively gruesome the next day, not to say totally dispiriting.

Some years ago my wife and I stayed at a small hotel in Biarritz and, while having breakfast, watched Madame taking every bottle off the glass shelves behind the bar, carefully polishing the shelves, then the bottles, and restoring all to good order. She told us she did this twice a week as part of her routine while guests breakfasted in the adjoining area. She had to be around to make sure everyone had what they wanted but, being French, she was unable to resist useful work. The rest of the building was similarly spotless, and we noticed it every time we walked in. It looked good and it smelled good, and there is hardly a better welcome than that.

A young *sous-chef* working for the THF group was sent to the Ecole le Nôtre for a month not long ago as part of his training and reported on his return: 'We had to wash everything down before we started, while we were working and when we finished.' I find the necessity for such a comment surprising. I would have thought it went without saying, and it is also true that, if your kitchen is clean, your dining-room will almost certainly be as well. Routine makes both go together.

But although the British public are stoic about their restaurants, and rarely complain, they are not by any means unaware or unnoticing.

A place my wife and I used to visit in south-west England, in which the food was very good, recently changed hands. For years, the dark, quarry-tiled floor had been lovingly washed once a day and polished twice a week until it shone with a deep, warm glow. Even the central-heating pipes were polished, and fresh flowers stood on every table. But the new owners could not see the point of so much routine, and within a few weeks of their taking over the tiles were scuffed and lustreless, the copper pipes were greeny-grey, and dusty plastic flowers had replaced the fresh ones. There was the inevitable smell of old chips.

That lack of regard for how their dining-room looked or their kitchen smelled had also spilled over onto the outside, where crates of empty bottles were stacked thoughtlessly in what used to be a pleasant area by the entrance. It did not seem much of a welcome to any passer-by, and certainly not to former regular customers. The new owners were either simply indifferent to, or ignorant of, the initial impression they were creating – a dangerous lapse because the public do notice these things. And although, alas, they will rarely tell the restaurant owners they will tell their friends. Yet so many restaurateurs wonder why their trade begins to drop off.

So the moral is: always start the day with a clean place of work, with everything in its proper place ready for use. Insist on this with whatever staff you have. Attention to detail causes everything else to follow naturally.

Everything in Its Place
The actual preparation of food cannot take place until you have ordered and had delivered, or collected, everything you need. Ordering is part of the routine, as was the *mise-en-place* system discussed in Chapter 13, which should be an essential routine for any kitchen.

In many cases your suppliers will ring you regularly at a similar time to suit you every week, or you may be lucky enough to be near a market for meat, fish and fresh vegetables.

Delivered orders should be checked in, to ensure that not just the quantities are correct but that the quality is up to the standards you require. This again is part of your regular routine. Not for nothing runs the old adage 'If you want something done, ask a busy man.' Someone who is routine-conscious, who works to a plan, can always cope with sudden crises or extra problems. It is easier to alter plans, oddly enough, when such plans are properly laid than it is to change no plan at all.

Rigid routine should not be stifling, however. It is a tool to use and use wisely. On those dreadful occasions when things do go wrong (and, however meticulous you are, things will go wrong now and again), the discipline instilled by routine comes to the fore without anyone's having to think about it. 'Discipline' is merely another name for 'routine', after all.

On one evening in my own kitchen in Scotland I was feeling rather pleased with myself, partly at the way we had completed the *mise en place* but also at the thought of our guests' enjoyment of their forthcoming dinner. I was leaning back against the main hob when one of our staff warned me not to burn myself. I smiled at her concern. How could I, *chef extraordinaire* and lord of all I surveyed, possibly burn myself against a stone-cold saucepan?

Ah yes, she had a point. In horror I suddenly realized it should have been full of simmering potatoes. All of us went as cold and as silent as the saucepan. In the meantime, we could hear my wife greeting the guests as they went to their tables in the dining-room.

Within seconds, three of us had knives in our hands and, because the kitchen was properly organized and disciplined, there was space for chopping-boards. We diced the cold, raw potatoes at break-neck speed and tossed them into a *sautoir* swimming in butter, and by the time the main course was served, the guests had that glorious dish *pommes-en-dés* instead of parsleyed spuds. None had any idea of the momentary panic 'behind the green baize door'. But had we been disorganized, had we not had an established, proper routine, with cleaned work surfaces, clean knives and everything set for service, the guests would have waited – and waited – for those potatoes.

To the Bitter End
Any kitchen worthy of the name, however big or small, is not for the weak-hearted when the cook is at full stretch in the middle of the *coup-de-fer*. Nor is it a place for the refined of manner, the sensitive flower. People get hot, 'lose their cool' just a little bit on occasion (especially the chef). That is how it has always been, and for sheer excitement and exhilaration it is unsurpassed. But

once the *assemblage* has been completed, once the dishes have gone in and service begins to slow down into the pudding and cheese courses, the tumult and the shouting die and, if the captains and the kings do not exactly depart, it is time to start cleaning up again. Yes, once again. For there is always tomorrow. And tomorrow is another day, as the famous last line of *Gone with the Wind* has it.

The same goes for the dining-room. No ashtrays, no empty wineglasses, no pools of spilled drink. However tired you are – and you will be, a bit of cleaning up now will reap rich rewards the next morning. After all, who wants to be reminded of the night before, like a hangover, when you start the following day?

'The List Ethic'
Of course, the admin. cannot be left to itself. Nor just to you. So we now come to the importance of lists.

It is no good running out of scouring-powder, say, and discovering it only when you take the empty container off the shelf. It is essential that anyone connected with the operation notes down, in a proper, pre-arranged place, what is going to be needed. This applies to everyone and everything, and under no circumstances must any excuses for failure to do this be allowed.

For a great many years our lives were lived with constant, often vast lists, and my wife became an expert, being responsible for their upkeep.

It started with a general information board in the kitchen – actually a blackboard on the wall upon which was written every conceivable item of information necessary for the running of the operation – from the names of people staying or booking a meal, with the daily menus, to small requirements like silver polish. Even chalk.

Everyone who worked with us wrote on that board immediately it was discovered something was wanted. My wife then transferred requests to a master shopping-list, and only then was it erased from the board. When the item was bought, it was erased from the master list. It sounds somewhat pompous but it worked, and it worked well. It was simple. Everyone knew the form. Everyone understood why. Nothing got forgotten. The routine had become established, and once it had become routine, it no longer occurred to anyone that there was a problem.

In this modern day I now have a new toy, a word processor which prints out requirements every week. The list habit dies hard, however – we still use a blackboard as a primary source of information.

Obviously a diary should also be kept, again for anyone working with you to look at if required. Unless you have a very large operation and can afford a telephone-answerer, so to speak, all reasonable staff should be able to take a telephone call and deal with it if it is a matter such as a booking for a meal and so on. Nothing irritates putative customers more than to be told to 'hang on a mo' while someone responsible is fetched, just to say there is a table for two free at one o'clock. Yet this is what frequently happens. Lack of routine again. Lack of trust in staff. Lack of involvement. A wall telephone is a must in any kitchen, I believe, as it saves a lot of trotting about, and the diary should be available near it, or all necessary information written on the board. And another plea: keep paper and pens/pencils by the phone.

Now, once again, I am sure this must seem to many readers idiotically obvious. Why bother to mention it in the first place? I am afraid that experience has taught me that in this trade it is by no means obvious to a great many caterers, who listen to me with mild amusement or superiority. So be it. Perhaps they are walking diaries and compendiums of knowledge in themselves. But I wonder whether they share that ability with their staff, or whether their staff even care.

On the other hand, more than one restaurateur we have met has said, 'What a good idea, that blackboard! How obvious – and how very simple!' Yes, simplicity is the key-note, and it works like a charm.

This 'list ethic' should run not only to shopping and bookings for meals. If you are going to run a restaurant with a changing menu, a menu list is essential. It is also a delightful source of reference in years ahead, and a cheap means of 'public relations'.

My wife and I have often envied, in our darkest moments, those restaurants with the same dreary, printed menu where nothing ever changes. It is undoubtedly easy for the restaurateur, and probably for the kitchen staff, to be able to prepare dishes 'in their sleep'. My own reaction is that it must be stultifyingly boring for any chef to cook exactly the same thing every working day of his or her life. But, no matter, perhaps some so-called chefs think that is normal and, indeed, desirable. Certainly the owners of such places do, otherwise they would not permit it. But then such restaurateurs are not exactly filled with imagination, are they?

But if you are going to have, say, a 'dish of the day' to lift an otherwise ordinary offering, or you are cooking something rather special for a party of diners, the menu book is a must.

To make the most of this, plan your menus well in advance and write them down in the book, even if it is just the one dish of the day which changes. And because it is planned, the dish can be altered if the supply of anything is unobtainable at the last minute, as it often is in Britain, where supplies are so irregular.

You can now use this menu book to enter the names of guests who have booked ahead, and set against them what they had and what they enjoyed. When they return – as I am sure they will, they will be delighted that somehow, as if by magic, you have 'remembered' their previous visit, even down to the food and wines they had. It is merely a trick of the trade, but none the worse for all that. All customers like to be remembered, and if there is another facet to that memory which you can introduce into their minds, they are overjoyed. 'Public relations' is what it is called, and it is very cheap and effective.

Now I know that, if you are running a vast restaurant, a 'card index' system is not practical. But I am assuming you are starting off in a smaller way. Remembering people's names, even if they have booked for the first time, and greeting them by those names, is a simple and very effective way of winning friends and loyalty.

Greeting and Seating

There is a charming custom in many great French restaurants of offering the *livre d'or* to their most enthusiastic guests – a visitors' book in which are recorded comments and observations, witticisms and even drawings or sketches, instead of the banal or tasteless jokes so many contain in Britain. Many of these books have become priceless treasures, such as that of the Rocher in Cancale with the signatures of Balzac, Victor Hugo, Baudelaire and Flaubert. There are seven volumes at the Camille Renault in Puteaux which contain paintings, water-colours and drawings signed by Picasso, Braque, Léger and many others. I do not imagine that you, the reader, will attain these heights, but at least it is worth dreaming about. It is marvellous PR, nonetheless.

But whoever your customers are, whenever they come in 'off the street', a warm greeting is essential not only from the 'greeter and seater' but from other staff too. I always aver that the reason so many big chains of hotels have 'Good Morning' printed on their breakfast mats, or 'Have a Nice Day' on their bills, is because it saves the staff from having to say anything personally to a customer. Otherwise there would be no point to it. Remember, a decent smile and a decent greeting cost absolutely nothing and yet reap a rich reward from the customer. Yet how often they are forgotten, or their importance not understood.

A little while ago I found myself, by chance, coming out of a London Underground station to see across the road a famous brasserie of which I had heard much praise. It was just before two o'clock in the afternoon and, as my Inter-City train had had no buffet car on it and I was hungry, I thought I would go in and try it.

The entrance area was very plush, with a long bar towards the right and two very glamorous 'greeters and seaters' standing towards the left, where the restaurant was. I realize that, because the place was so popular (though there were many empty tables), they were not over-concerned about 'casuals' in from the street. In any event, the moment I stood hesitantly inside the door, the barman to my right (who was polishing a glass) immediately walked away from me to the other end of the bar, and the two glamour girls also turned their backs on me and busied themselves elsewhere. I assumed I was not welcome, so left to go into a pub and have a pint of beer and a sandwich.

Well, so be it. That may be all right and correct for a popular place with a so-called good reputation – though much of the reputation stems from the well-publicized pronouncements of the owners – but it is not any good for the likes of you, just starting off and anxious for customers. Yet a great many places I have been into, some very new and some, like that London brasserie, well established, treat incomers with no great welcome.

We are in the 'hospitality' industry, according to most

pundits, yet that industry has spawned one of the cruellest (and true) 'punter' jokes known. The customer goes into a restaurant and asks for a table. The head waiter looks around a completely empty dining-room, sighs, inspects the diary and then says wearily, 'I can just about fit you in', leading him to a table right by the service doors from the kitchens, where the unfortunate then has to wait all alone for some time.

This view of our industry by the 'punter' is, alas, all too true and richly deserved. It is your mission in life to see you are the exception – as it is by not making excuses when something goes wrong, by not passing on your problems to the customer, by ensuring that that mountain of routine is designed to allow you to cope with their satisfaction and enjoyment. Running a restaurant is not about serving food: it is about selling enjoyment. However much I hate the American expression 'the meal experience', it is, like so many Americanisms, extremely cogent. Others dub the catering trade a 'leisure industry', but I prefer to regard it as a branch of 'show biz'. People do not come to your restaurant just because they have to eat to stay alive, nor do they visit a cinema or theatre because of any absolute need. It is up to you to persuade them for other reasons. Excellent food is one.

The Essential Balance
Mind you, no customer, after enjoying a 'meal experience' with you, is actually going to leap to his feet, shake you warmly by the hand and congratulate you on your fool-proof list technique, the clarity of your blackboard, the ineffable skill of your routines, your courtesy towards the VAT man by doing work he has elected not to do, the calligraphy in your account books, the lack of viscosity in your cash-flow forecasts or your faultless taste in interior decoration and design. No. But he will have had a happier meal, a better experience, because he will be blissfully unaware of that four-fifths of the iceberg which lies below the water-line. That four-fifths sank the Titanic, I know, and it could sink you if the customer becomes aware of it, but it keeps the iceberg afloat, and it will keep you afloat as well. It is a point worth remembering.

The routine should not be allowed to get in the way of your operation – it should be a prop and stay. It is to help you to help the customer, not get in the way of both. We have all come across those places where barmen and waiters and receptionists all seem to be shoving masses of paper around instead of attending to the customer. That is caused not by routine but by too much of it, not enough of it or bad design.

Anyone who has crossed the Channel on a ferry will have noticed the bar staff doing more paperwork than attending to their customers. It may be that currency problems cause this, but I doubt it. It is almost certainly poor routine, a routine which is unworkable by those at the 'sharp end' and which causes the customer unnecessary fury.

A nice balance is necessary. It is fun finding the essential balance. It will be no fun without it.

16 From Crate to Plate

The weariness, the endless pain of waiting for someone to come.

Longfellow

The previous chapter dwelt upon routine, with a small diversion about how to treat customers, which should not have been necessary – but I have more experience in these matters than you, dear Reader, and, regretfully, such a lesson is still not taught either in catering colleges or in life generally – at least not in the sort of life a great many people now running restaurants seem to have lived in previous years.

But we have not quite finished with routine, because we ought to take a look first at the whole business of how orders get to the kitchen, to the till, onto the customer's bill and into your record book for the accounts; and second, at the whole complicated (and often frustrating) business of finding suppliers and 'doing the shopping'.

Orders

As regards orders, there is simple, classic way in which this is done. You may not wish to follow it exactly, because yours is not a huge operation yet, but nevertheless the principles are the same and you should adopt some system (some routine) in exactly how you will deal with the matter.

In an ideal world, you or your waiting staff need an order pad which copes with three copies: one for the kitchen; one for the till, which, when priced and added up, will go to the customer; and one for the accounts, once that also has been priced and added up. For record purposes, disregard the copy which goes into the kitchen – it will get stained, covered in grease, torn up in a terrible rage if the chef makes a mistake, or used to wipe the edge of a pudding dish if the waitress is in a bad mood and no one is watching. But the kitchen must have a copy, for obvious reasons.

There are ways round this paperwork, and you can see it in action in many fast food establishments, where the customer is given a copy only if he specifically asks for it. In most cases, a customer does not actually want an itemized bill to take away, though he or she obviously wants one presented before getting a wallet out, being content with proof of the total amount – either for his or her own records or for an expenses claim at work. Personally, and unless you have highly automated accounting and bill-issuing systems in your restaurant, I think the itemized account for the customer is a waste of time and paper. It takes very little time for any member of staff to fill in the total cost of a meal on a slip of paper with the restaurant's name, address and VAT number already printed on it.

Assuming, then, that your accounting system utilizes pen and paper, the waiter or waitress merely has to write down the dishes ordered, giving one to the till, so to speak, and taking a copy into the kitchen. Pads which are made up for one or two copies are easily obtained from any catering suppliers and sometimes even from ordinary stationery outlets, where they are normally called 'waitress pads'. The entering of prices on the bill can be done, whenever there is time, either by the waiting staff or by whoever is in charge of the till when the customer wants the account.

Once the order goes into the kitchen, it can be dealt with in a number of ways, again depending on the size of your operation.

In larger places there are pegs, one for each table, and the order is hung on the peg to await filling. In smaller establishments you may not have pegs, the orders being put under a weight, or something similar, the last order underneath, each time. Table numbers for orders are essential but never really necessary on the tables themselves, as you or your staff should be able to memorize them. Customers do not like to be numbers, so avoid making them feel that that is exactly what they are when it comes to ordering, and getting, a meal.

It is essential, however, that staff call out the order when they enter the kitchen.

I know many chefs who hardly ever look at the pieces of paper but have a built-in 'ear' for the order being called out and the table number it is for, however busy the kitchen is. Calling the order out also helps other kitchen staff to prepare, say, starters, salads or other cold dishes. The order is left where it is until it has been filled, and then it *must* be 'spiked' out of the way so that mistakes do not occur. If you employ a chef, he or she will probably tell you the method he or she would like you to use, and if you are the chef, you can make up your own mind how the routine should go.

Ideally, all orders are dealt with in strict rotation, but this is not always possible when customers are asking for different things. The calling-out of the order often means that time can be saved by adding more potatoes, say, to the *sautoir*, because the previous lot has only just gone in. The essential thing is to get all one table's orders dished up together, and in the proper sequence, and if you are to be the chef and this is your first time in the 'hot seat', the better and simpler the kitchen is organized, the easier it will be for you.

Very little credit is given, or attention paid, to waiting staff in regard to the way they can help the kitchen work flow, and thus help themselves and their customer. I think this is because of the way in which waiting at table is 'looked down on' as an occupation in Britain, something which I mentioned in Chapter 12. In the great restaurants of the world, where a waiter's job is dignified by being thought highly skilled and therefore worth good money, the dining-room 'paces' the kitchen in such a way as not to put too great a load on it throughout any particular time of service. A good waiter or waitress can artfully manipulate the flow of orders into the kitchen as well as his or her work-load by an appreciation of everyone else's jobs. This is the point of having no proper demarcation in the strict sense: all your staff should be encouraged to realize that they are part of a team and that a person not interested in another's job or problem is a person not worth having.

To give an extreme example, but true nonetheless, I well remember the time when we became so busy that our gardener turned to in the kitchen, not only washing up but serving food onto plates. He had come into the kitchen just because he knew we were very busy and to offer a hand. That is what being part of a team is all about. And many a time a passing member of the dining-room staff has saved a sauce by moving a pan off the stove when it was in danger of 'catching' because I was attending to some other crisis. There can be such places as 'happy kitchens'.

But, as I said, you must make up your own mind what system you adopt, making adjustments to that system as you find other, better methods which suit you. Most of it, anyway, is just common sense: you need a record of what the customer has ordered, but you do not need a waiter or waitress to spend hours at a customer's table writing sheaf after sheaf of paper and snatching the menu up to put in the prices at the same time. You cannot rely on the kitchen to keep a piece of paper clean and readable, and you as the owner certainly must have a copy for your records, as well as for customers who may ask for one for theirs.

The Till

It may be that you are an expert at tills or very used to them. From the point of view of someone who is electronically inept, I do ask you to get a till suitable for your own type of business and one that will help you, rather than just sit there looking good.

What you really want to know, surely, is what you have taken each day in total and, preferably, how much of it was on food and how much on drink. You do not want to know what the time is in Melbourne, whether it is raining in Rangoon or what the Dow Jones Index stands at on Wall Street. I am sure you can get tills which will give you all this information but, I suggest, they are not for you.

Get the simplest one possible to start with – lease or buy – and learn how to use it and whether it is the correct one for you before you sign any agreement.

My wife and I were once plagued by a young man trying to sell us an electronic cash register. He was, we admit, a very pleasant chap, but eventually we got so exasperated that we said if he cared to install a machine right that minute, and show us how to work it, he could call back the following morning and either we would buy it or he would have to take it away.

The machine was incredibly complex, to us anyway, and about ten of our customers that evening 'had a go' trying to understand how to work it, which caused hysterical laughter.

The till area was eventually covered with rolls of paper, and the read-out showed we had taken an incredible £6,781 that one evening – just for about five simple meals and the odd drink or two. The young man returned the following morning to find the machine in the hall. We felt rather sorry for him, so blamed it all on our own stupidity. The fact was, however, that the machine was simply not suitable for us or our operation – a conviction we had held originally but had failed to get over to the young salesman. A simple test showed him more eloquently than words, and he left us alone after that.

You will certainly need a 'float' of money in the till, enough notes and coin to see you through the day, or the service, with enough spare change in the safe.

Change is always a problem in any cash-based business: you can never have enough of it, and nothing infuriates a customer more than having to wait while you rootle about for change when he or she is anxious to be away. The size of the float is something you will learn by experience, but it should be invariable, so that book-keeping becomes easier.

On a security note, many businesses I know leave some sort of float in an *open* till overnight, or at other times when they are closed, on the simple reasoning that the till, when locked, very often invites an intruder to break it open or take the till completely. Either way, the cost of the till or its repair tends to be greater than the money lost.

Any restaurateur can insist on being paid cash for meals taken on the premises, according to the law, but today that would be either a very rich or a very foolish man or woman, for the credit card has come to stay, whether we like it or not.

Perhaps the two most commom credit cards are Barclaycard/ Visa and Access. The commission deducted from total 'credits' each month varies but is around 2½ to four per cent, and they have an advantage over other cards in that the slips can be presented to your bank and are credited as cash, the adjustments for commission being made by the issuing companies at the end of each month.

Other cards, e.g. American Express (Amex) and Diners Club, deduct their commission and pay the restaurateur only after a delay, sometimes as long as six weeks. Only in situations where your business is very dependent on Americans, tourists or the flashier businessman should acceptance of such credit cards be necessary.

The terms and conditions of acceptance of all cards can be had from the organizations themselves, but your own bank will advise you as to the best course, and the details of each system.

There is some indication that customers who normally pay by credit card tend to spend more money in those places which accept them, making the commission the restaurateur pays of little account. This is debatable, perhaps, but the fact remains that most restaurants now accept some sort of credit card, and your business may actually suffer from not following along.

The checks which are necessary when accepting cards are fully explained by the various companies and obviously include ensuring that the card is in date and not 'void', that the signatures tally and that the card is not on the list of a Lost or Cancelled Card Warning Notice which is issued from time to time.

Fraud on credit cards is huge, about £20 million annually, but most of this is borne by the companies themselves (out of their extremely high interest charges) and very little, if anything, by the business which accepts in good faith the payment by cards and makes the proper enquiries as advised. A reward of £50 is offered to the man or woman who detects any card listed as 'wanted'.

Personal cheques will also be offered to you, for which you should ask for a cheque guarantee card. (Remember: a credit card is not, as such, a guarantee for a personal cheque.) You must write down, on the back of the cheque, the number of the card and not let the customer do it.

As a matter of interest, having mentioned the commission deducted by the credit card companies, you have to bear in mind that any customer's cheque you may pay into your own bank can attract an account charge of up to 50p per cheque – which is one very good reason for not cashing cheques for customers even if they are backed by a guarantee.

As one bank manager once pointed out to me, 'When you want to open your own bank, let us know. In the meantime, we cash cheques, you sell food.'

Pilferage
Having mentioned fraud, unless you are running a very large operation with a floating or transient staff as well as numerous regular employees, the problem of theft or pilferage should not trouble you.

I firmly believe that honesty flourishes where there are open doors. You must trust the people working with you – assume your staff are honest, and they will respond. If there is any sign of pilferage or theft, make quite sure any enquiry you make is fair and courteously conducted and then get rid of the culprit. Personally, I have never had any trouble of this kind at all, largely perhaps because of the way we have employed staff and the type of person we have chosen.

Remember, if you are a suspicious employer by nature, pilferage does not just mean the taking home of a pork chop or a can of baked beans; it is far more likely to disappear inside staff in the way of food eaten on the premises or, more common, I believe, alcohol swigged from a bottle in the dispense bar. As I say, I have never come across this, and I am always especially cynical when I hear stories from other restaurateurs about the way they have been cheated by staff.

The 'locked fridge' syndrome, as I call it, is more often the case of staff emulating their employer, who is often cheating the public – an unpleasant facet of the catering trade with which I shall deal in Chapter 18.

I have already mentioned that incoming goods should be checked not only for quality but to make sure you are getting what you ordered. If you deal with wine and spirit merchants, the cases should be checked anyway to make sure no bottles are broken, and not signed for until you are certain everything is in one piece.

Pilferage among such merchants is fairly rare – for some reason deliverymen always seem a very nice type of person. There is far more honesty lying about in Britain than dishonesty – a point which many people tend to ignore.

Only once have I ever detected a definite attempt to cheat me by a delivery driver, and that was in the case of a big brewery which supplied us regularly. Draymen, to use the old-fashioned term, are a super breed, but for some reason I did not like this company's drivers and mates, and over a period of a some weeks I found that at least two bottles, if not more, would be missing from the bottom crates of deliveries which they stacked in my cellar. I did not create any fuss at all. I merely told the brewery never to call again – their draymen would tell them why, and left it at that. It is all very well to blame deliverymen – I prefer to blame their employers for not taking enough care in their selection of staff.

Which brings us to the whole question of:

Supplies and Suppliers
Depending on your type of outlet, the supply position can be either very easy or exasperating.

If, for instance, yours is to be a burger-bar style of operation or one which relies virtually solely on 'bought in' or frozen foods, and if, above all, it is to be 'cheap and cheerful' there is bound to be a major frozen-food supplier quite near to you, as well as a cash-and-carry.

If, on the other hand, it is to be an 'up-market' establishment relying on good, fresh supplies of vegetables, meat and fish, there are definite problems, especially with vegetables and fish.

The first thing you should do, to help your cash-flow situation, is negotiate credit terms with main suppliers who will ask for a banker's reference and set an agreed credit limit to your account, which will be payable monthly. The difference between the credit limits for groceries and other supplies compared with those for wines, spirits and so on is, if you are licensed, instructive; that for your wines and spirits having to be very much higher than for food suppliers. In some cases, particularly greengroceries, which may be delivered, you may be asked to pay the bill at once, and receive a reasonable discount for so doing. In any event, many suppliers give discounts even on monthly accounts if the invoice is settled within a certain number of days.

Some suppliers, particularly of frozen foods, may be willing to provide freezers and the like, on a type of lease. If you agree to take a certain amount of frozen food for a year or two, the company will often let you have a freezer at a peppercorn rent, a nominal sum by which they own it for a certain time, after which it becomes yours. But, as I said before, do not tie yourself too much at the start. This arrangement also applies to ice-cream firms, who are always anxious to get their products into any new outlet but who, not unnaturally, take a rather dim view of the arrangement when their representative finds his company freezer filled with your own dishes and those of his competitors.

Which brings us to another subject: company representatives.

There is a curious 'bush telegraph' system that works in any locality of Britain by which reps automatically find out when places change hands or new ones open. There will be no shortage of men and women knocking on your door and per-suading you as to the usefulness of their company and its products. For the most part they are extremely pleasant and very helpful, but not necessarily in the obvious way you would think.

My wife and I enjoyed reps calling on us, although I know some restaurateurs dislike it. But we were choosy: we got rid of those whose products we disliked or whose manner irritated. We did deal with most of them, but it was the information they conveyed which was most useful of all, for although we never came across any who were less than judicious and tactful in what they said, they were founts of knowledge about their operations and other people in the trade once they got to know us. They are also very good at pricing-policy and advice, and many, especially the older hands, quickly became friends.

If you are a restaurateur, you cannot be blind to what other people are doing and buying in your district; you cannot be blind to new trends, new products, new ways, even, of making money. Reps call on more people than you ever imagined. A lot of leg-work and experience are yours for the asking.

If you are licensed, it may be as well to put into your mind how useful a reputable wine merchant can be to you, even if you put yourself into the 'wine buff' class.

When we set about opening our first venture in Scotland, we wrote to eight wine merchants explaining what we wanted to do and the sort of place we were going to run and asked them if they would care to set up the sort of wine list they would like to see in such an establishment. At the time they were 'boom' years, and our letters were ignored by all except two companies, Yapp Bros of Mere, Wiltshire, and Cockburn & Campbell of Edinburgh. We were extremely grateful to them for the help and advice they gave, for, although I thought I knew a fair amount about wine, I did not make the mistake of pretending that the experts who make their living from such knowledge could not teach me a thing or two.

In due course, one or two other suppliers joined our 'team', and we made sure that our wine list, which became, for the size and type of place, quite distinguished, not only credited the merchant by name but also contained their own notes on why the wine was good. We found that our customers enjoyed reading the notes almost as much as they did drinking the contents of the bottles.

As part of our pre-determined policy, we ignored those wines found on virtually every other list we had come across, believing that the well-known 'branded' wines acted as a block to the enjoyment of less familiar bottles by some customers, who, perhaps, were not as adventurous as they might be. With our experts, we therefore had a great deal of enjoyment in settling on a list which changed fairly frequently as the merchants suggested alternatives.

Our customers appreciated that they were being offered often unfamiliar wines but which were nonetheless distinguished in their own right. And to go with this policy we 'marked up' very much less than other places, in the belief that selling something was better than not selling it at all. Wine prices on restaurant lists are shameful, in my opinion, as well as their choice of wines – especially in this day and age when every supermarket worth its name displays extremely good wines at very competitive prices. Good wine merchants know very much more about their subject than, I would suggest, you do, and it seems surprising to me that so few restaurateurs even bother to consult them, let alone suggesting they construct a 'list' especially for their restaurant.

Incidentally, to go back to our first venture in Scotland, after some years of 'boom', the whole trading-picture altered and many of the original wine merchants whom we had approached and who had ignored us started calling for orders, as by that time we had earned quite a good reputation. We were able to tell them, with some pleasure, that they had missed their chance and should not have been so 'toffee-nosed' in the first place.

Obviously, the people who called on us from our regular wine suppliers were assured of a very warm welcome, as they always seemed to have 'something in the car which might be of interest'. I can remember washing down an excellent cottage pie one lunchtime with a very fine champagne, and on another occasion a spaghetti bolognaise absorbed a noble Burgundy. Heresy? Not at all. Proper wine merchants, like good restaurateurs, do not have those sacrosanct attitudes to eating and drinking which so amuse the French and Italians when they meet food and wine snobs in Britain. Wine is for drinking, not for fastidious sipping and pretentious discussion. And the fact that on both occasions we all ate together in the kitchen added to the piquancy.

One final plea: please do not 'dress up' cheap wine by using basket-work cradles. It is pretentious rubbish and fools no one.

You will also get other reps calling on you, those with the hard sell. Insurance, cash registers, computer accounting and stock control, vending machines, games machines, cleaning-equipment, machines for dispensing soap, condoms and sanitary towels, hand-dryers, 'in-house' music and a host of products you never even thought of or knew existed. Be polite, take their cards, say you will think about it. Never, never enter into any agreement without considerable thought.

Always tell any rep, whoever he or she is and whatever they are selling, what is the best time for them to call on you again. The better ones will appreciate knowing when you are less busy and can talk to them; the less reputable ones will soon give up – you hope.

Shopping
So what about normal 'shopping'?

Unless you intend to trade very much down-market, it is a foolish error to 'buy cheap', but you will certainly need a cash-and-carry. Such places are not noted for their up-market quality, but they are, to be fair, quite reasonable with their prices. Certainly for basic items of a household and 'larder' nature, as well as soft drinks and so on, most offer a good service.

To use the cash-and-carry you will need a trade card, as they do not like normal retail selling to private individuals, thus under-cutting their trade customers, for whom they exist. Obviously, 'private' customers do get in by borrowing trade cards, but this is unfair generally, and a trader who 'lends' his card to a friend could well lose the facility, and quite rightly.

Trade cards are obtained easily enough by going to see the manager of your local cash-and-carry and taking the VAT registration document which the VAT office will send you upon registration. This assures the manager that you are in bona-fide business, and he or she will ask for a bank reference and set an amount of credit agreeable to you both, which should cover any cheques you sign for goods.

If you are unfamiliar with this type of wholesaler, do not be concerned. The form is quite easy, and the manager or staff will explain anything you need to know, as well as the layout of the store.

In most cases you collect your own trolley going in, trundle it around choosing whatever you need (from your list, of course!)

and then go to a check-out. In some cash-and-carries they have loaders by the tills who transfer your goods from your trolley to a spare one, calling out the code numbers of the items as they do so. The man or woman on the till punches in the codes, and the price is automatically recorded on the till roll by the computer. Remember that all prices you will see on the storage racks are exclusive of VAT – the computer adds the total VAT amount at the end of the transaction.

In some stores the customer takes the till docket to a cashier on the way out; in other places the money is taken at the check-out itself. Sometimes your trolley is checked again before you leave, to make sure everything has been accounted for; specific amounts are not checked but just the number of items on the trolley, to see that it corresponds with the check-out docket.

Only in a few cash-and-carries do you get a specifically itemized bill, the computer printing out exactly what you are buying. This makes life very easy, especially if you are buying individual items – such as one bottle of a drink you do not serve often but feel you have to stock.

It is worth noting that, contrary to what many people believe, cash-and-carries always have shelves of individual items – you do not have to take a whole case of anything, whether it is alcohol or foodstuffs. Most stores have shelves of 'catering' goods, sold in large or medium-sized containers, as well as packs of items which are bought by shop-keepers for re-sale from their own shelves. In some of the bigger chains there are two, quite separate sections, one of which sells food and drink, the other a remarkable range of household equipment ranging from garden furniture to television sets and word-processors.

In such places you, as a restaurateur, would normally get one card allowing you to visit either section, but if, say, you ran an electrical shop or something similar, you would be allowed a card only for the non-foods department.

'Speciality Lines'
For 'up-market' restaurants, especially in the countryside or away from the major cities, good-quality supplies – and anything the catering trade considers 'special' – are a dreadful headache. There are few such caterers who fail to lament these problems. There is little advice one can give in such cases, other than to hunt around and hope you will find a good source.

In 1988 the first London Food Exhibition was held at Wembley, a tentative move to encourage quality food producers to become better known. It was backed by the Delicatessen and Fine Food Association, which had only recently come into being, and by the British Frozen Food Federation. The intention was to hold the exhibition every other year. In 1985 the British Culinary Institute was founded in an effort to encourage the use and supply of better food-stuff.

Another recent addition to the scene is the *Directory of Fine British Foods*, the first of which was published in 1987 by Henrietta Green. This costs nearly £15 (1988) and is, Ms Green claims, used by 'all great chefs'. Although this claim may seem a little extravagant, Ms Green hopes to make this an annual publication, with more than 5,000 all-British products featured.

However, the day is still a long way off when chefs can expect to get first-class, fresh, properly priced foods more or less in any part of Britain, as they can in France. There are one or two suppliers, notably West Country Game at Nether Compton, near Sherborne in Dorset, whose business has rapidly expanded because it detected a demand in south-west England for high-quality foods, which it satisfies by importing or by bringing in from other parts of Britain a great range of delicacies, from oysters to Parma ham. There are not many other such companies that I know of, but certainly one or two of the frozen food suppliers do specialize in what, alas, is considered in Britain to be 'speciality' lines.

17 Public Relations

With money, anyone can offer succulent dishes and fine wines, but courtesy and kindness cannot be bought.
                                                              Lucien Tendret

In previous chapters we have considered at odd moments not only the creation of menus but also the treatment of your customers, and what I described as 'getting 'em in through the doors'. But I think we should take a closer and more considered look at what, broadly speaking, must be classed as public relations.

This is a very wide field, and the term is used more often than not by skilled practioners acting for large companies – but it applies to you, the restaurateur, all the time, however small your business is. Without some form of PR, in the widest sense, there is no point in opening your doors.

Allure

In Chapter 15 I mentioned my own abortive visit to a famous brasserie in London. In their case, so far as I was concerned as a customer, the staff failed completely in any form of PR. We also saw in that same chapter that a pleasant smile and a nice greeting give an immediate impression of welcome – in other words, they are the cheapest (and among the best) forms of PR known to the catering trade.

It is also said that the best form of advertising is personal recommendation – it is effective and costs nothing. But it does take time for word of mouth to 'get around', and some restaurateurs may not be able to wait that long. So how do you set out to sell your 'meal experience' to the public at large?

Most people think first of some form of classified or display advertising in the local papers. But hold on a minute: the first piece of advertising you do is the sign on the front of your 'shop'. And, if it has a window or windows through which the public can see into your restaurant, the 'window-dressing' is very important.

Sit down and think just what image you wish to create. We have mentioned this before, I know, and I also know that you have already done that. OK, but the sign declaring your name on the front of the building also declares a lot more. The size and type of sign, the way the information is lettered and in what colour conveys very definite impressions to passers-by as to what they can expect once they open the door and step inside.

A coffee- and tea-room not far from where I live recently changed hands. It is designed to cater for what used to be called 'the carriage trade', even by the new owner, and the sign and lettering outside had been extremely well done by the local and very expert sign-writer. The interior too looked inviting and warm, with comfortable seating, flowers and nice table-cloths. The new owner, however, decided 'improvements' must be made but, instead of calling in the sign-writer to convey further information in a similar way, went to a catering suppliers and bought 'ready-made', black-on-white, plastic strips advertising 'home-made' foods and filled rolls to 'take-away'. In other words, the new owner destroyed in one adroit move the whole impression which the sign-writer had acheived so painstakingly. The reason for this was given as 'cheapness' – which is just what the signs conveyed: cheap, ordinary food of little distinction.

I am not saying that the goods sold in the shop were in fact cheap or ordinary, but the signs were in themselves cheap and ordinary and thus conveyed an impression which may have been totally at variance with what the new owner actually wished.

I do not want to be unfair by adding yet another point about this tea-shop, but it is important to you, in a new business, that you do not yourself make the elementary mistakes made by so many newcomers (as well as established owners) from just plain ignorance or, perhaps, a lack of knowledge of how the public see your product. Or even, let us face it, because someone like myself simply has not bothered to point out the obvious.

The very pleasant windows of this tea-shop faced south, and there were no blinds outside the premises which might have shaded the area immediately inside. Despite this, the new owner insisted – as, to be fair, the previous owner had – that certain 'fresh' foods be displayed in one of these windows. I can always remember looking in one morning at about eleven o'clock and seeing a plate of cheese-filled brown rolls which glistened waxily in the strong sunshine and were actually curled up all round. I have rarely seen anything more certain to put anyone off buying them. As a 'come-on', it was a disaster. Yet not only were such items displayed in full sunshine: just inside, one could see a whole area of counter top covered in side-plates, some balanced half-on-one, half-on-the-other, each bearing one slice of cake or pastry. There they stayed all day, getting staler and staler.

The owner did this because it seemed good salesmanship to cut up slices of very good, home-made cake at the start of every day, never mind that unwrapped, exposed pieces would inevitably get (and look) staler by the minute. Not surprisingly, cake sales never seemed to flourish, and the staff were given parcelled-up rolls and pieces of cake to take home at closing-time. Most went straight out into the garden for the birds or into waste-bins, needless to say.

Psychologically, you must understand that you will never sell anything that has not been cut into. People simply do not like 'spoiling' a whole cake, say, by asking for one slice, even though it is obviously for sale. But the perfect technique is very simple – you merely cut one slice from the cake and edge the segment forward, or even remove it altogether. In that way, the customer does not feel he or she is ruining some perfect symmetry but gets a fresh slice, and the owner gets the profit and no wastage.

It is these very simple, basic factors which so many people in the catering business do not understand or will not take the trouble to think about. I have said before that I reckoned to be able to 'sell' virtually any food I wished, but I do not consider myself a natural salesman. What I do know is that I could never have sold stale food or food badly kept and presented. I would not have wanted to, and my customers certainly would not have bought it. But there is nothing special about me, compared with anyone else, other than the fact that I have taken the trouble to study such matters because I regard them as important to my business. But I bet you that, if a number of well-established men and women in the catering trade read these words, they would say, 'Pouf! What a load of nonsense!' So they may, but that brasserie lost a customer that day (and forever), just as that tea-shop does, for similar reasons.

Advertising

Thus you have looked at the outside of your premises (and just inside) and decided that it tells the world the sort of person you are, the sort of food it serves and the sort of customer to which it appeals. Fine, if you are in a busy situation where you can rely for much of your trade on 'chance' customers walking in from the street. If not thus placed, what do you do?

Normal advertising in papers, even the 'freebies', is now very expensive and of doubtful value unless you have a very strong 'selling' line. You will probably read a great number of advertisements telling the public of change of ownership, 'home-cooked foods', 'extensive menus', Sunday lunch 'specials', newly redecorated dining-rooms. Indeed, in my own area, there is one restaurant which actually advertises that it has been in the same hands for more than twelve years – a woeful reflection on the British catering trade.

Are you to join that sorry band or try something new?

To succeed, advertising has to be succinct, well written and properly laid out. The layout is often suggested by the sales staff in the paper's advertising department, though bear in mind that their job is to sell space and not to write your advertisement for you.

You must first decide what it is you have to sell – whether it is going to be along the same lines as everyone else or to relate to something very special. Study all such advertisements very carefully before plunging in. My experience shows that for the most part they are badly written and much of a muchness. And, remember, you must not actually tell a lie in any advertisement or you are likely to call down the wrath of the Advertising Standards Association for misleading the public.

Only you can define what is special about you and your establishment. Only you can decide what will entice one customer or, you hope, a great many to enter your doors. Having decided on it, outline exactly what you wish to say and then set about saying that, and that alone. There is a French adage about cooking which says that, if you are reducing a stock, reduce it to the point where you are satisfied it is as you want it – and then reduce it again. Exactly the same applies to advertising matter. Remember that a whole industry is filled with very skilled people employed to do just that. They all spend considerable time defining and reducing. It is their whole life. You cannot hope to emulate those skills in a few minutes spent writing on the back of an old envelope. Good advertising copy takes time to write, and even then it may be a complete waste of time, and money.

As a perfectly true example, my own local weekly paper has more than once carried advertisements for catering-places without actually including their location. Yes, no mention at all of where it is, town, address or anything. That may seem very clever but I think it is very foolish. I also think it is carelessness – on the part of the advertiser and on the part of the paper for accepting such copy without querying it. These advertisements amuse my wife and me, who have spent a very great deal of time – but hardly any money over the years – writing good copy when we have felt we had something to say. But unless you feel very strongly that you do have something to say, leave the subject alone and spend your money elsewhere.

Free publicity, i.e. through the news pages of a local paper, is often difficult to promote. Many newspaper editors feel, and quite rightly, that their columns should not be devoted to 'plugs' for commercial operations at the expense of real news. This is by no means as widespread an attitude among editors as it once was, but you must not feel disappointed or 'put down' if, for instance, you ask a number of local luminaries to a party to celebrate the 'launch' of your new project, including the local newspaper editor, and see no result in its columns when it appears on the following Friday. The old saying that there is no such thing as a free meal applies equally well to local newspaper editors as to national ones.

Local companies may be a source of custom, but the preparation of a circular letter, or mailing-shot, needs as much care as any advertisement. It must set out precisely why you think the director or managers of a local company may be interested in your restaurant, and whether you would be prepared to consider credit accounts, to be settled either individually or by the company itself each month. If you have a special, private room where they can hold meetings and be fed at some stage, this should be mentioned, along with the number for whom you can cater.

But mailing-shots are a lot more effective if addressed personally, instead of a 'Dear Sir or Madam', and it will take you a long time to ferret those names out if you are new to the area. Again, printing and postal charges will be quite expensive, and you may not feel it is worth your while when you consider that the advertising industry works on a ten per cent success rate by way of 'return' for all expenditure.

But even if mail-shot is not within your means, the list of customers you will gradually build up is going to be of use to you in the future, as you will possess your own mailing-list which will be much more effective than indiscriminate mailing-shots in untried and untested directions. Such a list will be very useful if you decide to hold 'special events' or promotions.

Special Events
'Specials' can be a very useful tool to promote your restaurant, particularly during the often depressing 'off' months of gloom, such as February and November, when the entire catering trade seems to put its head in its hands and moan. But they should not be used too often or they will lose their appeal.

Because of our Scottish background we instigated special evenings on Burns' Night and St Andrew's Night when we came south, and they proved immensely popular, quite beyond our own expectations. Not unnaturally most of our English customers had never had proper haggis and, although we thought we had prepared enough, we soon ran out – a thing which happened on every subsequent occasion. Near Guy Fawkes Day we had a special 'Banger Night' at which we served at least six completely different types of sausage. Again a sell-out. And on another occasion, when our own village held a special week-end event, we put on a sixteenth-century meal, even down to re-creating as accurately as we could the bread for the 'trenchers' on which the meat was placed. Again this was a sell-out. Again we did not have enough food.

Now, the moral in the runaway success of these four 'specials' was not just the date of our celebration, of course, but the fact that it was closely coupled with an additional 'come-on' in the shape of curious or unusual food. But there was one other point.

Our customers turned up in droves because they trusted us and knew the food would be very good. In other words, we already had a 'track record' locally, and if we announced a special party, they knew it really was going to be special and not some gimmicky re-hash of another occasion. This means that you may only successfully promote a restaurant which is known and liked. It thus adds jam to a normal helping of bread and butter. And it may not be a wise way for you at the start of your catering life to set out to promote something which is an unknown quantity.

Incidentally, we did not advertise our own special nights except by writing a simple announcement of them on our blackboard in the bar. We always used this board as a 'news sheet', and very effective it was too. One of our other successes was our announcement in mid-November that under no circumstances would turkey be served in our establishment except at Easter. This may sound idiosyncratic – as, indeed, our whole operation was – but it brought us many customers simply for the curiosity value of finding any catering outlet in the 'festive season' refusing to serve what every other single outlet always served at that time of year. An example of how successful the 'negative sell' can be.

But, as I said, do not rush into any form of special promotion too early in your days.

Take a very careful look at what the opposition is doing, and when, and then think very carefully whether you should emulate them or come up with something of your own. All too often the simple copying of one idea by someone else is merely laziness and lack of imagination.

Commercial pressures, perhaps, but certainly lack of imagination by many has led to that awful sameness you now get in country pubs, where each has to have a 'beer garden' or a 'children's play area' with those gaudy plastic Mother Hubbard boots or a plastic tree over which the kids can scramble. I look forward to the day when the only thing that will persuade me to visit a pub is the very fact that it does *not* have any such 'attractions'. Similar items of quite startling stupidity are now cropping up all over the country alongside restaurants, in the mistaken belief, perhaps, that anything is better than the actual food offered therein. But what a plastic tree has to do with a 'meal experience', I, for one, cannot see.

On the other hand, if such gimmicks or appurtenances really do add to your profits, you may well feel bereft without them.

There is nothing wrong in making money, and I hope this book is going to help you make a great deal of it, or at least attain a comfortable standard of living, but it is dangerous to copy slavishly what other people do, otherwise it will become meaningless.

But whatever you do, make sure that it is absolutely within the image you are striving to create. Any gimmick or promotion which departs from your image drives a coffin nail into it – you will upset your loyal customers and probably fail to attract any new, worthwhile trade. It is a curious feature of catering that customers get very possessive about 'their' restaurant and feel upset if it apparently lets them down by departing from what they expect of it. The proper image is going to take a long while to achieve, so nurture it tenderly.

It is also a bad idea, I believe, to introduce into your 'calendar' too many special promotions. Keep them few and far between. There is one woman restaurateur who apparently racks her brains inventing more and more and writing about the success of them all. From a customer's point of view, I would hesitate ever to go there in case I found myself in the middle of an Edwardian-song-evening, a Victorian-menu-evening, or even a Ruritanian-fancy-dress-and-cookery-demonstration-evening. Indeed, it may in fact be a more clever ruse than I thought. There may come the day when a no-gimmick evening will be advertised and people like me will flock in.

However, it is horses for courses, and only you can judge what works for you.

A chap I know who runs a very successful restaurant in a seasonal village in the Highlands of Scotland is very good at his special promotion evenings, even buying job lots of china for customers to smash at his 'Greek Night'. He is an amusing man with an inventive turn of mind, and his 'specials's always raise a laugh – often of envy among those less adroit at PR. The number of such specials does not matter, because during the summer his customers are in the area for only a week or two and therefore do not get bored by their repetition, whereas if the area was more permanently residential, his trade would undoubtedly suffer. In the winter he goes in for more traditional ways to get custom, such as Burns' Night and St Valentine's Night, opening specially for the occasion. These become very attractive to those people who live all the year round in such a remote area, where there is little to do in the evenings, so the fellow pleases both ways and makes useful extra money in the 'shoulder months'. He is a man who either studied his market very closely or simply possessed a natural sense of business acumen. If your place is in a predominantly holiday area, you would do well to study in just what sort of way you can promote extra profit without necessarily slavishly copying your competitors.

On occasion the trade seeks to promote itself, either nationally or locally, with something like a National Eating-Out Week. Whether you go along with the idea is up to you, although its adherents swear it increases their trade by leaps and bounds – an assertion of which I am doubtful, as it seems yet again to smack of doing something because you are afraid you will 'miss out' by not going along with the herd.

This tendency to copy others is rife in the catering trade, and if one is not careful, one falls into it unconsciously. In our own case, as an amusing example, we used to have very regular customers who turned out to be successful restaurateurs from a village some miles away from us. They came to eat whenever they had a day off and were shopping in our local large town. After lunch one day, when we had got to know them, they remarked that they did not want to seem rude but would like to ask why we never ever served chips. We explained the answer, which you know now yourself. There and then they apparently decided that, if we could get away with it, they could. They took chips off their menu at once – and have never served them since. I am happy to report that they are among the most successful restaurateurs in the whole area in terms of profitability and in quality and imaginative food.

A footnote to this – for they ran an operation very similar to ours – is that they tried to stop serving any form of 'Ploughman's Lunch' in their bar area, which we had never actually put on our bar menu, telling people that, if they really wanted something like that, why not try some bread and cheese?

Anyway, our friends felt that, with the total abolition of chips, they had better proceed with caution when it came to the dreaded 'Ploughman's' so they increased the price of it to a phenomenal £3 and waited for the item to die a natural death. Unfortunately, no such thing happened: they sold more 'Ploughman's' at that price than they ever had before.

Nevertheless, within a month or two the ploughman plodded his weary away off the menu and into obscurity. Few people seemed to notice his demise.

Guides to Good Eating

Without doubt, the proliferation of various Guides to eating out may have irritated some caterers but they do seem to fill a need among their customers. The trade press is full of anger and hurt feelings when each of the more prestigious Guides comes out, especially those like the *Good Food Guide*, which is somewhat blunter in its criticism and praise than some others, which tend to pussy-foot about.

Perhaps I have been very lucky, for I have found the better Guides to be a fantastic help.

On the whole, those caterers who get a good 'mention' find no fault in the publication; those who get a bad one find no time (but a lot of excuses) for that particular Guide. It is human nature – we all like praise, and many, especially caterers, resent criticism. I have scarcely known another industry which is so 'touchy' when the spotlight of publicity is turned on it, or on parts of the body corporate.

But a good 'mention' does have one drawback, and this seems to be ignored by those who complain that their 'rating' has changed or disappeared altogether. It is the simple fact that a good Guide entry is a Sword of Damocles over your head: you really do have to maintain that original standard or improve on it. You cannot, and you must not, allow yourself to 'rest on your laurels' and say, 'I've got a good mention, I need not worry any more.' To continue to please the Guides, you must adopt the saying about marriage: it needs to be worked at. And criticism should not be resented – after all, you are taking the public's money, and the public is entitled to its say. Use the criticism wisely and get cracking again at what you are doing.

We had one or two rather splendid Guide mentions, and then one year we were criticized (albeit mercifully mildly) for 'occasional lapses': one guest was apparently served 'dry' crab vol-au-vent and another 'rare' pork, and I was ticked off for sometimes being dictatorial about wine. I had not been aware about the crab or the pork but certainly remembered who criticized me about the wine; but I wasn't humbled by being thus castigated, for I regarded the man as a fool. On the other hand, I do not dispute his right to tell the Guide about it.

However, though it came as quite a shock, instead of telling everyone that we did not agree, and writing rude letters to the trade press putting forward our excuses and condemning the Guide, we realized we had erred and strayed in our ways and were about to become lost sheep if we did not attend. The following year, happily, told us that we had indeed come back into the fold. But we took the lesson to heart.

Briefly, there are three sorts of Guide to eating-places.

Those who seek out such places, either by their own efforts or by reported discoveries by members of the public, inspect those establishments incognito to start with, and do not attempt to charge, coerce or obtain any favours for a good 'mention'. *The Good Food Guide* and *Michelin* are probably chief among these.

The second type of Guide charges the restaurant for an entry, and the restaurateur can write his own 'puff' as he wishes. These are, without qualification, worthless. As a caterer you will probably be approached by this latter category. Some of the publications are well known, some just fly-by-night businesses anxious to make a quick buck out of a gullible caterer. They often do just that.

Be extra careful about these tricksters. The latest form of fraud is to come out with a Guide similar in size, lettering and title to a well-known one, with perhaps just one word altered. It is difficult for me to give you an example without treading on the toes of those lawyers engaged in trying to stop one or two recent, and allegedly spurious, publications, one of which appears to use the famous lettering of a motorists' organization.

But, to invent an example totally from my imagination, you may one day get a circular from, say, the *Egg On Ronay Guide*. It will show a Guide with a type-face similar to that of the better known, and only the quick-witted will see that it is nothing like the original it is pretending to ape. The circular will enclose a form asking you to write down details of your business and to return it, together with a cheque for about £50, 'so that entry to our new Guide can be considered at once'.

Alas, very often the Guide does not appear at all or, if it does, it is immediately challenged in the courts. Either way, you will have wasted your money. However tempted you may be, do not, repeat not, pay for any entry in any Guide unless its credentials are impeccable and you are quite satisfied that it will assist you to become better known to a wider public.

The third type of Guide is, to my mind, a curiously grey area of publishing but quite legitimate.

For the most part this third section applies mainly to hotel-owners, though, as most of those have restaurants (and you may yourself be thinking of becoming, eventually, a 'restaurant with rooms'), it is legitimate for them to be covered in this book.

A prime example is that of Miss Elizabeth Gundry, who made her original reputation more than twenty years ago with her *Shopper's Guide* and who, as the winner of the British Travel Writers Jubilee Award, founded that guide known as *Staying Off the Beaten Track*. Miss Gundry does not ask for payment for any entry but she does ask for a voluntary contribution of four per cent of any trade resulting from entry in the Guide.

I am not entering into the legal or moral arguments about such behaviour, but it would strike me, as an ordinary hotelier/restaurateur, that any Guide which claims independence should not expect its publication to be supported financially by that trade. If it does not make enough money by its sales, it can hardly be termed independent if it asks for contributions.

On the other hand, any criticism of Miss Gundry should well be tempered by a look at other Guides which charge in some way for an entry.

The Automobile Associations's *Hotels and Restaurants in Great Britain* not only insists that owners apply for inclusion but also charges a fee for 'registration' of between £65 and £150 (1988), and annual 'inspection and administration' charges come to a further £30 to £180. This publication accepts advertisements as well but makes no mention in its book that it charges fees.

The *RAC Hotel Guide* also insists on applications for entries, also charges fees for 'inspection', also accepts advertising and also makes no mention that it charges owners.

The *Where to Stay* publications by the Tourist Boards in England, Wales and Scotland also charge fees for entries and do accept advertising, but they state quite clearly that fees are charged, as does the English Tourist Board's *Let's Go*, which is not true of the British Travel Association's *Commended Country Hotels, Guesthouses and Restaurants*, although this does not accept any advertisements.

As I said before, you must make up your own mind on the value to your business of inclusion in any Guide, but it is proper of me to say that neither the *Michelin Guide*, the *Good Food Guide* nor *Egon Ronay's Cellnet Guide, Hotels and Restaurants* charges any fees, though the last does accept sponsorship and company advertising.

But where no 'invitations to apply' exist for one of the Guides, and entry is entirely on your own merit, just how do you get into them? Do you have to wait years to be stumbled upon and achieve some recognition? Providing you are not too 'pushy', there is no reason why you should not write a courteous letter to one or two of them telling the editor that you are in business and, very briefly, describing what it is you are doing.

Once again, choose carefully. It is no good writing to the *Good Hotel Guide* if you do not have any rooms to let, or to the *Good Pub Guide* if you are not a pub and do not hold a licence. Make sure you get hold of a copy of the Guide which interests you and ask yourself honestly whether it caters for the likes of you. If not, do not waste your time or that of the editor.

Under no circumstances suggest that the editor or an inspector calls round for a free meal! However courteous and well-meaning your letter is, it will go straight into the waste-basket. You simply have to wait.

Most Guides have a team of staff inspectors, backed up by a number of part-timers. None of them is authorized to cadge anything off you or to make promises of any sort. They will normally have a meal and pay for it. He or she will then say who they are and what Guide they represent, and they will produce proof to that effect. If you have pleased them, they may ask you to fill in a form, or fill it in themselves and ask you to check whether it is accurate as to detail. You then have to wait until you hear from head office as to whether you are to be included. You may receive a list of supplementary questions to answer; you may get a further visit from the same inspector or a different one, who may or may not reveal who they are beforehand. If they take any meal or drink, they will expect to pay for it. Either on the first visit or on a subsequent one, they may ask to inspect the kitchens and accommodation (if you have rooms) and other areas. Do not tell them to wait a minute until you have cleared up, or ask if they can come again some other time. It makes them suspicious.

But is it all worth it? Yes, it most definitely is in the case of those Guides which do not make charges for entry. It is truly 'free' advertising, and the books are used by thousands of people, not only tourists but people living locally and business travellers, who are always anxious to find somewhere new, agreeable and good. And do not fly off the handle at the first whiff of criticism. It may be fair, and it may be designed to help you help yourself. To the best of my knowledge and experience, most Guides are anxious to be of as much service to the caterer as to the public who support their efforts. They have done much to improve the standards of catering in Britain and have come a long way since the editor of one Guide was accused of being so élitist that the only thing he enjoyed was 'eating yoghurt on a Greek mountain while listening to the music of a set of Pan pipes'.

As regards those Guides which seek to charge you money for entries, I can only repeat that you must make up your own mind as to whether you can afford their fees or approve of their policy. Morality, however, has little to do with business: if you are going to get a handsome return on the fees you have paid, it becomes part of your legitimate 'advertising expenses' and as such is perfectly acceptable both to your conscience and to HM Inspector of Taxes.

But before we leave the subject of Guides, we should perhaps make mention of food writers and critics, about whom I had harsh things to say briefly in Chapter 13. It is a mixed blessing if any of that band decides to take an interest in your establishment.

For the most part, and unlike the better Guides, the food critics tend to be destructive or choose to damn with faint praise. Their wallets are heavily filled with their employer's money by way of expenses, and their judgements are correspondingly weighed down.

On the other hand, they can claim that they represent not the restaurateur but the public – though in my opinion the public they actually represent tends to be that section to whom money is of as little consideration as it is to them. Unless you are very expensive and very 'up-market', you will mercifully be left alone. There seems little interest, and therefore no 'media value', in the ordinary small restaurant, however good the food is and however reasonable the charges. Quality, or value-for-money, is not their concern, alas, for if it was, we would hear a lot less about the catering trade's 'big guns' (i.e. those most adroit at their own self-promotion) and a lot more about the hundreds of decent, honest chefs and restaurateurs who strive to give the public at large a fair deal.

There are, of course, some exceptions among the critics, and if you do chance to attract the attention of one such, they can undoubtedly lead to a quite startling increase in your business. But be careful not to 'cash in' too quickly. Many caterers have seen in some form of public recognition a chance to increase their prices dramatically while lowering their standards. The attempt is bound to fail, for they succeed in destroying those very qualities which first attracted the writer/critic.

Regulars or Cliques?
Care should also be exercised if your restaurant is likely to be 'taken over' by one set, clique or type of person – what I call 'the works canteen syndrome'. This is difficult to deal with, for becoming 'fashionable' can, in certain respects, help profits no end in the short term but lead to a restaurant empty of other customers in the long term – and completely empty when the 'fashion' changes or your popularity wanes in favour of another exciting 'discovery' elsewhere.

If you are 'adopted', however, by a particular company or organization, you will have to work doubly hard at reassuring other customers that you are not exclusively reliant on any particular clique and that their own presence is as welcome as ever. The loyalties of single groups of people are notoriously fickle, and you do not want to become 'typed' as always being full of one set of customers at the expense of others. This is a very real consideration if you own a restaurant in the country but near a large town or, say, near a Services establishment which has a large caucus of money-spending men and their wives, who tend to move every two years, often in great 'blocks'. A very busy restaurant can find itself over-night without any 'regulars' if the trade has been based on either a transient population or very much a specialized one.

Opening-Hours
However busy or slack you are, there is still the question of the hours you are going to be open and shut. This needs careful consideration. Once again, it depends where you are and the sort of operation you are running. Of course, if you are a

franchisee, these hours will be dictated to you, and the terms of the contract must be adhered to, but if you are a one-man business, you must study the local market, find out when other places shut and try to gauge whether to fall in line with your competitors or open when they are closed, in the hope that you will pick up some of their trade.

But whatever you do, you must be absolutely consistent. You must start as you mean to go on. This is very important.

A restaurant in my local town (which had, admittedly, never been very successful) was taken over by yet another new owner who tried various combinations of opening and closing for the first year. It was a disastrous experiment. No one knew when the place was open or likely to be shut. First of all it was lunches from Tuesday to Saturday and dinners from Wednesday to Saturday, then lunches from Wednesday to Saturday and dinners from Thursday to Saturday. There followed an experiment, in high season, with Sunday lunches, but this stopped after about six weeks. And so it went on. Most months the restaurant advertised its 'New Opening Times' in the local paper, but all of them were so complex that I was not surprised that no one ever went for a meal. Only after at least a year, as I say, did the owner settle down to a regular pattern – more to suit her than to suit the public.

Not surprisingly, the place soon went back on the market, and the owner had enormous difficulty in selling it. When she did so, the new owners started the same thing all over again, and at the time of writing it has been closed and shuttered for the past six months. It is hardly likely to appeal to any experienced buyer, with a record like that. As I said right at the start of this book, a catering outlet with a bad reputation is a worse buy than a place with no reputation at all.

Depending on the area, do not stick slavishly to what you think are the hours people want to eat. Some restaurants which stay open all afternoon pick up a surprising amount of trade from those very people who have to work during lunch hours – other caterers, for a start. And if your competitors close mainly on a Monday, a traditional 'black' day in the trade, especially for dinners, ask yourself whether it is because of knowledge or because they have never thought about it properly. But whatever you do, do not chop and change.

When you become popular, of course, you may open on a day

you have always been closed. Fine, providing you stick with the decision for a good long time, at least until word has got around. But do not even do that until you are quite certain that the restaurant will be run as you would want it run in your absence, for it is essential that you do have a day off. Unless you are absolutely sure about the maintenance of standards, do not risk it. Stay shut. We all know places where the excuse (see Chapter 15) that 'It's the chef's day off' is quite commonplace, or where we can detect that the owner is away, because of behavioural changes in staff attitudes. Do not risk your reputation. It is going to be too hard-earned to throw away casually.

I can think of a number of caterers who make a lot of money out of the closure of their competitors, particularly among the tea-shop group who think that the local 'early closing day' (now gradually disappearing) means that no one will be about on a Wednesday or Thursday afternoon. In my own local country town, at least two such places stay open and are always busy – and the same goes for Sunday lunches. Now, it may well be that the owners of the outlets which close actually do so because they want to, and why not? That is their prerogative. But you must not make the mistake of assuming there is no trade at such times.

What you have to do is undertake yet more research. Walk about the town; look at it on early closing day, in the evenings, at weekends, especially on Sunday. If in the country, is there a market day, and would it be worth opening earlier than normal or staying open later than normal on other days? There is no easy answer, no easy advice worth proffering. Local conditions vary not only from one part of the country to another but from one town to another, and even within towns if it is a large conurbation.

In country towns, particularly, most of the 'tea-shop' operations seem to close between 5p.m. and 5.30p.m., and the pubs open at 6p.m. There has always been a gap, it seems to me, which could be used profitably. Careful observation often reveals people aimlessly drifting about, waiting to meet others or to catch a bus or train. In most towns, the only places open are the off-licence chains. They must find it worthwhile. I wonder why the tea-shops do not. Or perhaps they have never actually looked at the question – just shutting because everyone else does.

You have learned enough from this book to know that the catering trade is a very hard trade indeed in which to make money – do not make it even more difficult for yourself by throwing away possible sources of extra profit just because you have not looked at opening- and closing-times and suited them to local conditions. Careful research may reveal all sorts of unexpected misconceptions about when customers want feeding. There is no reason why you should not literally 'cash in' on it.

But you must, must, must give yourself a decent day off, otherwise you will go under with sheer exhaustion. And once again, unless you cannot trust your staff, you must have a holiday. So shut then – but only when you know, from research and careful thought, that it is the best time. The best time not from a purely selfish point of view but from that of your business.

18 Expansion

Always beware of a thin chef.

Fernand Point

The fruits of success, to many restaurateurs, result in – expansion.

This course is fraught with almost as many problems and difficulties as you faced when you first decided to go into the catering trade, with possibly one exception. Money.

There are, in reality, three forms of expansion. The first is by an increase in the size of your present premises – by extension, perhaps, or by the conversion of those parts of your property which are under-utilized, by building on, if there is the space, or by taking adjacent premises should they become vacant.

The second is by a move, lock, stock and barrel, to larger premises, preferably in the same locality.

The third course is to open another restaurant, either by buying an existing one or by starting up anew elsewhere.

There are fairly obvious advantages and disadvantages to all three.

Extension and Moving

First of all you must ask yourself whether you are truly equipped, mentally and physically, to have a go at any expansion. For expansion is not merely a question of money; it is also a question of yet another 'stretching' of your time and energy, an extension of problems in every single aspect of running a better restaurant.

If you are a born businessman or woman, these challenges will merely be grist to your mill, and you will revel in all of it. But you are nevertheless only 'one person', so to speak, and will that 'one person' be elastic enough to cover the new challenges?

If the answer is 'yes', expansion within your present site is the most desirable course, and there is no point in dwelling upon it here. It is merely a question of gaining planning (and licensing) permission and of the inevitable building work, which should be done, so far as is humanly possible, while your present operation remains open for business and thus still attracting the public. There are dozens of examples of success in this field, but you do need a builder who will understand your problems and work within reasonable parameters agreed in advance between you.

There are also many successful examples of businesses moving to larger premises locally. The upheaval this entails is often minimized by the fact that the new premises can be readied without any problems of interruption to your existing operation, and in many cases it is usual to move certain items of essential equipment over a weekend or within one or two days, so that your daily revenue does not suffer unreasonably. The added advantage is that your clientele will remain as it was before. You do not have to go out and get a new 'set' in again.

In fact, in many cases, a move to larger, but nearby, premises is often the best way to expand. In a great many high streets in Britain, leases of better and larger properties become available quite often, and your own local knowledge will tell you in advance which ones may become empty, so that you can start negotiations ahead of the field when it comes to outsiders. If your operation is in the country, however, it is more problematical. There are not that number of truly local properties changing hands all that often, and if you are not able to expand by building on, because you do not have the land or cannot get it, or you meet up with planning opposition, you may be faced with the third choice – an additional restaurant elsewhere. I think this needs a lot more thought than the two alternatives above.

A Second Restaurant

I do not want to dampen enthusiasm or curtail any desire for greater success, but another restaurant in some other locality means that inevitably you are going to be an 'absentee landlord' at one of them, for you simply cannot be in two places at once.

The natural tendency will be to spend more time, to start with, anyway, at your new premises, seeing it is working properly, that it is on the right lines, that it is just as you wish it to be. It will take a great deal of time, and you are going to need expert and trustworthy staff at both places to ensure that your interests are protected fully.

It is (like marriage) something into which you should enter not lightly or wantonly but discreetly, advisedly and soberly. And you must decide from the start whether the new business is to be a copy of your present one or something quite different, aiming at a different market and serving different food.

Of course, there are a great many such ventures, and a lot of them are very successful, because they are being run by people who are successful with their initial operation. They are 'old hands', in other words, and the chances of failure are thus reduced.

Certainly, because you have become adept at cash-flow forecasts, budgets and money-management generally, your bank manager is going to look upon you with greater kindness and considerably less scepticism than he did when you appeared, hesitantly, in his office the very first time. But even then you will need to convince him that you are not over-stretching yourself both physically and mentally, apart from financially. And in order to assure him – and others – of these three things, you are going to have to go back to school and start trudging the pavements again, doing the sort of research I was urging upon you right at the start of this book. It will be necessary, nay, essential, believe you me.

The main problem will be one of reputation. Reputation does not travel very far in Britain; in fact, probably only as far as just around the corner of the block. There are a great number of instances in which well-known, successful restaurateurs have decided to set up anew elsewhere, flushed with their own wine-pride in the form of 'hype', only to discover that their newly adopted part of the world cares little for them. In other words, they had not done their research carefully enough. Their success and fame had gone to their own heads but not to the pockets of a different public. They thus retired 'hurt', as they say.

So, although your bank manager may know about you, no one else necessarily will in your new area. You thus have to start all over again, putting your own stamp on the new business. It is not going to be any easier than your first step into the catering world. Success in one place certainly does not guarantee success anywhere else.

So, if you are determined upon opening another business elsewhere, the only bit of advice I can proffer is to go back to the beginning of this book and refresh your memory. It may bring back all sorts of problems you had forgotten about. It could be a timely reminder. But if it does not change your mind, I am sure you have every chance of making a go of it.

Perhaps the most difficult success to achieve is a copy of your original business. Without you, the host or hostess, the restaurant will almost certainly lack some personality, and the 'image' will suffer. For the most part, customers like the feeling of permanence and continuation, and even in the fastest food franchise operations regular patrons actually appreciate that someone they know, or have got to recognize, is always in charge. De-personalization of a restaurant is not a recipe for a profitable venture, even though a great many 'chains' have no personality at all, which is why they always seem to be searching for new 'themes'.

One idea that does often seem to work is for your prime business to sire a satellite operation, different and perhaps simpler in style, which can be 'serviced', so to speak, from your present kitchens.

Modern catering equipment will allow the adoption of batch cooking for two places in one central kitchen. The food, either chilled or frozen, can then be taken to the satellite operation and reheated or regenerated in microwave or conventional ovens, thus saving on staff, particularly in the form of a chef. But the drawback of constant to-ing and fro-ing with supplies remains.

It is this single factor – travel – which seems to irk the most and which more often than not leads either to failure or to disenchantment, however successful or appealing the new operation becomes.

In any event, you will have to ensure that you set up and exercise the tightest management controls for your new outlet. A reliance upon 'casual' staff will not be wise. You will have to have at least one permanent manager and perhaps others, and you will have to pay them well – perhaps even offering a share of the profits to ensure that there are fewer hands in the till than there might otherwise be.

You may need to consider detaching one of your own staff

whom you can trust and who is ready for the challenge, for he or she will know how you want things run better than any newcomer. But I think I am wasting my time and yours in stating obvious problems. You will be experienced enough by now to know about them and to cope with them.

There is one point, however, that I think is worth mentioning. It is the possibility – if you have lived 'over the shop' for years – of using the fruits of your success to buy a place of your own in which to live, thus releasing your own living-quarters as possible money-earning space. And I do not necessarily mean as an eating-space.

'Restaurants with Rooms'
Over the years, there has been an increasing tendency in Britain, following the lead of Europe, to create 'restaurants with rooms', particularly in country areas. This can often be a cheap and easy alternative to expansion elsewhere, and it is profitable too. Not for nothing is the old hotel-keeper's phrase so often quoted: 'Bums in beds make money'. They actually do, too. The cost of servicing letting bedrooms is way below the cost of servicing any other form of catering or leisure operation. And if you are to use what were hitherto your own living-quarters, you are half way there anyway.

It is in this field of 'restaurants with rooms', rather than in expanding into a second restaurant elsewhere, that you can retain control of the operation you have created, that you remain an owner, rather than something like a company director. I think it takes a special type of person to cope with the double operation rather than having it all under one roof, so to speak. It is not something that appeals to me, but then I am a chef and not a businessman, and the day-to-day running of a very personal restaurant provides all the challenges and excitements I need. I am not criticizing in any way those men and women who seek further successes in the industry – but, remember, two restaurants are the start of a 'chain', and chain restaurants are never the same as the 'owner-driven' one. If you are more of a business person than a restaurateur and have been fired by the enthusiasm of monetary success rather than profitable satisfaction at remaining small and very good, the new challenges you will be facing will be welcome. It is entirely a matter for you to decide.

Bigger is not always better. Running a good restaurant is not just a matter of making money – it is a way of life, and making people comfortable and happy creates enormous personal satisfaction. Do not sacrifice what you have created because of dreams of avarice.

'A Con Man's Guide to Catering'

Having used that noun above – avarice – I feel it is time to come to a somewhat sorry section of this book. For avarice is rampant in the catering trade, and I find it very sad to have to say so. But you are going to come across such people, and I feel it proper to warn you about the whole question, so that you will not be as 'dewy-eyed' as I was when I started. In simple terms, I shall dwell for a few paragraphs on 'how to cheat the public', or 'A Guide to Con Man's Catering'.

Although 'portion control' is a proper and acceptable way of controlling your costs, as we have seen, another 'acceptable' way of controlling the amount a customer eats is by ensuring that the plate he is given is small enough to look filled with food, however strict you are about portion control. It is a simple, and for some an acceptable, method of 'packaging' used the world over by many businesses, such as perfumiers, washing-powder manufacturers and so on. Only when you open the box do you realize that the contents are somewhat smaller than you thought.

The smaller dinner-plate size is very popular, almost obligatory, for those catering outlets of a 'buffet' or 'carvery' nature where a member of staff serves a meat or fish course and the customers help themselves to the 'trimmings'. However high the plate seems to be heaped, it actually holds very much less than appears. Other types of places can operate this way too. A heap of chips (the cheapest and most profitable food there is to serve) can be piled higgledy-piggledy onto a plate to hide a miniscule portion of, say, ham or fish. Any complaint a customer may feel like making will quickly die on his lips because his stomach will be over-filled with what is, in fact, a specious food. There can, therefore, be no question of not feeling satisfied.

This practice was, however, cleverly reversed by the hype-merchants who adopted the *cuisine-minceur* fashion, which we have already considered. In their case, 'artfully arranged' small portions on large plates, preferably white and hexagonal, were made virtuous by their high cost, and the customer was challenged, like Oliver, to dare to ask for more, risking an accusation of gluttony instead of a simple desire to get value for money.

The 'bulking' of portions can be obtained by the use of salad stuffs, again very cheap, or batter, which, if skilfully applied, as it is in most commercial 'bought-in' products, helps to hide the actual size of the meat or fish being sold. The adroit chef can use 'extenders' for sauces, creams, jams, soups. We all know those stories about how unscrupulous transport-café owners used to 'top up' tomato ketchup bottles with vinegar and water, or mix in the cheapest margarine with the butter. Such practices are not likely to exist in a transport café, I can tell you; they certainly do in a number of 'posher' outlets I know of.

Coffee, too, can be adulterated by simply putting in less than the recommended amount. A visit to any catering exhibition, where the coffee suppliers are extremely generous with their product, will convince you of this. Quite rightly, they insist that their pre-packaged product requires an exact amount of water to produce a very acceptable brew. Yet I have seen blatant examples in some restaurants, using the same equipment and package as have been demonstrated at an exhibition, whereby only a portion of each packet is used, thus increasing the profit margin even further.

In a restaurant local to me, I have seen a waitress go to the two 'wine boxes' on the dispense bar and fill a glass half with red and half with white because the customer had asked for a *rosé* wine. And I know of another one where the Spanish sherry bottles are filled solely with British-type sherry.

The dispense bar is an enormous source of illicit profit. If serving 'mixers' at all – say, tonic to go with customers' gins, it is common practice to collect bottles with any left-overs, pour them back into one of the bottles and then re-cap with a crown cap, leaving that particular bottle as 'first off the shelf' for the next service. In a busy restaurant bar the 'heel-taps' account for a very acceptable slice of extra profit, as does the pouring back of all 'slops' into one of the barrels in the case of those establishments selling draught beer. In fact, catering suppliers actually sell narrow-necked funnels which will fit the spile-hole of any barrel.

And, of course, by not stating the size in which you serve wine by the glass, you can ensure that only miniscule drinks are served, while charging an exorbitant price, the poor 'punter' expecting a large measure of wine because of the large price.

The list is endless. The catering trade is a haven for the fiddler. But not for long.

The 'punters' are not that stupid, and even if the British do not complain in public, they certainly complain in private, and eventually they will boycott your establishment, and you will go to the wall.

You will deserve all the bad luck you will get.

Just one true example in my own experience:

Some years ago we had a new, and very good, member of staff who was clearing up after service. She approached me with a number of bottles containing 'heel-taps', some more than half full, and asked me what she should do with them. Such was my innocence that I told her somewhat sharply that she knew where the sink was and where the bottle-skip was. Use both.

Thankfully she was good-humoured enough to laugh. 'That's not what they did where I've been working,' she told me, naming a well-known local drinking- and eating-place. I had to confess to her that I was totally ignorant, and slightly disbelieving, of what she had to say. 'How can he do that?' I heard myself indignantly asking.

'I don't know *how* he can do it but I do know he does, and all the staff are instructed to do it too,' she replied. 'On the other hand he's got a new BMW, which is more than you've got.'

Point taken.

Mercifully enough, that man is now actually 'looking for work elsewhere', though he at least has his new car to console him.

Cheating the public can last for only a certain amount of time, and even if the Weights and Measures people, or the Trades Descriptions Act, or even the police do not get involved, the ordinary 'punter' will one day have his own, private say – and you will be out of business. It may take some time, but Abraham Lincoln's famous words on fooling people are especially applicable to the catering trade. It is well to bear them in mind.

19 Success?

The discovery of a new dish does more for the happiness of mankind than the discovery of a star.

Brillat Savarin

As you may already have realized, there are no hard-and-fast rules, no items of essential advice, no finite number of hints, tips, adages or anecdotes which can assure the success of any restaurant. There is no single area, part of a street, town or village which will guarantee custom. There is nothing in the whole wide world as uncertain as the future of a restaurant, either in the continuation of its life or in a sentence of its death. In the strangest parts of Britain, from the far north-west of Scotland, where there is only a single-track road and where property and people exist in a permanent wind-tunnel, to the far south-east, where restaurants of quality jostle within an area of streets only just one up from a London slum, there is nothing to be learned which will absolutely, irrovocably and certainly confer the accolade of profitable distinction upon you.

There is one certainty, however, among all this doubt: you cannot hope to please everybody all the time, but if you just manage to please some of them, some of the time, and instil in others a sense of joyous well-being, you are on your way to finding some sort of magic formula.

In order to attain just some part of this paradise, you must, as I have tried to demonstrate, stick to what you know, what you like, what you regard as acceptable. It is no good, I am afraid, trying to guess what I like, what I regard as acceptable – or anyone else. As I said before, you are not unique; neither am I. It is true there are thousands upon thousands of customers out there with the same tastes and attitudes as you yourself, as well as myself. But it is equally true, in every sense in the catering trade, that one man's meat is another man's poison.

You must create an atmosphere which you would like to find in any place where *you* want to eat. And, just as I am entitled to stay away from it because I find it disagreeable, you are entitled to discourage people like me from eating with you. Too many people tend to say, 'The customer is always right.' He may well be, but I firmly believe that a certain customer may not be right for you, and if you think this to be true in any particular case, I do not see why you should 'grin and bear it'.

For, if you 'grin and bear it', you are not being selfish: you are, in fact, being caring about the customers you do want, you do like and who, you hope, enjoy themselves immensely by being with you. If you are false, other people will detect it. You are going to need superhuman powers of tact, diplomacy and forbearance anyway, just to cope with the sort of people you do like, so why add to your problems by tolerating those you do not?

The Awkward Customer

Any restaurateur will face awkward or unpleasant situations. Bores and bad behaviour are not the prerogatives of those in the catering trade. I have had to cope with verbal abuse (often well merited, some of my detractors would say), physical assault, fraud, drunkenness, customers' heart attacks, marital rows and even a court appearance on the accusation of serving alcohol to minors, a charge which was trumped up and mercifully seen as such by the magistrates and thrown out. Yet I still adore the whole business of running a good restaurant. It can be fun, it can give you some standing in the local community, it rewards you with a great number of very good friends, often from all walks of life, and because making other people happy is happiness in itself, there may be easier ways of making money but there are precious few more satisfying.

There is little boredom in dealing with the public and, as we saw, if you dislike people, you should not be in the catering trade. You will quickly get to recognize in advance potential trouble-makers – one develops a sixth sense, as one does about those who come in quite determined to be unpleasant, to find fault. Under no circumstances allow a customer to get the upper hand – he is in your 'home', so to speak – but equally never lose your temper or resort to abuse. If you do either of those things, you have sunk to the level of the customer, and you cannot hope to win anything, only to lose your self-respect. Deal quietly but firmly with people out to upset you, your staff and other customers. If a nuisance is caused by anyone's behaviour, make sure you apologize to all the other customers personally. They will be on your side, and you will win friends rather than alienate them.

Remember, too, that trouble-makers are normally to be found in quantity among what is now called the 'yuppy' class, especially when hunting in packs, and, although it hurts me to say so, the 'club' type of man who plays rugger or cricket can be a perfect pest when he is with his mates – largely because of booze. Have no hesitation in banning such people from your restaurant. I have had to ban many such in my time and have been thanked for it by regular customers. If a group of people are unable to enjoy themselves without throwing their weight around, politely tell them they are not welcome now or any time in the future.

If anyone arrives obviously the worse for wear from drink, you have every right to refuse entry, and, indeed, you have a moral obligation to do so. I know of at least one restaurateur who asks drivers for their car keys if they have drunk too much and, if any driver refuses to hand them over, warns them that, if they remove their car from the car-park in such a condition, he will telephone the police. And he does so. I see nothing wrong in this. It is not 'sneaking'; it is a defensible policy. What people drink and in what quantity is nothing to do with you, perhaps, but if it is on your property, your proper responsibility lies towards the public at large. After all, to put it selfishly, it may be one of your regular customers whom that driver injures and, although it may be difficult to prove your culpability in law, it is not going to do you any good at all in the community.

There are other tiresome people you may come across, one of whom is the deliberately fraudulent, and, regrettably, they are invariably from among the so-called 'professional' classes and, if clever, are beyond the law.

The trick is simple and well known.

A party of 'respectable' people will eat and drink expensively and seem very good customers, well worth having. But one of them, at the very end, will complain about some aspect of service, or food, or some rudeness or off-hand attitude of a member of staff or yourself. He will ask for the bill, look at it, immediately query it, then do one of two things. He will either write out a cheque for the full amount, throw it down and tell you are lucky to get any money at all, or he will cause considerable disturbance by saying that under no circumstances is he going to pay such a monstrous sum for a lousy evening and hand you a card with his name and address, inviting you to put the matter in the hands of your solicitor.

Now, this behaviour places you in a difficult situation. If you accept the cheque (which will always be for more than £50), you will have to do so without asking for his cheque guarantee card or you must ask him to write enough cheques to cover the bill, each one of which must be for £50 or less, for the guarantee to be operable. Only a very brave and determined caterer is going to do this and risk more trouble and abuse in front of other customers. This particular customer knows that. He also knows that, theoretically, you could call the police even if he supplies a bona-fide name and address, for he has obtained goods and services fraudulently, in itself a criminal act. Once again, he is pretty certain that you will do no such thing, and, indeed, it would be a difficult charge to bring, because at no time has he actually refused to pay for anything.

So now what? You let the party leave. There is nothing you can do. Almost certainly, if you have accepted the cheque, it will be stopped. This means that the customer has in fact refused payment. But he will be one jump ahead. You will receive quite quickly a replacement cheque for an amount of money considerably lower than the bill, but not so low as to make it worth your while to go to your solicitor and start proceedings for the balance. The legal costs, even in a small claims court, will ensure that you lose money anyway, even though 'costs' will almost certainly be awarded to you if you win. Winning such a case is a problem. A judgment on whether the customer did receive sufficiently good food and wine and skilled, attentive service to make such a total bill correct and reasonable is not a legal one, it is a qualitative one, and the resultant publicity, if you pursue your case into the court, is not going to do you any good at all. You have actually been 'caught', and it is immaterial whether you are right or wrong. Put it down to experience.

Ah, you might be saying, but no one can go on doing that sort of thing for long. You are wrong. For the most part, this trick is played by people on holiday. If four of them, touring, let us say, play that trick every night for two weeks, they will end up paying in actual money at least a third less than the holiday would have cost them otherwise. For they will certainly be doing it in hotels where they are staying. Their 'savings' are considerable, for they stay in the better places and eat in the better restaurants, although careful to avoid the 'chains', most of which are linked by telex and always report customers like that throughout their network.

There are also the people who, having eaten, discover they have come out without their wallet. They are always pleasant and plausible and, indeed, we all know it can actually happen, though unlikely in the case of going out for a meal. You can only take their name and address and hope you will get the money. In most cases you will, because not paying at all, as we saw above, renders them open to prosecution. If you are very suspicious, however, you can always ask a man to leave his wristwatch, perhaps, as 'security', or a woman her handbag. Quite often the necessary money is found quite quickly.

Free Meals and Split Meals

Be careful too about the 'free loaders', including your so-called friends. All small, personally run catering outlets tend to suffer from quite innocent and well-meaning friends who tend to think to themselves, 'I'll just pop in to old so-and-so for a chat and a cup of coffee – he won't mind.' Very often old so-and-so does not mind, for he forgets that it is his living which suffers. But look at it another way. If a close friend of yours was a bank manager, would you 'pop in' for a chat and a fiver? Or if someone else ran a clothes shop, would you feel able at any time to 'pop in' for a cup of coffee and a free blouse? It is only when it is put in these terms that many caterers understand that they are being taken for a ride, however unwittingly and innocently.

You have to be very firm about this point right from start. No 'freebies' so far as you are concerned, and if you do want to entertain some friends (and why not?), try to do so on your day off, in your own living-quarters. Under no circumstances permit 'landlord's cliques' to grow up around you, where the owner or chef can be seen sitting with his cronies enjoying themselves 'on the house' while other customers have to pay for their own and your pleasure, which is how they will see it.

You will also come across the 'split meal' eaters. When a couple come in, one says he or she cannot eat anything at all but will keep their companion company. So they will – by sharing everything served to the person who ordered. I have even known one such couple to ask for an extra roll, as 'One isn't enough.' There is little you can do about it, for no amount of remonstration will cure them. Such customers actually do not see that what they are doing is morally wrong. After all, they are only keeping their friend/husband/wife company, and if that someone cares to share their plateful, no restaurateur can charge 'extra', because the person who ordered is, after all, eating only half the food. There is, as they say, no answer to that.

The 'No Shows'
Another problem which exercises the minds of all restaurateurs are the 'no shows'. These are the customers who book a meal and either never turn up or telephone to say they cannot make it. The first of these poses a problem, although the law is quite specific and makes no distinction between them.

Technically, if a customer has booked a meal (or a room in a hotel) and either cancels or does not turn up, that customer is liable for any loss of profit the restaurateur/hotelier incurs, unless the latter can re-let the table or the room to someone else.

If more staff have been brought in to cope with, say, a large party of people who have booked, the wages can be added to the loss of profit and so on. It will, obviously, be necessary to prove to a court that you did, in fact, incur these losses – but do you want to take that extreme step? You may, possibly, get a cancellation from a very good and regular customer who brings many people into your restaurant and who otherwise contributes substantially to your business. Would you want to sue such a person? Probably not, but here again you are very much on your own. You must make the decision alone. You must decide what your policy is to be.

I have heard of some restaurateurs who claim the money lost willy-nilly, no matter who the customer is and, if they do not get it, immediately go to court. You may agree with this course. I do not. Unless the circumstances are extreme, I think it is all a matter of swings and roundabouts. Very few people deliberately book meals or rooms with every intention of cancelling them or never turning up. And if such people do in fact occur in your life

– and they well may, they are not likely to do it again. In any event, if they used the same name, you would not accept the booking the second time around, because your diary would reveal what they had done.

The restaurateurs who make a claim whatever the circumstances say they are protecting others in the trade by their actions – that if everyone, without question, took proceedings against 'no shows', the entire habit would die out. Maybe so. I am simply not prepared to set myself up as an arbiter of anyone else's attitudes.

A quite legitimate course of action by any restaurateur is to ask anyone booking a table by telephone for their name and address, which could well make a follow-up easier in the event of their not turning up. Although I am in principle against legal action in such cases, a polite enquiry as to what happened may well win you a confirmed booking at a later date or, at the very least, have the effect of making that person think twice before he does such a thing again.

We have suffered a few 'no shows' and many cancellations, often at the last minute, in our life in the catering trade. It is annoying, to say the least, disappointing certainly, but I do not think we have ever suffered in the long run by a tolerant and understanding attitude. Indeed, I think we might well have gained by it. There are very few of us who, having decided to do something at a certain time, such as going out for a meal, have not discovered, often at the last minute, that one of us is unwell or that our friends simply cannot turn up. In that case, most of us telephone the restaurant, surely, and apologize. We would certainly go there on another occasion if we could. We would never go there at all if the proprietor sent us a bill for his loss of profit.

Children
You will also have to make up your own mind whether you wish to encourage small children into your restaurant if it is of the type where bad behaviour might irritate other diners.

Some children, of course, are very well behaved, but there is no telling in advance. (Actually, all children are well behaved, very few are evil; it is the parents who are to blame.) I have always dealt with the matter of bad behaviour quite simply by telling the child very firmly to sit down at his own table and be quiet. No parent has ever actually hit me for such a liberty, though they have looked rather pained.

I make it clear, however, that well-behaved children are more than welcome but others definitely not. If attracting children, however, is going to form a deliberate part of the operation you intend to run, and where they will be definitely welcome, then it is worth considering special menus similar to those offered in many fast-food places, and at a special price. Once again it is a matter of 'targeting' your market from the start.

It strikes me as sounding rather sad that I am ending this book on what some may feel to be a slightly sour note about the peccadilloes of some customers but I do not mean to be sour – far from it. Without such customers, life might be easier for you but it would certainly not be as interesting. And it is this inexhaustible supply of interest which makes the whole catering trade so fascinating. It attracts to it some misfits, it is true, but they are greatly outnumbered by the amusing, competent men and women who, once they have a whiff of the gun-shot, so to speak, simply cannot do without it.

People who find the trade unsuited to their own personalities will not last very long and they will certainly not make any money at it; but I find it quite impossible to define why it attracts so many varied types of people.

Catering has all the disadvantages you can imagine – hard work, poor rewards, long hours, evenings and weekends, an endless succession of strangers eating your food, sitting at your tables, even criticizing your efforts. Why on earth do you want to join us? What on earth are you doing reading this book? Surely I must have put you off by now?

No?

Then I think you are going to succeed in your new career, and I think you are going to enjoy it more than you have ever enjoyed anything in your life before.

I wish you every success – and I hope one day to be a (very well-behaved) customer and, I am sure, a satisfied one in your new restaurant.

Bon appetit.

Useful Addresses

I am indebted to Croner Publications Ltd, Croner House, 173 Kingston Road, New Malden, Surrey KT3 3SS (01-942 8966) for all the help and information contained in, and freely offered by, their publication *Croner Catering*.

British Franchise Association
Franchise Chambers, 75a Bell Street, Henley-on-Thames, Oxon
    RG9 2BD (0491 578049)
Franchise Opportunities Directory
Franchise Concepts Ltd. Enterprise House, Buckingham Road,
    Aylesbury, Bucks HP19 3QQ (0296 433135)
Delicatessen and Fine Food Association
6 The Broadway, Thatcham, Berkshire RG13 4JA (0635 69033)
Hotel Catering and Institutional Management Association
191 Trinity Road, London SW17 7HN (01-672 4251)
Hotel and Catering Industry Training Board
PO Box 18, Ramsey House, Central Square, Wembley,
    Middlesex HA9 7AP (01-902 8865)
Catering Equipment Distributors Association
25 Ecclesbourne Drive, Buxton, Derbyshire (0298 79307)
Caterer & Hotelkeeper
Quadrant House, The Quadrant, Sutton, Surrey SM2 5AS
    (01-661 3500)
British Hotels, Restaurants and Caterers Association
13 Cork Street, London W1X 2BH (01-499 6641)
Cookery and Food Association (Craft Guild of Chefs)
1 Victoria Parade, By 331, Sandycombe Road, Richmond, Surrey
    (01-948 3944/3870)
Council for Small Industries in Rural Areas (CoSIRA)
141 Castle Street, Salisbury, Wiltshire SP1 3TP (0722 6255)

The Academy of Wine Service
8 Hanover Street, London W1R 9HF (01-493 1552)
Microwave Oven Association
16a The Broadway, Wimbledon, London SW19 1RF (01-946 3499)
Transport and General Workers Union
Transport House, Smith Square, London SW1P 3JP (01-828 7788)
Performing Rights Society
29-33 Berners Street, London W1P 4AA (01-580 5544)
A Directory of Fine British Foods
Rich and Green Ltd, 1 Moorhouse Road, London W2 5DH
    (01-727 9808)
British Culinary Institute
33 Longfield Road, Bristol BS7 9AG (0272 424045)
West Country Game
The Old Dairy, Compton Park, Nether Compton, Sherborne,
    Dorset DT9 4QE (0935 73247)

Further Reading

How to Live with VAT – an easy-to-follow Guide (McGraw-Hill, 1987) Brooks, J., and Copp, A.

Fowler, Deborah *The Woman's Guide to Starting Your Own Business* (Thorson's, 1988)

Helling, Jack, *Accountancy for Small Businesses* (Sphere, 1983)

Williams Sara, *Lloyds Bank Small Business Guide* (Penguin, 1988)

Williams, Sara, and Willman, John, *Lloyds Bank Tax Guide 1988/89* (Penguin)

How to Set Up and Run your own Business (Daily Telegraph Business Enterprise Book, 5th edition, 1986)

Starting Your Own Business (Consumers Association, 1986)

Index

accessibility, 36-9
accountants, 70
accounts, 69-70, 83-4
    books, 62-4
advertising, 202-3
advice, 55-7
air-cleaners, 102-4
Appert, Nicolas, 62
assets, 63-4

balance sheets, 165-6
banks, 29-30, 65-8
blackboards, 180-1
Byron, Lord, 93

capability, 16-17
capital, 19-20
Capital Gains Tax, 80
Carême, 72
cash and carries, 196-7
cash-flow, 75-7
catering colleges, 131
catering statistics, 13
change-of-use, 85-6
children, 231-2
cleaning, 176-8
competition, 33
concessions, 47-50
con-man's catering, 222-4
Copeland, 80
credit cards, 190-1
customers, 213
    awkward, 226-9
    drunk, 227
    fraudulent, 227-8
    free-loaders, 229-30

delicatessens, 51

Des Essarts, 142
dining-rooms, 114-26
    furnishings, 117-22
    smoking, 120-1
    stations/still-rooms, 122-4
    temperature, 121-2
    'themes', 115-16
Dumas, Alexandre, 156

Environmental Health, 42, 82,
    91-2, 94
excuses/apologies, 174-6
expansion, 217-22

fads and fashions, 151-2
fire safety, 40, 87
fixed overheads, 156-9
flair, 14-15
food writers, 212-13
Forte, Charles, 31
franchizing, 43-7

green wellie syndrome, 30-1, 39
gross profit, 171
guides, 208-13

health – *see* Environmental Health
Hilton, Conrad, 31

image, 22, 200-1, 206
insurance, 170-1

Job Centres, 74, 140
job experience, 15, 57-60

kitchens, 93-113
    air cleaning/ventilation 102-4

cleanliness, 100, 104-5
equipment, 101-13, 105-8
equipment exhibitions, 101
equipment suppliers, 102
floors/surfaces, 104-5
fuels, 106
orders to, 186-9
planning, 96-9
refrigeration, 113-14
second-hand, 102
storage, 108
water/washing-up, 109

landlords, 80-1
leases, 81-2
legal status, 83-4
liabilities, 63-4
Licensed Victualler's Association, 88
licensed trade, 47-9
licensing laws, 86-90
   Scotland, 89-90
limited companies, 84-5
lists, 180-2
Longfellow, 186
luck, 18-19
Lytton, Robert Bulwer, 127

mailing shots, 203-4
menus, 145-55
   language, 153-4
   planning, 145-8
   selling, 148-51
money raising, 62-71
   assets and liabilities, 63-4
   bank loans/alternative sources, 72-4
   ingoings, 64
   presentation, 64-8, 79
   previous accounts, 69-70
Monselet, 35, 55

'no-shows', 230-1
notebook – *see* workbook

opening hours, 213-16
outdoor catering, 53-4

parking, 36-9
partners, 23, 83

performing rights, 125-6
pilferage, 191-2
planners and planning, 40-2, 85
Point, Fernand, 217
pricing policy, 157-9
private cooking, 54
profit/loss forecast, 77-9
promotions – *see* special events
properties
   basic requirements, 40-2
   buying, 23, 26, 80
   in the country, 39-40
   leasing, 24-5, 80-1
   location, 31-4
   own home, 51-2
   reasons for selling, 26-8
   renting, 23
   searching, 23
   specialist/ethnic/vegetarian, 52-3
public relations, 199-215

reading up, 60-1
research, 24-34, 55-7
restaurant with rooms, 10, 221-2
routine, 176-85

seasonal/special restaurants, 34, 52-3
self-motivation, 67
smoking, 120-1
solicitors, 70-1, 80-2
special events, 204-7
spend-per-head, 160-1
staff, 127-41
   'casuals', 133-7
   foreign, 138-9
   law, 140-1
   sixteen-hour rule, 128-9
stairs, 38-9
stock-taking, 164-5
supplies/suppliers, 193-8

take-aways, 37, 51
tearooms/shops, 37, 51
Tendret, Lucien, 43, 114, 199
TGWU, 128
tills, 189-91
tips/*tronc*, 139-40
toilets, 91-2

VAT, 77, 85, 157, 162, 167-70
  tables, 173
ventilation, 103

wastage, 142-5
wine merchants, 194-5
workbook, 35, 55-7